Teaching Primary Programming With Scratch

Teacher Book – Research-Informed Approaches

PHIL BAGGE

Published in 2022 by University of Buckingham Press,
an imprint of Legend Times Group
51 Gower Street
London WC1E 6HJ
info@unibuckinghampress.com
www.unibuckinghampress.com

Copyright © Phil Bagge 2022

Published by arrangement with Hampshire Inspection and Advisory Service (part of Hampshire County Council)

All rights reserved. No reproduction, copy or transmission of this publication may be made without written permission.

Except for the quotation of short passages for the purposes of research or private study, or criticism and review, no part of this publication may be reproduced, stored in a retrieval system, copied or transmitted, in any form or by any means, electronic, mechanical, photocopying, recording or otherwise, now known or hereafter invented, save with written permission or in accordance with the provisions of the Copyright, Design and Patents Act 1988, or under terms of any licence permitting limited copying issued by the publisher.

This book is sold subject to the condition that it shall not, by way of trade or otherwise, be lent, resold, hired out, or otherwise circulated without the publisher's prior consent in any form of binding or cover other than that in which it is published and without a similar condition including this condition being imposed on the subsequent purchaser.

Any person who does any unauthorised act in relation to this publication may be liable to criminal prosecution and civil claims for damages.

ISBN 978-1-91505-4-203

OVERVIEW

FOREWORD

I am delighted to be able to offer a few words to introduce this incredibly useful book for primary teachers wanting to teach programming. This book represents a much-needed, very accessible introduction to teaching programming with Scratch – it's going to be a valuable resource for teachers – and for all those involved with introducing young children to the essentials of programming. It has links to many of the excellent resources developed by the author himself, available at http://code-it.co.uk.

Scratch, the language used throughout this book, was developed as a programming language nearly twenty years ago and was released in 2007. Even in its original form it was a game-changer for learning to program, as the drag-and-drop nature of Scratch blocks reduced learners' reliance on correctly typed syntax commands and made programming genuinely accessible to young children. Since then it has evolved and developed and become even more intuitive and user-friendly, as well as incorporating concepts such as blocks and variables, which mean that learners can gain more understanding of the key programming concepts and develop more efficient programs.

Scratch is the ideal language in which to situate early programming, but this book offers much more than that. It's not just a tutorial for teachers on how to use Scratch, and neither is it a set of resources, although it does offer both of these. In this book, Phil draws on this wealth of experience to explain the rationale behind research-informed approaches to teaching. He has drawn on specific strategies from the research literature and taken them into the classroom, adapted them for primary education, iterated them through his own practice and now is sharing them with other teachers. Moreover, he is able to illustrate it with examples of learners' work, which I believe teachers will find incredibly useful.

The range of topics addressed in this book is very impressive. As well as covering key programming concepts including sequence, selection, loops and procedures, the book covers specific strategies for using in lessons, including concepts before code, Parson's problems, PRIMM and faded worked examples. The importance of design, collaboration and reading aloud (all close to my heart!) are highlighted, and there are specific examples to support teachers with assessment. What a treasure trove!

Finally, I can't finish this short foreword without expressing my huge admiration and respect for the author, Phil Bagge. Phil has been one of the leading lights of primary computing education in England since it started to evolve ten years ago, creating research-informed and classroom-tested resources and generously making them available for primary teachers everywhere. He is incredibly open to new ideas and sees himself as a lifelong learner, whilst able to critically engage with research and transform it into useful practice. He thinks deeply about how learners learn, and as a reflective professional is invested in each and everyone of his pupils and their progress and well-being. Thanks Phil for everything you have contributed to the computing teaching community!

Sue Sentance
University of Cambridge & Raspberry Pi Foundation

INTRODUCTION

Who is this book written for?

This book is aimed at KS2 primary teachers and KS3 secondary teachers.

Why was it written?

To introduce a range of research supported programming methodology that works in the classroom in a way that non-specialist teachers can action in their own classrooms.

To share the joy and creativity of block-based programming through knowledge that leads to greater progress and higher pupil agency.

How should I use it?

If you have little programming knowledge, I suggest you start with the concepts before moving on to pedagogy.

If you have some programming knowledge, I suggest you dip into the chapters that are new to you.

If you are frustrated with your current methods of teaching programming, start with concept before code and then move on to code comprehension.

If you are struggling to support pupils in your classes, then the More Support section will be a good place to start.

Is it complete?

No book on programming with younger pupils is complete. We are still at such an early stage in our understanding of this area. I am pleased to announce that Hampshire's Inspection and Advisory Service will be turning any profit from this book into further revisions and more research informed writing.

Are there modules of work to use with my class?

There are four companion books to this which include fully resourced modules to use with your class

Scratch IT–Teaching Primary Programming in Year 3

Scratch IT–Teaching Primary Programming in Year 4

Scratch IT–Teaching Primary Programming in Year 5

Scratch IT–Teaching Primary Programming in Year 6

This volume has been designed to help you gain a depth of knowledge in teaching block-based programming regardless of whatever programming scheme of work you choose.

Is this book still useful if you choose other resources to teach?

Yes, research-informed methods are always useful in improving the knowledge you choose to teach, the order or progression you choose to teach it in and the methodologies and support strategies you choose to use.

Who knows, you may even be inspired to write and share your own modules of work.

Phil Bagge
01/02/2022
@baggiepr
code-it.co.uk

CONCEPTS

Sequence

CHAPTER 1

Dictionary Definition

Sequence

A particular order in which related things follow each other (Oxford English Dictionary)

To combine things in a particular order, or discover the order in which they are combined (Cambridge Dictionary)

Simple Sequence

Programming is about sequence, and sequences can contain all other forms of programming concepts, loops, conditions, variables, procedures, etc. For the teacher introducing programming to the novice it helps to distinguish between simple sequence, where one command follows another with no other programming concepts used, and complex sequence, which combine sequence with any other programming concepts.

Precise Instructions, Proper Outcomes

Watch this Jam Sandwich Algorithm video to discover the unintended consequences when instructions are not precise enough. https://youtu.be/leBEFaVHllE

People are often very imprecise, relying on others to fill in or end sentences or interpret instructions using common sense. Digital devices can only follow precise instructions and predefined rules. This is because they don't have the ability to interpret instructions that a human has. Even AI is only a way of teaching a computer to make a simple decision based on clear criteria learnt from exposure to multiple examples. It still depends on the programmer asking the right question and establishing the right set of criteria to be useful.

Everyday Precision

We shouldn't leave precision to the coding stage to introduce, as block-based programming commands are as precise as they can be.

It is most easily introduced when thinking about everyday algorithms. Consider these simple instructions and how we can make them more precise. Pupils can engage with precision without any programming knowledge.

Everyday Algorithm Example

Good	Better
Stand up	Stand up
Clap	Clap for 10 seconds
Sit down	Sit down

13

Algorithm Precision

        Triangle
        Start drawing
        Three steps forward
        Turn right 120 degrees
        Three steps forward
        Turn right 120 degrees
        Three steps forward
        Turn right 120 degrees
        Stop drawing

Take away the last three instructions one by one. Although it only fails to draw a triangle once the third from bottom is removed, if the other two instructions are removed, drawing other shapes after this one becomes much more problematic, as you are still drawing and not facing in the same direction as you did when you started.

Wait

The most important code block to the novice programmer is the simple wait command. Even simple sequences on a digital device can run so quickly that a human is unable to follow them.

A wait command slows the program down and allows the user to see what is happening.

Create these code blocks and then left click on them to run them one section at a time. At most you will see only one change, but mostly you will see no changes. Now introduce wait commands between each block. Now you are able to see the effect of each command.

Built in Pauses

Some blocks will have their own built-in pauses. Separate wait blocks are not needed for these.

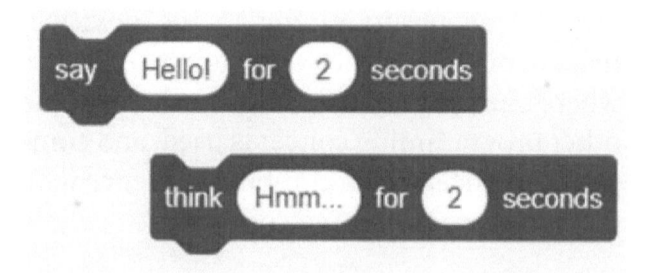

Helping pupils to identify blocks that run as quickly as possible and those that have their own time to execute is an important part of using simple sequence effectively. Say and think commands are useful for this as they have both types.

This code when run would only show, Good to hear!, And that would only be displayed if there was no other block underneath.

Different Instructions Produce Same Outcome

There are many different ways of coding an outcome. Consider these two sets of simple sequence instruction to draw a square in Scratch.

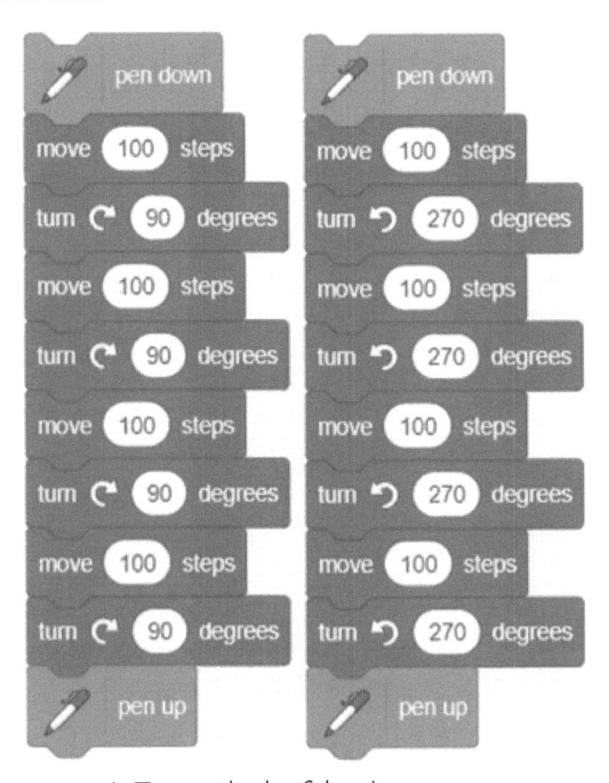

A, Two methods of drawing a square

These are not the only possible permutations to draw a 100-pixel-length square: they are not even the most elegant or adaptable.

The Best Method

Lets digress from simple sequence as we think about what methods produce the best code and the order we might introduce these.

This is important from many different perspectives. Pupils should be encouraged to find alternate ways to produce the same outcome, to compare methods and ask which was the best.

Programming is not a one-solution-only subject and at best can have many answers depending on the criteria that teachers are wanting to introduce or emphasise.

1. **The shortest code,** both examples in diagram A would not be the shortest, as a count-controlled loop would reduce the number of blocks

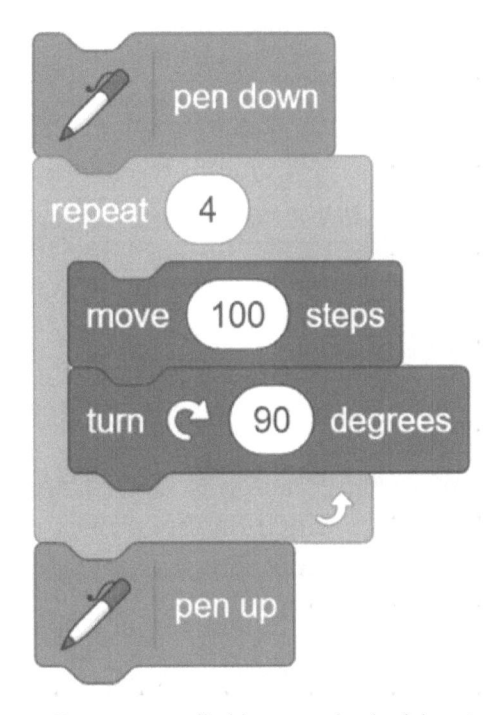

Count-controlled loop method of drawing a square
see chapter on repetition for more detail

2. **The most elegant** code uses the best programming concept suitable for the task. In the case of a simple square then a count controlled loop would make these programs more elegant.
3. **The most easily adapted** would involve the use of either variables for length and turn, so these can be easily changed or a procedure with parameters that can be changed with every instance used. (See chapter 4 on variables, and see chapter 5 on procedures.)
4. **The most efficient** uses the least memory and processing power. Both of these in diagram (A) are very efficient, as no other extra processes such as loops need to be processed by the device running this.

Clearly we can't introduce all these criteria straight away, my recommendation is a gradual introduction of the first three in primary and elementary practice, with the fourth being left to programming at a higher level.

Order is Important

The two square scripts in diagram (A) on the last page are an example of simple sequence where the order is important. Whilst we can find a few simple programming scripts or algorithms where the order is not important, in the vast majority of cases the order is very important.

Control Flow

Another aspect of sequence is the control flow, the order in which instructions are acted on by the program. You can find out more about that in chapter 27.

Sequence Research

The only research into sequence at primary/elementary level is that by the Everyday Computing Team based at the University of Chicago. You can view their excellent sequence trajectory on the next page. Do visit their website to learn more about their research.

Conclusion

It can be tempting to rush through simple sequences to get to the more exciting

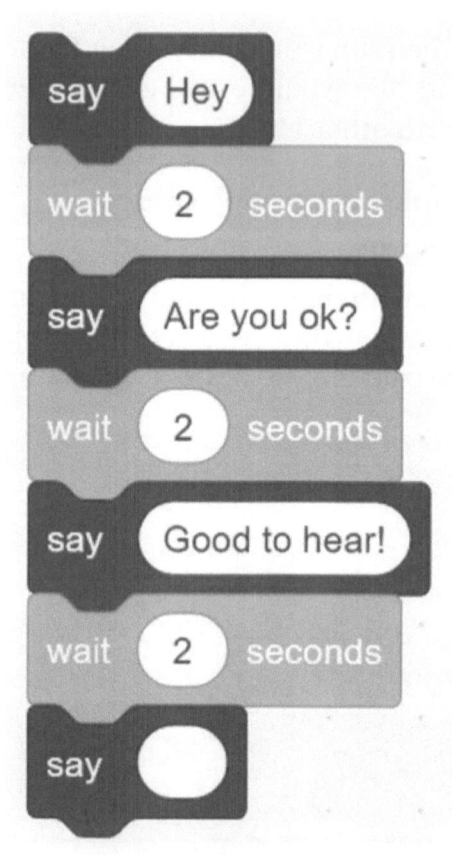

Conversation with separate pause blocks

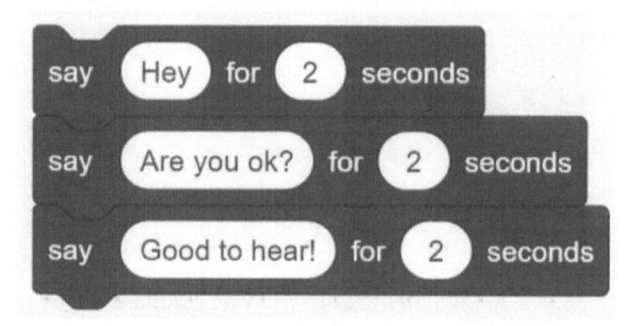

Conversation with built in pauses

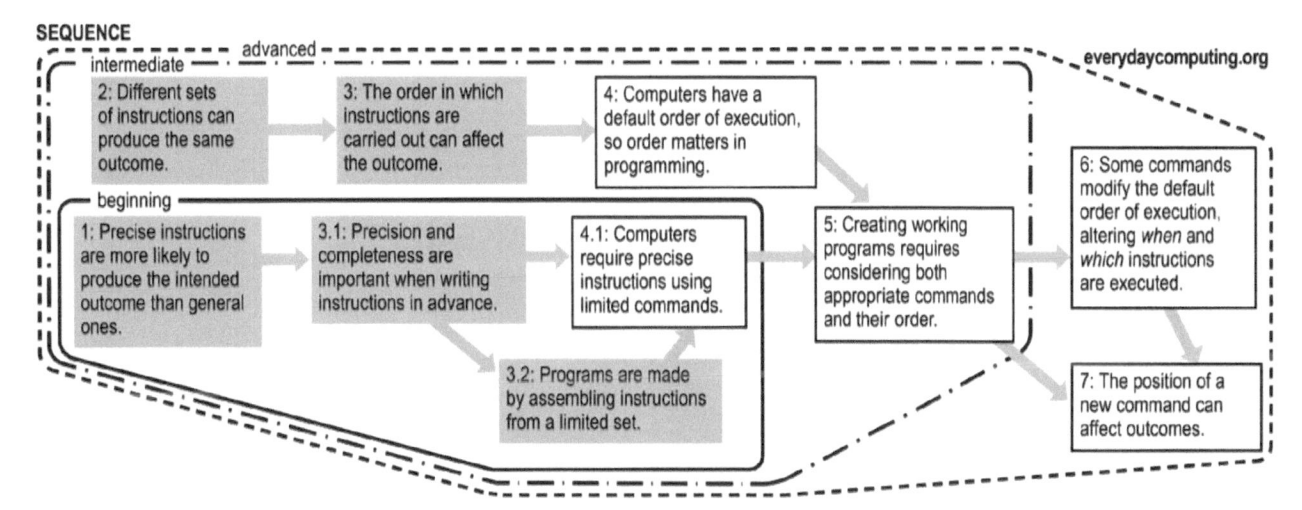

SEQUENCE

everydaycomputing.org

intermediate — *advanced*

2: Different sets of instructions can produce the same outcome.

3: The order in which instructions are carried out can affect the outcome.

4: Computers have a default order of execution, so order matters in programming.

6: Some commands modify the default order of execution, altering *when* and *which* instructions are executed.

beginning

1: Precise instructions are more likely to produce the intended outcome than general ones.

3.1: Precision and completeness are important when writing instructions in advance.

4.1: Computers require precise instructions using limited commands.

5: Creating working programs requires considering both appropriate commands and their order.

3.2: Programs are made by assembling instructions from a limited set.

7: The position of a new command can affect outcomes.

Published with the permission of the Canon Lab at the University of Chicago. You can view the original at http://everydaycomputing.org/public/visualization/ and find out more about their research.

programming concepts. I recommend that you pause to explore: precision in algorithm; time elements and different ways to program the same effect in code. These will help your pupils to make greater use of more complex programming concepts when they are introduced to them later.

Key Sequence Knowledge

A sequence is the order in which actions/instructions follow each other

Algorithmic Knowledge

I can make my instructions more precise so that they are more likely to be followed exactly as I wanted them to be

I can finish my instructions so no one will be in doubt as to what they do

When planning an algorithm that will be converted into code I will consider what type of instructions can be turned into code and use these

Programming Knowledge

I am careful to order my sequence as I know that the same blocks ordered in a different way will produce different outcomes

I can include wait commands in sequences to slow down the speed that blocks without timings are run in Scratch

I can choose a way to start my sequence that might involve a keyboard, mouse or trackpad input so they can be run

---

Types of Knowledge Key

Declarative Knowledge

Static facts or knowledge stored in your memory

Procedural Knowledge

How to perform a specific skill or task

Conditional Knowledge

When to use declarative and procedural knowledge

Further Reading

What is a sequence in programming (simple)

https://www.vedantu.com/coding-for-kids/what-is-sequence-in-programming

What is a sequence in computing (simple)

https://www.theschoolrun.com/what-sequence-computing

Control Structures (Complex)

https://www.britannica.com/technology/computer-programming-language/Control-structures

Repetition

CHAPTER 2

Definition
Loop: A sequence of instructions that are repeated.

Language of Loops
Looping is not the only word used for this concept. Other popular ones include iteration and repetition.

Everyday Repeating Actions
Pupils already have a basic knowledge of everyday repetition. This may be the lyrics of a chorus in a popular song or the actions in a dance craze. Then there are the many mundane tasks that involve repetition: washing up, cleaning, decorating, to name a few. Making these links with pupils' established schema of understanding grounds our new interpretation of repetition to established knowledge.

Programming Loops

Count-controlled loop
A count-controlled loop is one that has a number that controls how many times the loops will run for. This loop might have one or many instructions that are repeated.

Count-controlled loop in algorithm
Fill glass with water
Loop 5 times
    Drink water
    pause

Count-controlled loop in code

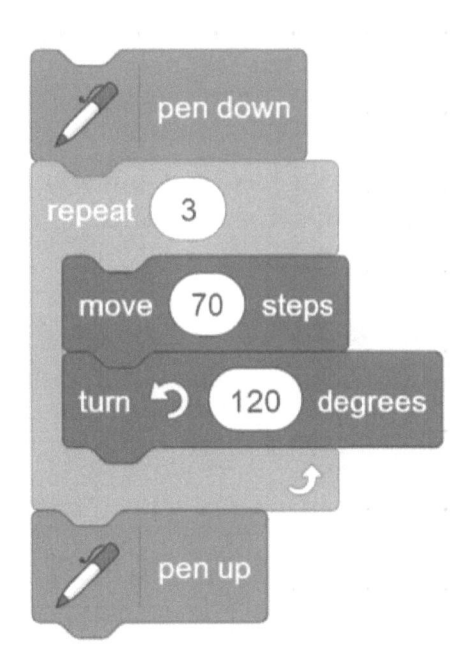

```
pen down
repeat 3
    move 70 steps
    turn ↺ 120 degrees
pen up
```

Act Two Times Same as Act, Act
Helping pupils see that a sequence of the same commands can be replaced with a

count-controlled loop and vice versa is important for understanding both why we might choose to loop (less instructions, more elegant code) and how it works.

Jump
Jump
Jump

Same as

Loop 3 times
    Jump

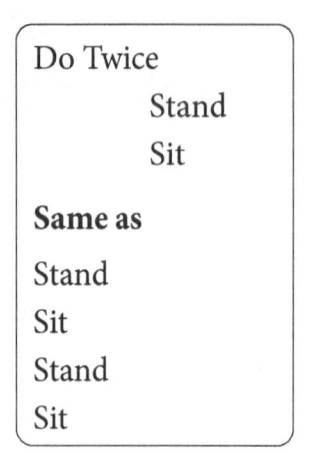

Do Twice
    Stand
    Sit

Same as

Stand
Sit
Stand
Sit

Role-playing simple count-controlled loops in this manner before writing their own to test their understanding, followed by converting a simple sequence to a loop and vice versa, are useful steps in comprehending how a simple count-controlled loop works.

Count-controlled loops have a definite end. Once the number of loops defined by the number is complete they end.

Indefinite Loops

Indefinite loops are ones where we don't know when they are going to end or how many loops they will complete.

The simplest indefinite loop in Scratch is the forever or infinite loop.

Infinite loop in algorithm

Loop always
    Check your phone

Infinite loop in code

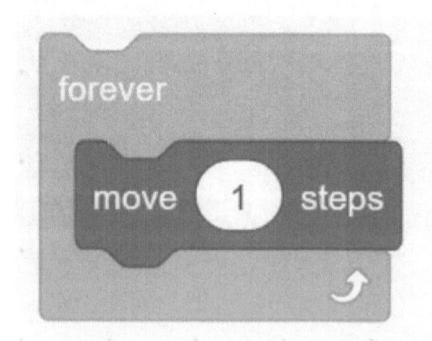

[forever { move 1 steps }]

Unlike a count-controlled loop, the infinite loop has no ending, which means that no programming structure can be built after it. Most programming languages do not have infinite loops, but it is a very useful stepping stone towards greater complexity.

Condition-ends-loop

A condition-ends-loop is also an indefinite loop in that we do not know when it will end or how many times it will repeat.

Unlike our infinite forever loop there is a way of ending the loop using a condition.

Condition-ends-loop in algorithm

Start eating food
Loop until full up
- Eat

You might have noticed that I have chosen to indent each action inside a loop algorithm. This helps the reader to know what is inside the loop. An algorithm can be written in any way the writer chooses, and so it is possible to choose some other way to show what is inside a loop, such as bullet points, as long as it is clear to another human reading it.

Condition-ends-loop in code

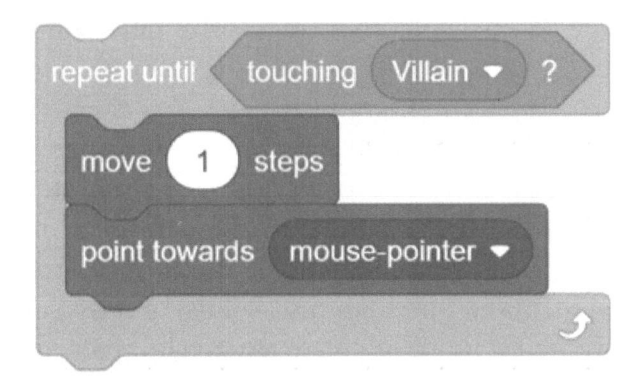

Loop Ended by a Condition

Condition-ends-loop flow of control

Many pupils believe that as soon as the condition is met the loop will end. Whilst this is generally true, it actually only ends if the condition is true at the moment it is checked in the flow of control.

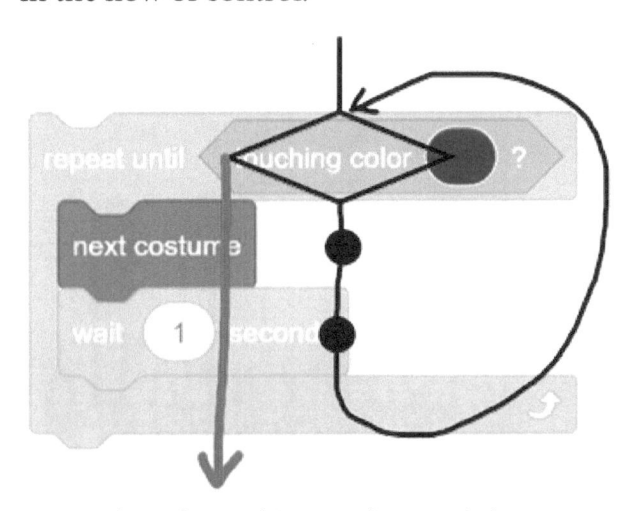

Flow of control in a condition-ends-loop

In our flow of control example above, if our sprite was touching the colour purple while waiting one second but was not touching purple when the condition is checked, the loop would not end.

The condition is checked represented by the diamond, as we have not touched the colour purple we proceed down the black line to run next costume (dot) and wait (dot). The loop then goes back to check the condition (diamond) if we are touching purple we would exit the loop via the green line. (To help you understand this more, read chapter 27 on flow of control.)

Cumulative effect

Repetitive tasks such as washing up, cleaning and decorating, all have a cumulative effect, they all build on the previous action to achieve a greater purpose be that clean dishes, clean home or fresh painted wall. Some, but not all, programming uses of repetition will share this attribute. In this counting program a count-controlled loop has a clear cumulative affect, as the number increases from 0 to 9.

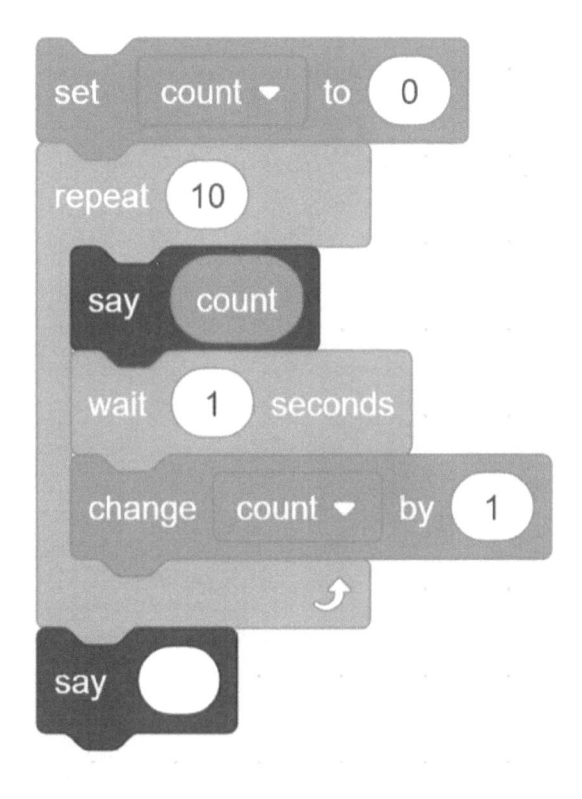

(You might want to read chapter 4 on variables, to help you understand this more.)

Variables Used to Control Loops

We have already seen that a variable can be used to create a cumulative affect and it can also be used to control the number of times a loop repeats.

In this example the user is asked how many sides they would like the shape to have. Their response is assigned to a variable called **no_sides**, which is short for number of sides. The value is then used to set how many times the count-controlled loop repeats and to divide 360 by the number assigned to the **no_sides** variable.

So if 3 is input by the user then the loop will repeat 3 times and turn 360 divided by 3, which makes 120 degrees, drawing a triangle.

A variable controlling number of repetitions

Loops Can be Nested

The everyday computing team put nested loops as their highest complexity aspect of primary/elementary repetition. You can view their trajectory at the end of this chapter. It is useful to reclassify this as more complex, as it was often taught soon after introducing count controlled loops in many primary/elementary curriculums. Whilst pupils can often nest loops to create wonderful patterns, they are often unable to explain how they work if introduced too early on.

Nested Loops Multiply

Loops that are nested inside other loops have a multiplying effect.

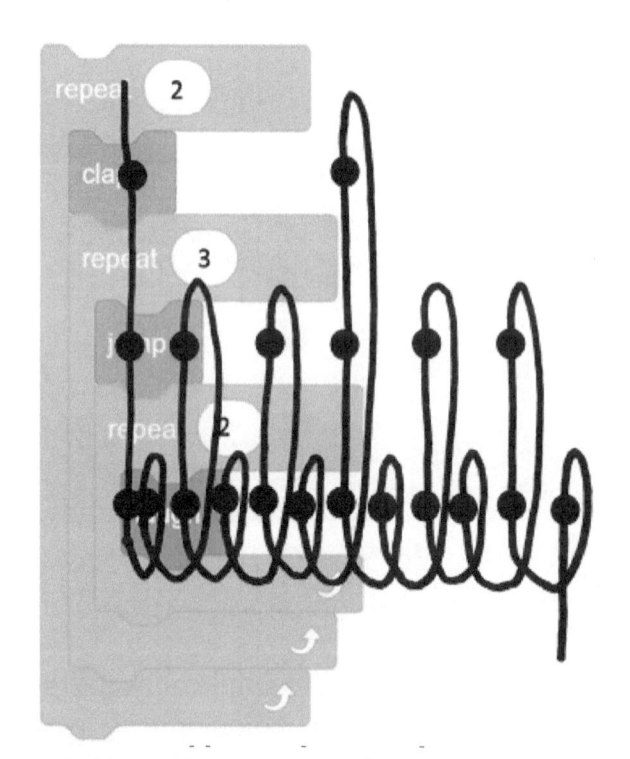

Nested loops shown using one flow of control notation

In this example we can see that the jump command is within two loops, and the repeat 3 loop is inside the outer repeat 2 loop. This means that both loops count values are multiplied by each other for the jump action, leading to 2×3 = 6 jumps.

Action	Maths	No. loops	Times run
clap	2×	1	2
jump	2×3	2	6
laugh	2×3×2	3	12

Can you calculate how many laughs (bottom purple block) there would be?

How Does it Stop?

Once you have more than one type of loop in your programming backpack you can ask pupils how the loop stops? This is more than just a formative assessment opportunity as it gets to the heart of what type of loop to use when. Count-controlled loops are useful where you want something to take place for a limited amount of time or distance. Infinite loops are useful if you don't want something to end.

Loops & Conditions

Loops have a very close relationship with conditional selection. They allow conditions to be acted on indefinitely. So much so that early Scratch had a block called **forever-if** that combined both aspects. Once conditions and indefinite loops have been introduced separately, the next step is to combine them to use them in gaming modules of work.

(You can read more about this on the chapter 3 on conditional selection.)

Order of Introduction

1. Count-controlled loop
2. Indefinite-loop
3. Loop-ended-by-a-condition
4. Conditions-checked-within-a-loop
5. Loop-controlled-by-variable
6. Nested-loops

This is my research-informed order to introduce loop types. This is based on my interpretation of the repetition trajectory from the Everyday computing team which is printed at the end of this chapter. It is also informed by the complexity of role-playing and writing repetition algorithms and working with flow of control for each of these loop types.

In my opinion, 3 and 4 are of a very similar complexity; if I have reduced time I leave out 3.

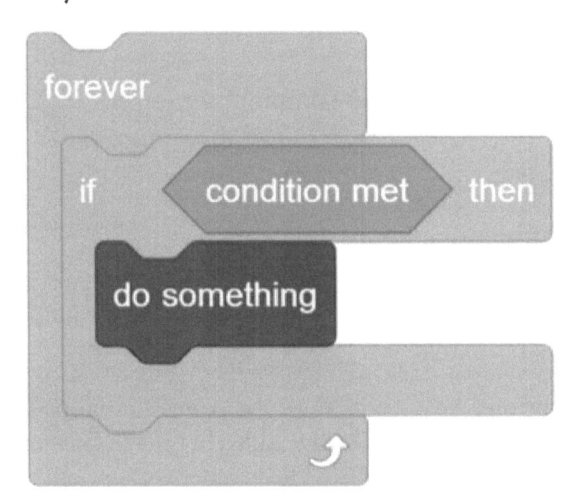

A condition checked inside a loop

REPETITION

everydaycomputing.org

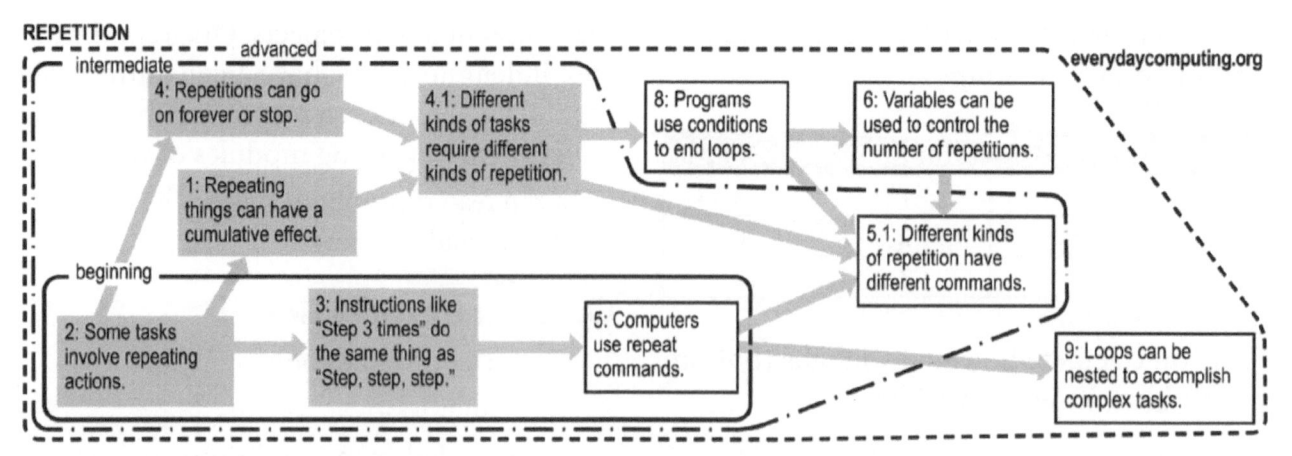

intermediate / advanced

- **4:** Repetitions can go on forever or stop.
- **4.1:** Different kinds of tasks require different kinds of repetition.
- **1:** Repeating things can have a cumulative effect.
- **8:** Programs use conditions to end loops.
- **6:** Variables can be used to control the number of repetitions.
- **5.1:** Different kinds of repetition have different commands.

beginning

- **2:** Some tasks involve repeating actions.
- **3:** Instructions like "Step 3 times" do the same thing as "Step, step, step."
- **5:** Computers use repeat commands.
- **9:** Loops can be nested to accomplish complex tasks.

Published with the permission of the Canon Lab at the University of Chicago. You can view the original at http://everydaycomputing.org/public/visualization/ and find out more about their research.

Key Repetition Knowledge

A loop is a sequence of instructions that are repeated

Indefinite means that the number of loops completed will not be known by the programmer.

Definite means the number of loops are known.

A **count-controlled loop** ends after the count is finished and is a definite loop

An **infinite** loop never ends and is an indefinite loop

A **condition-ends-loop** is ended by a condition and is an indefinite loop

Algorithmic Knowledge

I can write a loop as an algorithm using appropriate loop language such as do so many times, loop always, loop until or repeat x times.

I can indent actions inside a loop to make it clear they are inside the loop

Programming Knowledge

I can use a count-controlled loop where I want an sequence of actions to take place for a specific amount of time or over a specific distance

I can use an indefinite infinite loop where I don't want the loop to end once it has started

I can use an indefinite loop that is ended by a condition when I need the user or another program mechanism to interact with the loop end

I can nest count-controlled loops where I want to take advantage of the cumulative affect on inner loops

Types of Knowledge Key

Declarative Knowledge

Static facts or knowledge stored in your memory

Procedural Knowledge

How to perform a specific skill or task

Conditional Knowledge

When to use declarative and procedural knowledge

Further Reading

Definition of a Loop (simple)

https://www.thoughtco.com/definition-of-loop-958105

Programming Loops vs Recursion - Computerphile (complex)

https://www.youtube.com/watch?v=HXNhEYq-Fo0o (History of loops first 5 minutes)

Computer Science in K-12 An A to Z handbook on teaching programming edited by Shuchi Grover Chapter 18 Repetition and Recursion by Dan Garcia & Joshua Paley

Conditional Selection

CHAPTER 3

Dictionary Definition of Conditional

subject to one or more conditions or requirements being met (Oxford Dictionaries)

Dictionary Definition of Selection

A choice of something (Paraphrased from Cambridge Dictionary)

When we combine these we find that a condition or conditions met or not met lead to a specific choice.

A condition acts as a switch

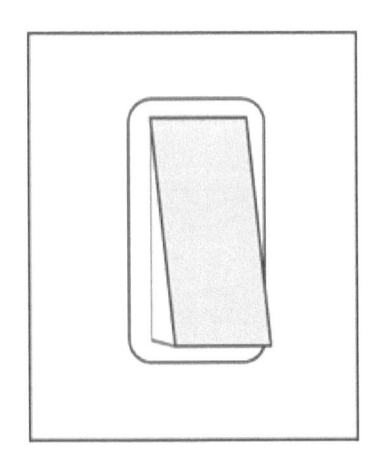

Alternate Words

Sometimes computer scientists talk about conditionals.

Actions Often Result from Specific Causes

The language of school, home and playground is full of conditional selection if only we look for it.

If you work hard
   you will do well at school

If you eat all your vegetables
   you will grow big and strong

If you don't finish your school work
   you will need to stay in to finish it!

Each of these examples has a specific condition (in red) that will trigger a specific event tied to that condition (in green).

Recognising everyday conditional selection and being able to identify which part is the condition and which are the actions is a good first step.

Condition-starts-action

In the simplest examples, if the condition is met events follow, but if the condition is NOT met, no actions will follow.

In this example, if we are NOT touching red, the program will proceed without saying anything. If we are touching red, it will say touching red.

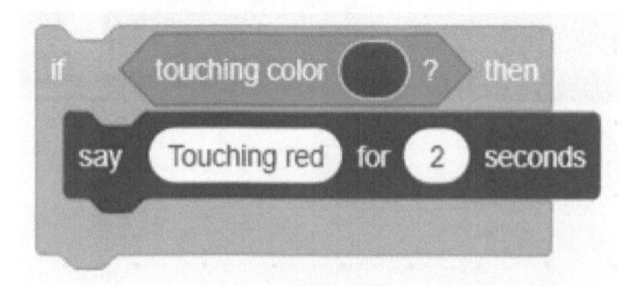

Another way to understand these pathways is through a flow chart such as the one below.

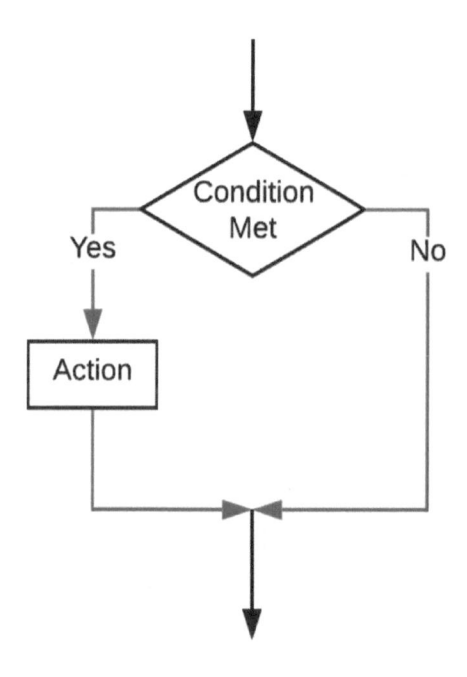

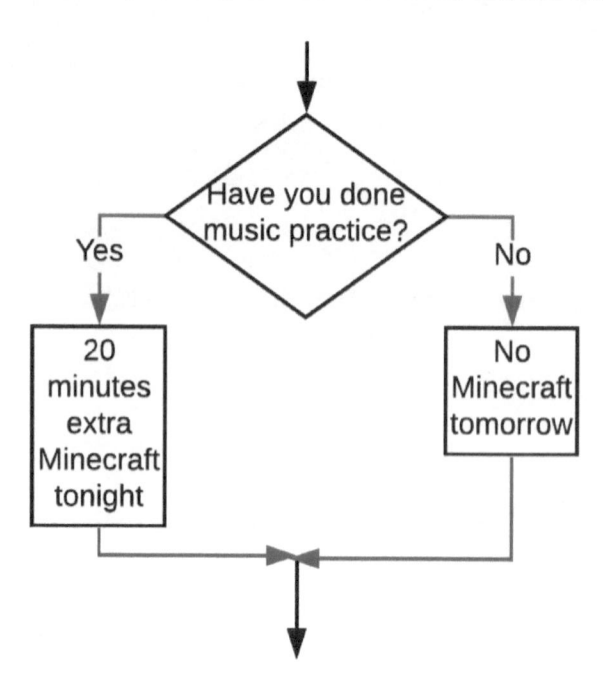

A simple Scratch example might look like this.

Condition-switches-actions

In the previous example, actions proceeded after the condition was met. If you didn't touch the colour red, no actions occurred.

We know that failure to meet many everyday conditions lead to actions.

If you do your music practice you can have an extra 20 minutes on Minecraft. If you don't do it tonight then no Minecraft tomorrow.

If you answer Adina to the question, then you are welcomed to the game. If you type anything else then you are warned off and the game is stopped.

Met or Not Met

For a programming language this decision is totally binary. You have either typed Adina or you haven't! If a computer was analysing if you had done your music practice, probably if it detected music for 20 minutes, then that example would be binary as well and you would only proceed down the red or blue path. You would be unable to do both at the same time or achieve some mix of both. Humans are less precise, and a parent might give part of a sanction or part of a reward. It is important to help pupils to understand the binary nature of conditional logic. A condition is either met or not met: there are no middle states.

Computers are Pedantic

For many programming languages, if you typed adina without a capital letter it would not be the same, as the condition would not be met. Scratch is more forgiving, but somewhere there is a hidden bit of programming telling the program to accept lower or upper case, so errors are reduced for novice programmers.

Understanding that precision and accuracy is essential in a program will help the programmer spot errors and think precisely and pedantically.

Logical Operators

It is far easier to start with simple easily understood conditions when beginning programming.

Scratch has many of these handily arranged in the same hexagonal shape.

However at some point you will wish to use logical operators to create more complex conditions. You have already seen an example of the easiest of these with our answer is the same as Adina in the code on the last page.

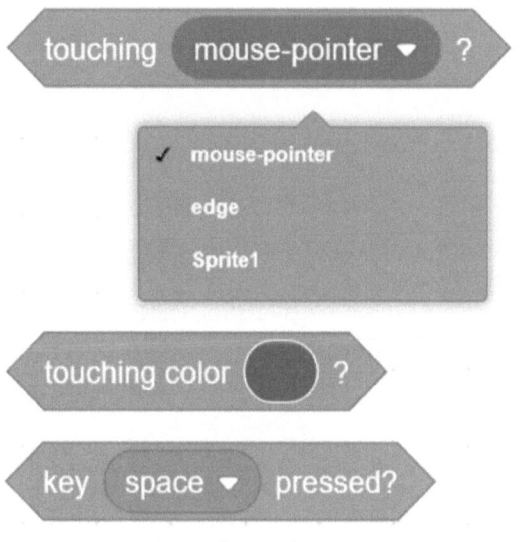

Hexagonal simple condtions in Scratch

Combining blocks

Created by combining more than one block as shown above, it compares the answer stored in an answer block to see if it is equal or the same as something, in this case the number 50.

The opposite of any condition can be created through the use of the NOT block.

Not block to check opposite of condition

Greater than or less than can be compared with any number stored in the answer[1] block.

---

[1] The answer block is used to demonstrate how conditions can compare data in different ways such as = < > etc. Any variable block could also be used. In fact the answer block is a type of variable block although we often don't introduce it as such to very young users.

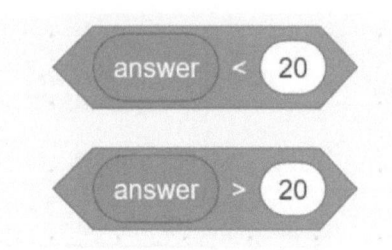

Scratch IT — Teaching Primary Programming with Scratch

[answer < 20]

[answer > 20]

Condition checks answer is less than or more than

As well as the four rules of maths, a wide range of mathematical operators can be used.

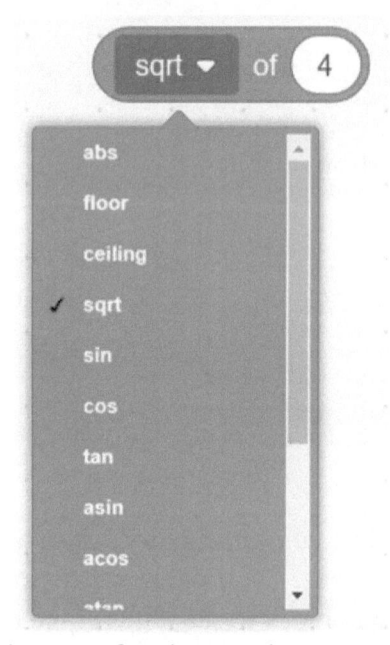

[sqrt ▼ of 4]

abs
floor
ceiling
✓ sqrt
sin
cos
tan
asin
acos
atan

Wide range of mathematical operators

Logical Operators Can be Used to Combine Conditions

In the top if-then block example below an OR has been used to combine two simple conditions that use an = or same-as operator. The OR means that only one of the conditions need to be met for the condition to be fulfilled.

In the second condition greater than and less than operators have been combined with an AND. This means that both conditions have to be met for the condition to be fulfilled.

In the example OR and AND are only used once in each condition, but they could be used many times if they are needed.

Stupid Humans

You might have noticed that if you type a number less than one or above four, in the example below, then nothing would happen. Programmers try to provide error messages if humans go outside of the things required. Whilst not immediately important for novice programmers, it can provide extension for those ready for the next challenge.

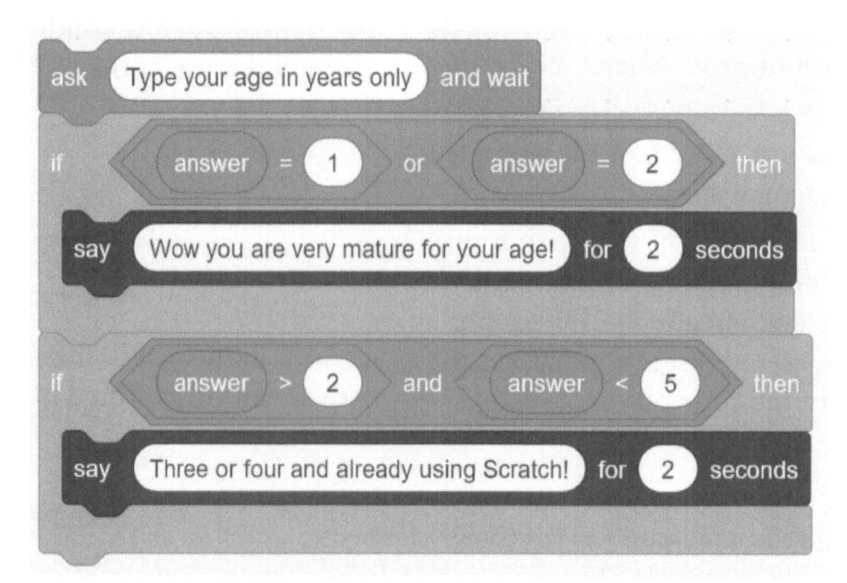

```
ask [Type your age in years only] and wait
if <answer = 1> or <answer = 2> then
    say [Wow you are very mature for your age!] for 2 seconds

if <answer > 2> and <answer < 5> then
    say [Three or four and already using Scratch!] for 2 seconds
```

Conditional Selection Can Create Branches in the Programme

Often when we are looking at simple novice use of conditional selection, the branches created by the conditions being met or not met join back again.

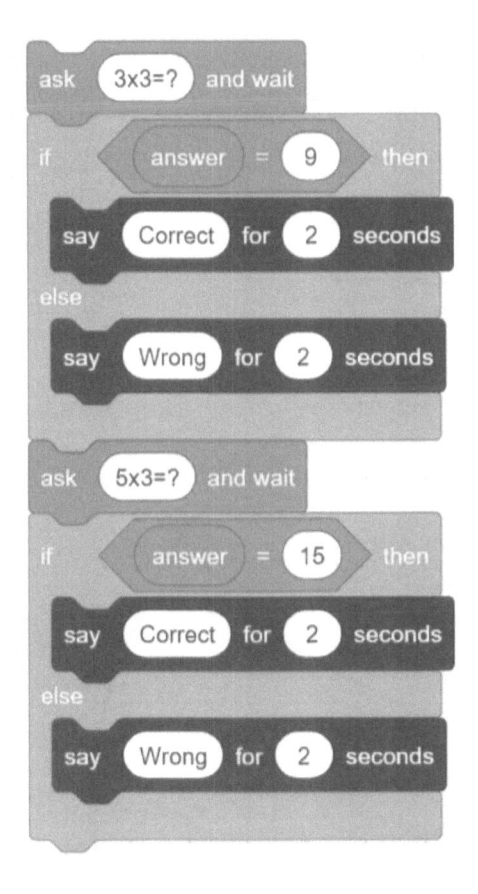

In the quiz above the second question will always be provided whatever the answer to the first question.

However this is not always the case and meeting or failing to meet a condition can lead to a totally different programming branch being activated.

In the quiz on the right, the user's answer to the first question will determine if they get a harder or easier question.

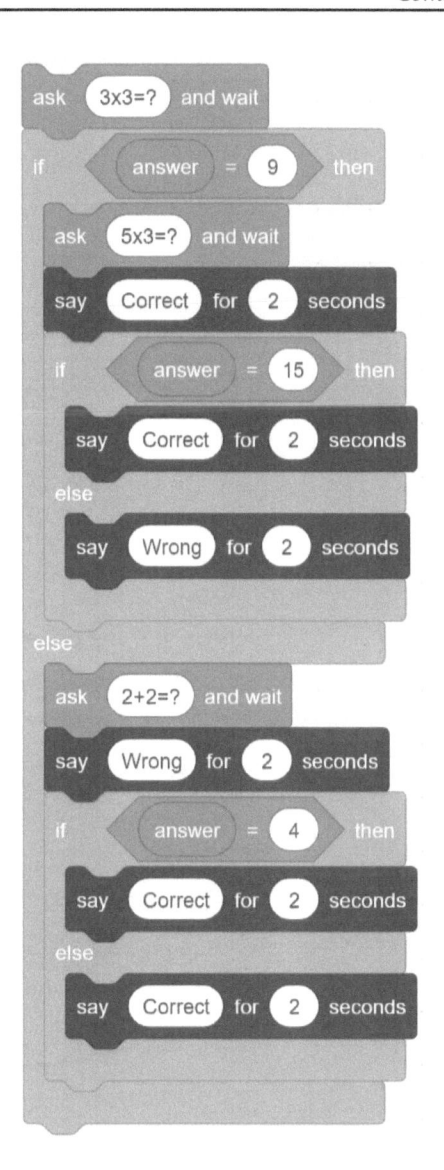

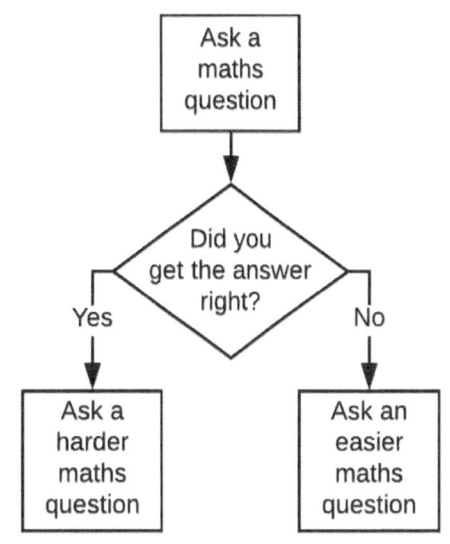

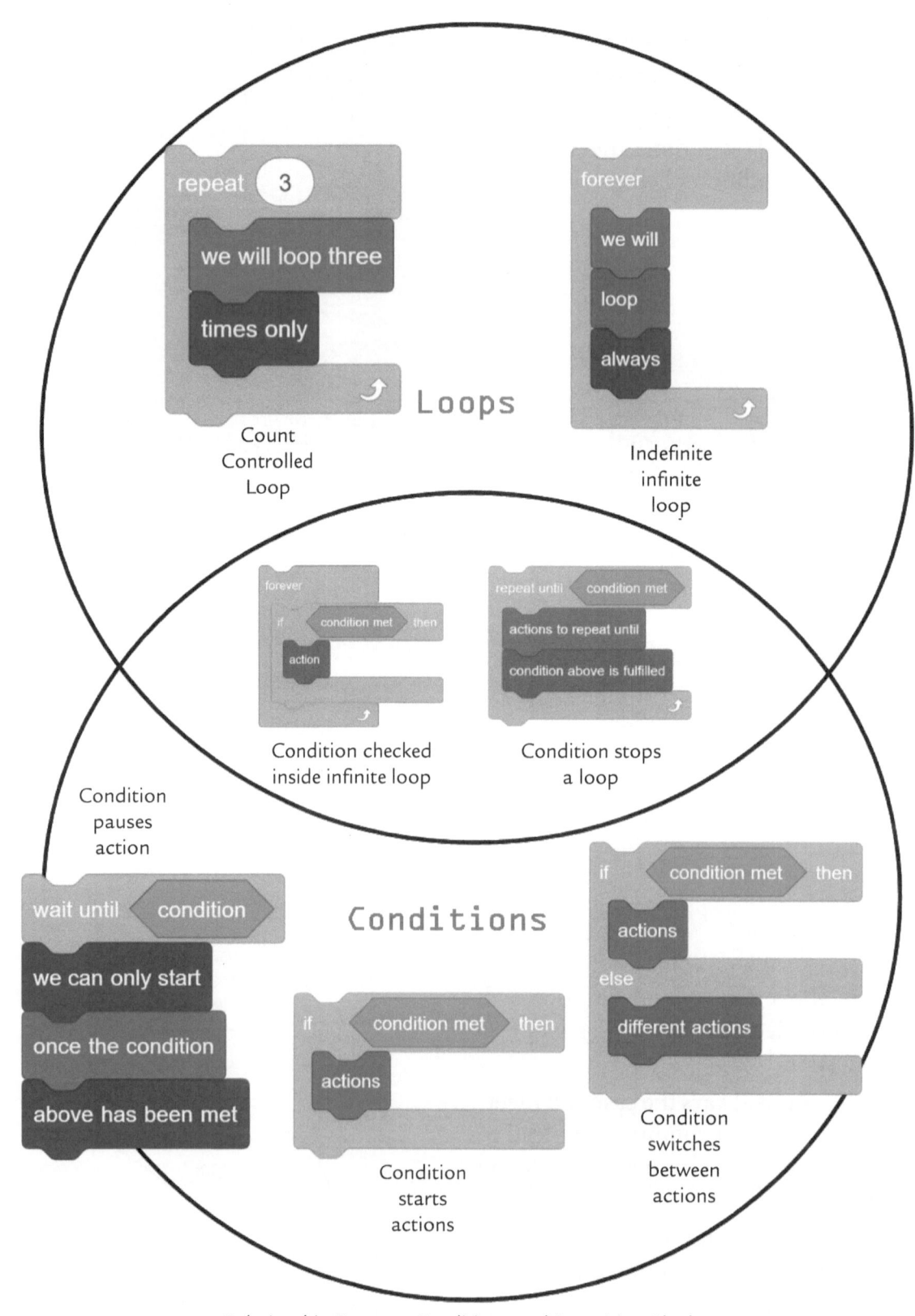

Scratch IT — Teaching Primary Programming with Scratch

Loops

repeat 3 — we will loop three times only
Count Controlled Loop

forever — we will loop always
Indefinite infinite loop

Conditions ∩ Loops

forever / if condition met then / action
Condition checked inside infinite loop

repeat until condition met / actions to repeat until condition above is fulfilled
Condition stops a loop

Conditions

wait until condition — we can only start once the condition above has been met
Condition pauses action

if condition met then / actions
Condition starts actions

if condition met then / actions / else / different actions
Condition switches between actions

Relationship Between Conditions and Repetition Blocks

Flow of Control

You may wish to read chapter 27 about flow of control to examine a simpler notation than flowcharts to show pathways when introducing conditional selection.

Complexity

As teachers we always have to decide what is the easiest thing to introduce first and what is a little harder, which we might leave as the next step. The Everyday Computing research published on the next page can definitely help us.

I have found that the simplest **condition-pauses-action** can be used by younger children as part of simple sequence if it is not introduced as a condition. This might be because it reads easily and makes simple logical sense.

These are also easy to concretise and act out physically. Wait here and only wave your hands when I touch you on the shoulder.

In my experience conditions are a little more complex than simple count-controlled loops and simple infinite-loops.

Condition-starts-actions are slightly less complex than condition-switches-actions, but only very slightly.

My order of complexity

1. Condition-pauses-actions
2. Condition-ends-loop
3. Condition-starts-action
4. Condition-switches-between-actions
5. Condition-starts-actions-within-a-loop
6. Condition-switches-actions-within-a-loop

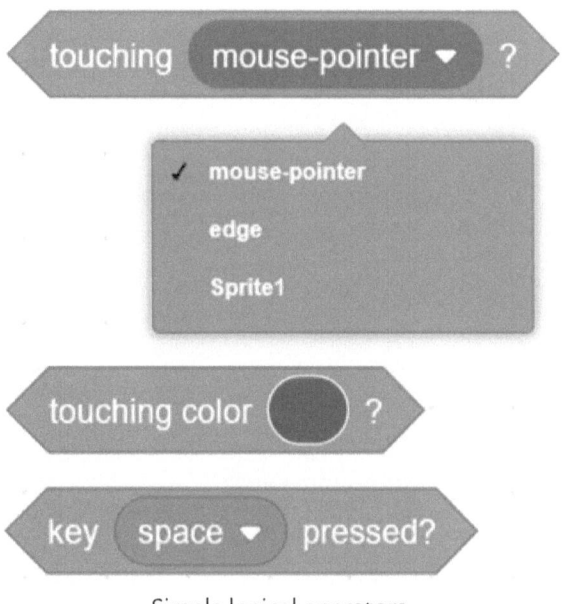

Condition-pauses-actions that might be used by younger pupils without being introduced as conditions

Simple logical operators

Earlier in this chapter, we mentioned simple logical operators as conditions but in reality points 3 and 4 above will need to use much more complex logical operators which compare data using = < and > to build conditions. These simple logical operators only become useful for points 5 and 6 when we have combined conditions with loops. Ideally we would use the simplest conditions when introducing 3 and 4 but useful projects are very limited.

Of these the least useful for simple novice programs is the condition-ends-loop, so if pushed for time it is the element I leave out.

Conditions inside loops

One of the most complex things to explain are points 5 and 6 in our order of complexity.

Here the flow of control diagrams and role-play really helps.

Loop always

    if touch shoulder

        turn right 90 degrees

Flow of control diagram and role-play

The teacher can explain that they are going to act out this condition within an infinite loop. They can point out that every time they get to the decision diamond they will ask the question: is my shoulder being touched? If it is, they will go down the orange pathway and turn right 90 degrees. If it is not being touched, they will go down the blue pathway. This and similar algorithms help pupils to see how conditions can interact within loops.

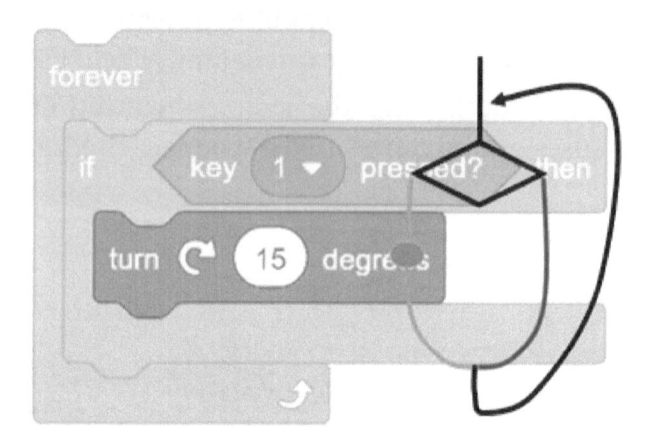

Flow of control diagram and code

If you act out this loop, make sure you go through the process lots of times to illustrate the infinite nature of the loop. Pupils enjoy acting these out as well, but often need to be prompted to ask the condition question out loud.

Conditional Selection

CONDITIONALS

- - advanced - -
- — intermediate —
- ···· beginning ····

everydaycomputing.org

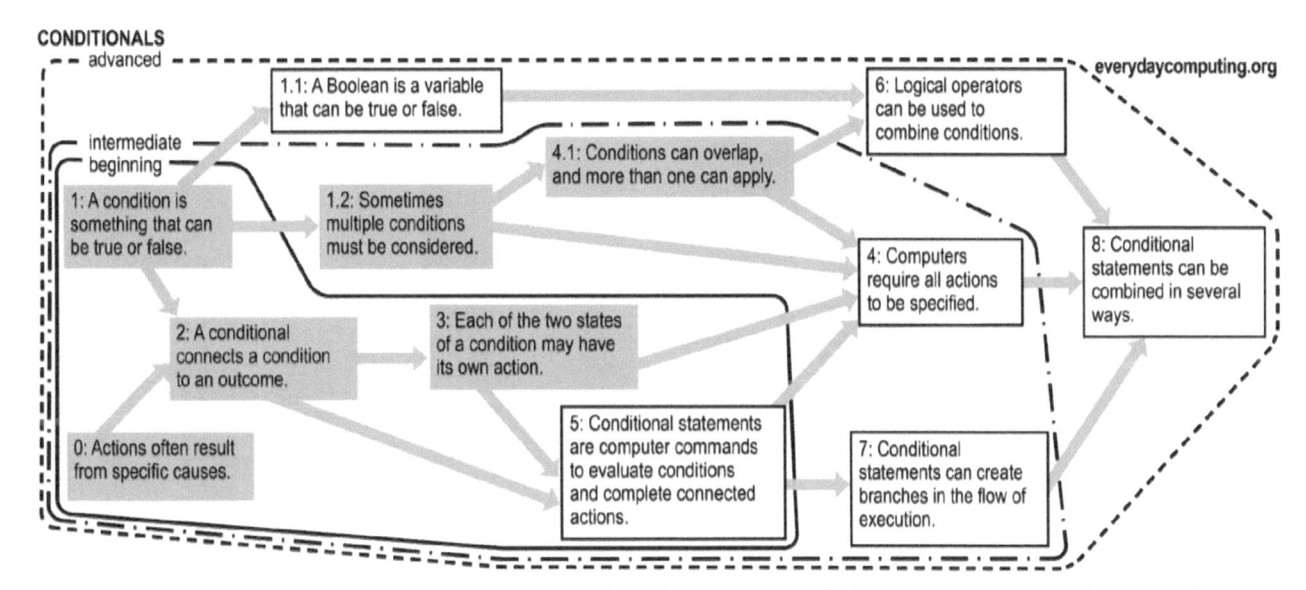

- **1.1:** A Boolean is a variable that can be true or false.
- **1:** A condition is something that can be true or false.
- **1.2:** Sometimes multiple conditions must be considered.
- **4.1:** Conditions can overlap, and more than one can apply.
- **6:** Logical operators can be used to combine conditions.
- **2:** A conditional connects a condition to an outcome.
- **3:** Each of the two states of a condition may have its own action.
- **4:** Computers require all actions to be specified.
- **8:** Conditional statements can be combined in several ways.
- **0:** Actions often result from specific causes.
- **5:** Conditional statements are computer commands to evaluate conditions and complete connected actions.
- **7:** Conditional statements can create branches in the flow of execution.

Published with the permission of the Canon Lab at the University of Chicago. You can view the original at http://everydaycomputing.org/public/visualization/ and find out more about their research.

Key Conditional Selection Knowledge

Conditions can be met (true) or not met (false); there is no middle option

A condition branches outcomes into two paths

A condition is only checked when it is reached in the flow of control

Conditions can be combined using AND or OR (KS3+)

Conditions can be inverted using NOT (KS3+)

Algorithmic Knowledge

I can indent actions that result from a condition being met or not met to separate them from actions not affected by selection

I can use if to indicate that a condition will follow in my algorithm

I can draw a flow of control diagram to show how a condition branches and what actions are on each branch

Programming Knowledge

I can use a condition-starts-action selection block to run code where a condition is true

I can use a condition-switches-between-actions selection block to run code where a condition is true or false

I can combine multiple condition-starts-action selection blocks to create multiple branches

I can use a selection block within a forever loop to check a condition over and over again

Types of Knowledge Key

Declarative Knowledge

Static facts or knowledge stored in your memory

Procedural Knowledge

How to perform a specific skill or task

Conditional Knowledge

When to use declarative and procedural knowledge

Further Resources

Flocabulary Conditions Video (includes Else if)

https://www.flocabulary.com/unit/coding-conditionals/

Computer Science in K-12 An A to Z handbook on teaching programming edited by Shuchi Grover Chapter 19 Selecting pathways with conditionals by Shuchi Grover.

Variables

CHAPTER 4

Many Aspects

Before we look at ways to introduce variables, let us briefly examine the range of information a programmer will need to fully understand variables in three simple examples in our table on the next page. A simple score that might be used in a quiz or game, a user input word such as a name that could be used to personalise almost any project and a variable that changes within a loop.

Name and Value

Variables have two parts: a name which we can use to refer to them in algorithms and programs, and a value. In the past I have often referred to this as like a box with a label on the side and objects inside. The concreteness of this analogy appealed to me because pupils can put real objects into a box to increase the value and take away physical objects to decrease the value. However, as soon as you try to move into negative numbers the box analogy falls apart. You also inherit other box-like traits such as their ability to accept lots of different types of objects at the same time, whereas a variable will only accept one type of object at a single time. A better, more universal introductory analogy is the whiteboard.

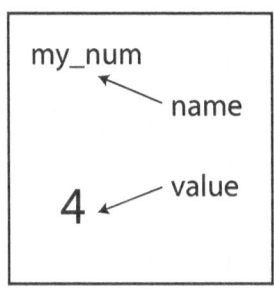

Variables are like whiteboards

Variety of Data

Whiteboards easily display a variety of different types of values such as numbers, strings (numbers, text, punctuation, etc.) and True and False. Unlike the values put into a box, which often couldn't be seen, a whiteboard's variable value is clearly visible.

Assigning

When I used the box variable example, I often used lots of box language. Values were inside the variable/box, the variable contained a number or word. I now use the word 'assign' right from the start. 'Assign' has no unwanted connotations: it implies something linked to something else but

Variable to collect a score	Variable as a placeholder for a name	Variable using a loop to count
Variable consists of a name and a value	Variable consists of a name and a value	Variable consists of a name and a value
When a value is linked to a variable, we call it assigning	When a value is linked to a variable, we call it assigning	When a value is linked to a variable, we call it assigning
Variables are named after their role	Variables are named after their role	Variables are named after their role
Values are assigned to variables at the beginning of an algorithm or program. This is called initialisation	Values are assigned to variables at the beginning of an algorithm or program. This is called initialisation	Values are assigned to variables at the beginning of an algorithm or program. This is called initialisation
In many programming languages the programmer has to decide if the variable is local or global	In many programming languages the programmer has to decide if the variable is local or global	In many programming languages the programmer has to decide if the variable is local or global
Number values can be assigned to variables	Text values can be assigned to variables. These are strings of characters which include text, digits and symbols	Number values can be assigned to variables
Read the name get the value. Variables can be used in place of numbers in any part of an algorithm or program	Read the name get the value. Variables can be used in place of string values in any part of an algorithm or program	Read the name get the value. Variables can be used in place of numbers in any part of an algorithm or program
Number values can be retrieved from variables, combined using mathematical operations and the results can be stored back in variables.	Variables can be assigned by the user through a keyboard input. *Some languages automatically store the most recent keyboard input in a variable called 'answer'.*	Number values can be retrieved from variables, combined using mathematical operations and the results can be stored back in variables.
		The value stored in a variable can be repeatedly changed each time through a loop

that this might not always be the case. A value may be linked ('assigned') to a variable at a given point, but at some point, the value might change or nothing might be assigned.

Not like a whiteboard

As with any analogy, it is important to explain how a whiteboard is not like a variable. You don't need to name a whiteboard you do need to name a variable or the digital device will be unable to recognise it as a variable.

Named after their role

Some pupils will not have encountered a variable in Maths or Science yet, but if they have, then their variables will have been letters rather than a description of what it represents. Encouraging pupils to name variables sensibly after the role they take is important. It makes their algorithms and programs much more comprehensible and aids the finding of errors (bugs). For the primary pupil novice programmer, their language understanding, is far in advance of any programming logic understanding, so readability is important. So, if a variable is used to collect a user's score, then 'score', 'points' or 'total' would be good names. If there are multiple scores we need to keep track of, then 'player_score' or 'users_points' are good names, because they further refine what the variable is being used for. Good habits are also important in naming variables. Text-based programming languages won't allow a space in the name, so using examples that link the words helps to encourage good practice. My thanks to Jane Waite for the use of the underscore example. In our normal writing we rarely use an underscore for anything else, so it makes multiple word variables stand out in algorithmic use as well as in programming. camelCase is another option.

Start well

Assigning value to a variable at the start of a program is called initialisation

What value will the score have before the quiz starts? What number will we start with when we start to count? Encouraging novice programmers to think about this in their planning improves their projects and leads to less frustrations in the programming and execution stages (see chapter on planning).

Scratch does not insist on initialisation of variables, but many later programming languages will, so teaching this early establishes good habits.

Types of Data

For the novice programmer we want them to know that we can assign numbers or strings (text that can contain punctuation and even numbers although they won't be treated like a number) to a variable.

One Type Per Example

On the previous page, we looked at the complexity of three uses of a variable: to collect a score, as a placeholder and to count using a loop. When creating variable examples for novice users it really helps to stick to one type of variable used in any code example rather than mixing them in the same example.

Keep it Simple

If we choose to assign numbers for our introductory examples, let us keep to low values to reduce cognitive load and keep all pupils with us. If we choose textual values, let us keep writing to a minimum for the same reasons.

Read the name, get the value

Part of the difficulty with a variables is seeing one thing (variable name) but acting on something hidden (variable value assigned). Part of our job as educators is to make the hidden visible, so that pupils can understand what is happening clearly. Your whiteboard can really help with this as pupils can see the value of the variable and see it change if it needs too.

Role Play Examples

Reading and acting out a few examples can be a great way of making sure pupils are really concentrating on how variables work without the complexity of code.

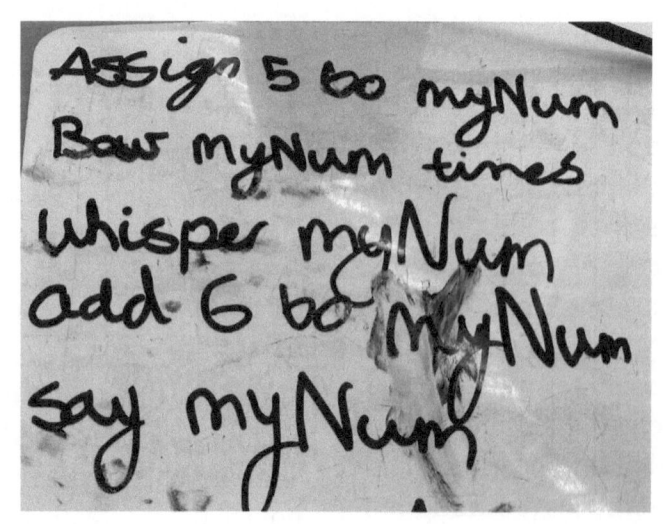

Year 6 (10-11) years old pupil creates an everyday algorithm with a variable called myNum that changes

String Example

Assign Florence to variable called best_friend

Say Hello best_friend

When we follow this algorithm we would say

Hello Florence

We read the name but act on the value

Number example

Assign 3 to variable called my_num

Stand up

Bow my_num times

Sit down

Wave my_num times

Say my_num

When we follow this algorithm we would

Stand up

Bow 3 times

Sit down

Wave 3 times

Say 3

Writing Everyday Examples

After acting out the teacher's everyday algorithms with variables, a great next step is to write their own like the one above. This also helps the teacher to spot any pupils who have faked understanding by copying their classmates' actions during the roleplay earlier.

Changeable Variables

The weather is variable, my moods are variable. Variable is a word that many pupils will have encountered already which will allow us to link to their pre-existing knowledge that 'variable' means 'changeable' before we introduce that variables can change during an algorithm or program. We can introduce how some variables can be constant (not changing) and others can be variable (changing).

Roleplay Variables Changing

The simplest introduction to changeable variables involves roleplay using everyday algorithms whilst tracking the changes using a whiteboard.

Assign 3 to variable called my_num

Stand up

Jump my_num times

Subtract 2 from my_num

Say my_num

What is changing in the story?	What might you call the variable that changes through the story?	What would the variable start at (initialisation)?	Can you say what value the changeable variable might have after walking in school?	What maths might be happening in the story?
Amount of steps	Steps	0	2002 + 945 = 2947	Add.

Every day variables examined with Year 5 Pupils

Sit down

Wave my_num times

Add 1 to my_num

Say my_num

When we follow this algorithm we would

Assign 3 to variable called my_num

Stand up

Jump 3 times

Subtract 2 from my_num

Say 1

Sit down

Wave 1 times

Add 1 to my_num

Say 2

Pupils enjoy writing their own examples and challenging their neighbours to act them out.

Real World Examples

The Vela project[1] by Grover and others explored how variables work in the world around us, in a drinks purchase, T-shirts for different ages, weather patterns over a day and the score at a basketball match. The questions prompt thought and discussion before using variables in programming.

Thinking about the concept before programming using a story is a really effective method of helping pupils to gain understanding before they use them in code.

Steps Example

In the example shared at the top of the page a simple story was told before pupils had to identify what the variable was, what was changing and the value of the variable at different stages of the project. This helps to build up a picture of variables as an everyday concept that affect our lives as well as a programming concept, something which I believe gives a concept more value.

Hidden Variables

Have a look at chapter 32 on more clues to find out about hidden built in variables in Scratch.

Rating Complexity

Of our three examples in the table, I would rate the placeholder variable as the least complex, followed by the variable collecting a score and then the variable in a loop. However, this is purely based on teaching all three rather than any research.

[1] http://csforall.sri.com/

Variables in Scratch

Scratch 3 comes with a singe pre-created variable called my variable, which I dislike because it breaks the rules. It is not named after what it does and there is a space in the name.

You can create your own variable easily by clicking on the make a variable button.

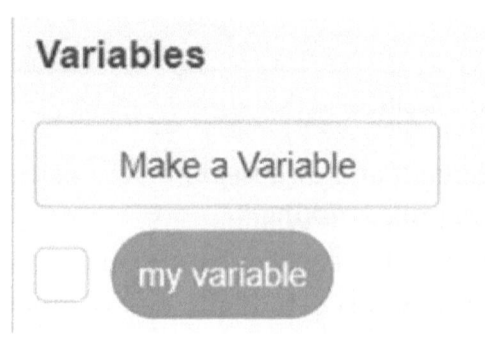

Make a Variable Button

Variables can be shown on the stage screen by checking the box next to their name.

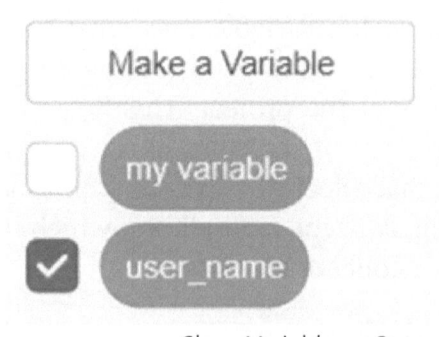

Show Variable on Stage

You can adjust the way a variable looks on screen by double clicking in the orange value area. The second view includes a slider, so the program user can directly interact with the variable.

You can decide if the variable is shown or hidden on the screen by using the show or hide variable blocks.

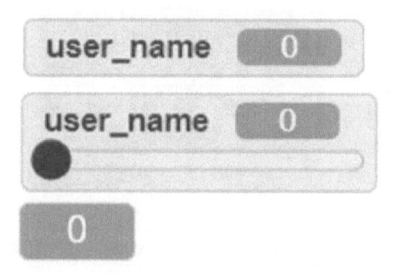

Three ways a variable can be displayed

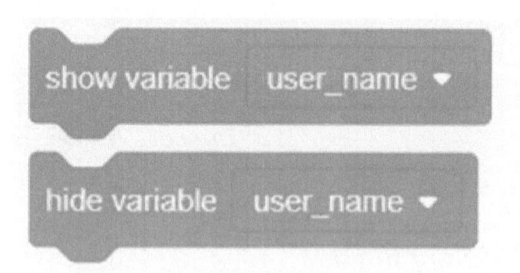

Show or Hide a Variable During a Program

Global or Local

When you make a variable you have to decide if it will be global, which means it can be used by any part of the program, or local, which means it can only be used by the sprite it was created in. For most primary project the global default is best.

Table Examples

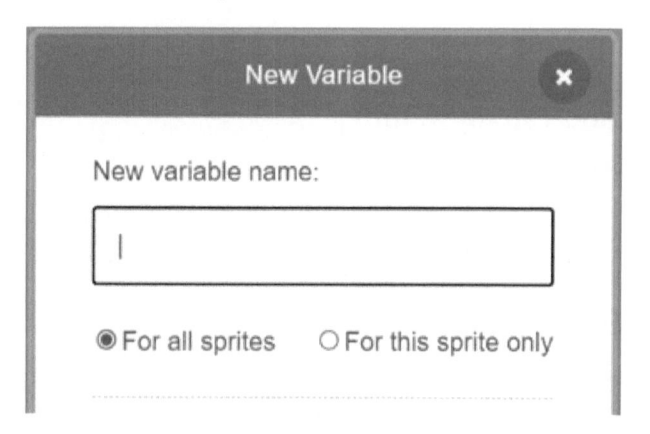

Global or Local Variable

Set or Change

Set removes the previous value and assigns whatever you tell it to. Change adapts the

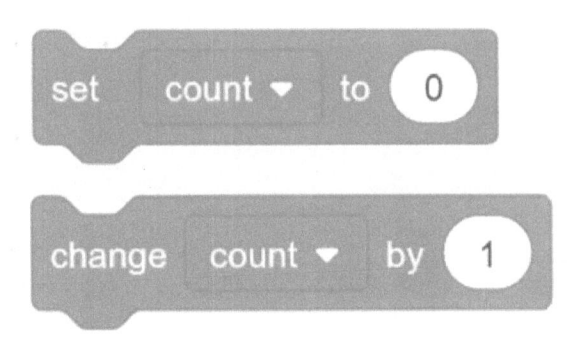

Set or change a variable

previous value assigned and can only be used with numbers.

Real World Placeholder Variables

Reserving a place for someone or something using a generic title such as Parking Bay or Bride, Groom and Best Man at a wedding are all example of placeholder variables that we assign values to at different times in life outside computing. Parking Bay 1 might have no value attached to it at 3am and then have Red Ford Escort assigned from 7:18am until 4:33pm. Drawing pupils' attention to these real world examples can help them to situate placeholder variables within their established worldview.

Although these examples are useful, I have yet to find a simple universal placeholder example that every pupil will instantly relate to. If you find one please do share it.

Placeholder Examples

In the first example below, we have assigned Flo to the variable called name in the first block and then in both say commands we have used the value of name in our text statements.

First Example Variable as a placeholder

Second Example Variable as a placeholder with value assigned by user

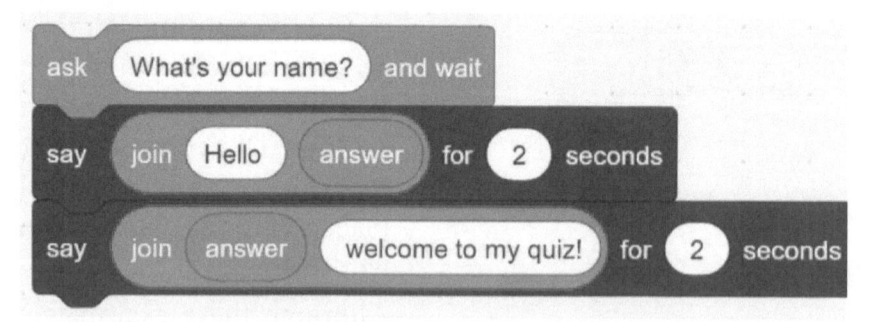

```
ask  What's your name?  and wait
say  join  Hello  answer  for  2  seconds
say  join  answer  welcome to my quiz!  for  2  seconds
```

Third Example answer Variable as a placeholder (not recommended)

The code when run would then read
Hello Flo
Flo, love what you are creating!

A small tweak to this code would ask the user to assign their own name through the use of the ask and answer input blocks as shown in Example 2.

Sometimes pupils try to use the answer block instead of a named variable block. This will technically work if the ask block is not used at any other point later in the program, as answer is a special variable assigned through the input ask block.

If the input ask block is used later in the program the value assigned to answer will be changed invalidating its use as a placeholder variable.

I would advise that you don't show this to pupils as it causes more problems than it solves and means the input block can't be used again in that program. The Third Example shows this imperfect solution.

Score Example

In Example 4 on the next page we can see score variable being assigned 0 on line 2. This initialisation ensures that every time the program is run the user will start with the same starting score of 0.

In line 4 the user is told that their score is 0 points.

They are then asked a question and if they get it correct a point will be added to the score on line 7 and if they get it wrong a point will be subtracted from the score on line 9.

Whilst we might find it harsh that a point is subtracted it is helpful to learn that the number assigned can be changed in many mathematical ways.

Finally on line 11 the score so far is reported to the user by reading the score variable and showing the value assigned at that point.

Collector

Sometimes this way of using a variable to collect a total is referred to as a collector variable.

Multiple Variables

A placeholder variable could also be added to this example so that the quiz is personalised, as shown in Example 5. I would recommend that you leave examples that combine variable uses to a later stage in pupils development.

An element of personalisation has been missed out of the example. Can you spot what this might be? The answer is at the end of the chapter.

Variable in a Loop

When I first started programming, I asked Professor Les Carr from the University of Southampton what variable examples we should show pupils. He said that the ability

Variables

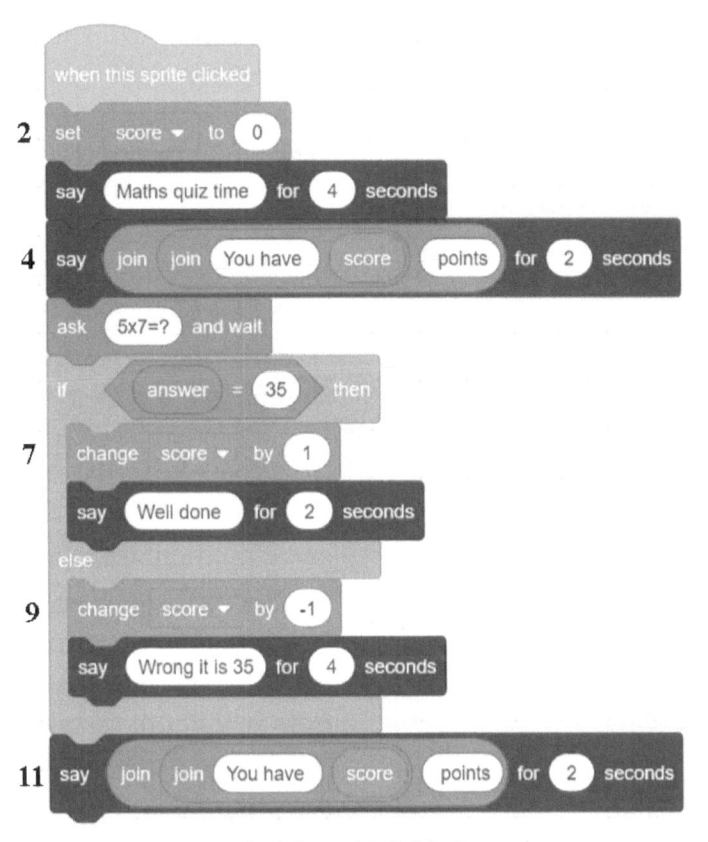

```
when this sprite clicked
2  set score to 0
   say Maths quiz time for 4 seconds
4  say join join You have score points for 2 seconds
   ask 5x7=? and wait
   if  answer = 35  then
7    change score by 1
     say Well done for 2 seconds
   else
9    change score by -1
     say Wrong it is 35 for 4 seconds
11 say join join You have score points for 2 seconds
```

Example 4 Score Variable Example

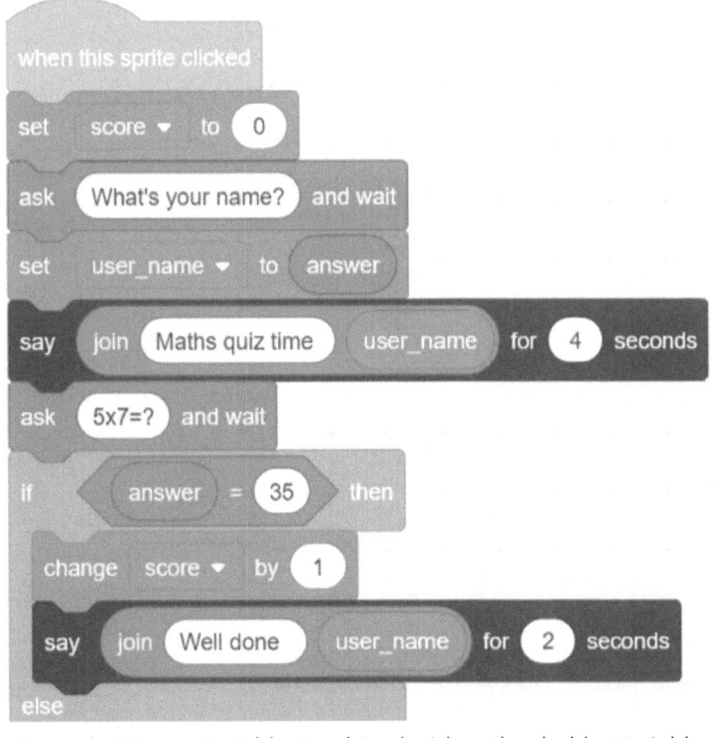

```
when this sprite clicked
set score to 0
ask What's your name? and wait
set user_name to answer
say join Maths quiz time user_name for 4 seconds
ask 5x7=? and wait
if answer = 35 then
  change score by 1
  say join Well done user_name for 2 seconds
else
```

Example 5 Score Variable Combined with a Placeholder Variable

to change a variable within a loop was a really important programming concept. As time has gone on I have seen how important a concept this is.

This seemingly simple idea can be used to count to 10 or adapted to count in any pattern you can think of.

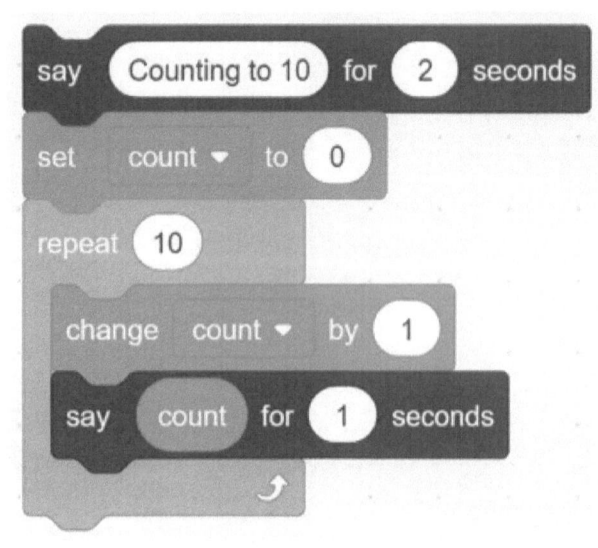

Using a variable to count to 10

One of my favourite lessons is asking pupils to modify code like this to make it count faster, backwards, in 7s, from 30, in multiples of 10, in halves, etc.

Flow of Control

To explore how the flow of control affects variables please see chapter 27 this is particularly important when examining a variable being changed by a loop.

Variables to do Maths

Another common use for variables is to complete mathematical operations.

In this example below all three variables are initialised to 0 at the start of the program. The user is then asked to type in two numbers which are assigned to num1 and num2. num1 and num2 are then added together and assigned to the total variable. The question and answer is then reported via the variables that they have been assigned to in the say block at the end.

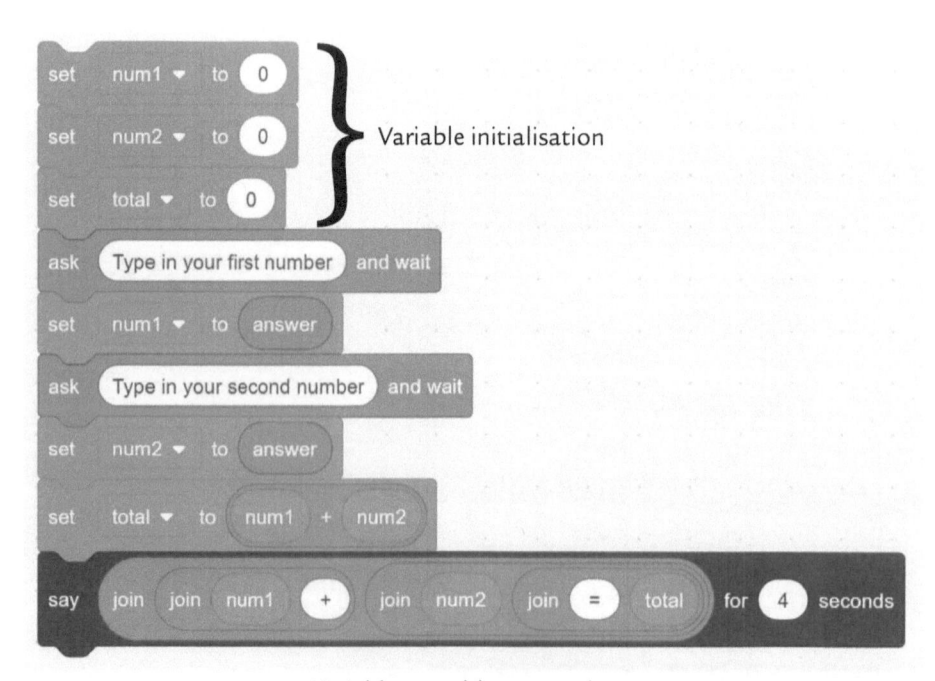

Variables to add two numbers

Redundant Initialisation

Because every variable block is using set rather than change any previous values are wiped out and our new values are overwritten. This means our initialisation is redundant. However, I would encourage you to teach pupils to initialise anyway, as this will help them establish good programming habits, and few programming languages are as forgiving as Scratch.

Key Variables Knowledge

Variables are used to store information to be referred to and changed in a computer program or algorithm

Variable have a name and a value

Read the variable name but act on the variable value

Variables can be global, affect the whole programme or local only affecting a part

When a value is attached to a variable we call it assigning

Algorithmic Knowledge

I can name a variable after the task it performs in my algorithm plan

I can name a variable using one word and camelCase or under_score to avoid confusion later in text based programming languages

I can avoid naming a variable using names used for other variables, procedures or lists to avoid confusion later in text- based programming languages

I can assign a value to a variable at the start of my algorithm plan so that the algorithm always works in the same way every time (initialisation)

I can add or subtract value to a variable where the variable is a number

Programming Knowledge

I can create a variable and show the value on the screen in Scratch so either I or the user can see the value

I can use a variable as a placeholder to refer to a value input by a user

I can use a variable to interact with other blocks using join blocks where needed

---

Types of Knowledge Key

Declarative Knowledge

Static facts or knowledge stored in your memory

Procedural Knowledge

How to perform a specific skill or task

Conditional Knowledge

When to use declarative and procedural knowledge

Further Resources

What is in the box

Hello World 7th Edition by Jane Waite, Felienne Hermans and Efthimia Aivaloglou

Concepts before coding: non-programming interactives to advance learning of introductory programming concepts in middle school

Shuchi Grover, Nicholas Jackiw & Patrik Lundh (2019):

Science Education, DOI: 10.1080/08993408.2019.1568955

Answer to question on p42

Ask user_name what is 5x7=? and wait on line 6

`ask   join   user_name   what is 5x7=?   and wait`

Procedures

CHAPTER 5

Dictionary Definition
A procedure is a small named section of a program that performs a specific task. Procedures can be used repeatedly throughout a program. (BBC Bitesize)

Language of Procedures
Procedures can also be called subroutines, subprograms or functions.

Everyday Procedures
Our bodies perform many procedures automatically such as breathing, cooling our skin using sweat or reacting to something painful that touches the skin. These bodily subroutines are programmed into the brain and either run continuously, e.g. breathing, or wait for an external stimulus such as a hot day or pain to trigger action. During the course of our life (program) these procedures will be run many times.

A more useful everyday example for helping primary pupils to understand procedures is training animals. Once a dog has been taught to beg or roll over, that subroutine can be accessed by saying 'beg' or 'roll over'. The quality of the animal procedure will only be impaired by age or lack of interest, which is where our analogy breaks down a little as a programming procedure will continue to operate uniformly whilst the programming is running.

Dog Sitting

Define sit
Bend rear legs
Lower bottom to floor
look up

Sit Procedure Algorithm

sit

Calling the sit procedure algorithm

47

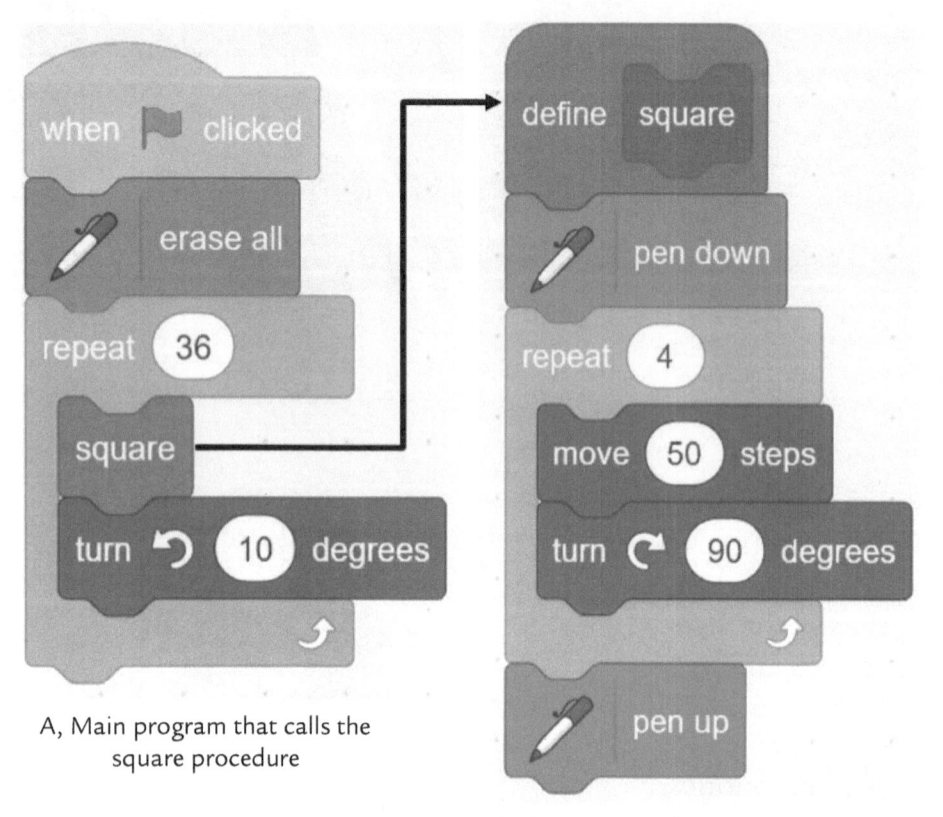

Scratch IT – Teaching Primary Programming with Scratch

A, Main program that calls the square procedure

B, Square procedure

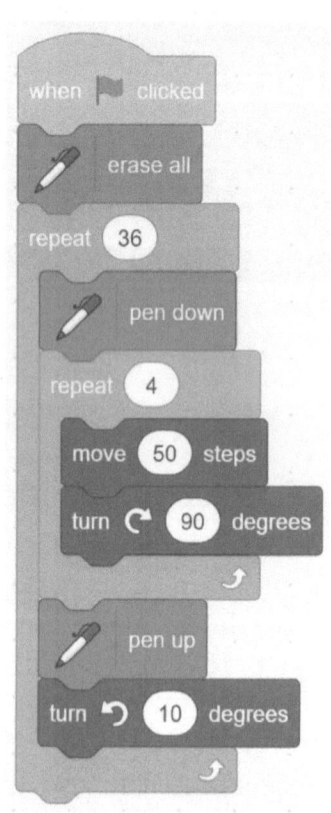

C, The same pattern coded without a square procedure

Procedures used multiple times

One of the useful aspects of a procedure is that it can be run or called multiple times. This makes it especially useful for repetitive code that might need to be used frequently.

In the example above a procedure called square has been called by the main program 36 times, which will produce a pattern when run.

Procedures make it easier to think about complex code

We might have coded our pattern without a procedure like the program script on the right called C.

Compare this with the main program above A, which calls the procedure in B.

The pattern drawn by A & B or C

Procedure called by square block

Procedures

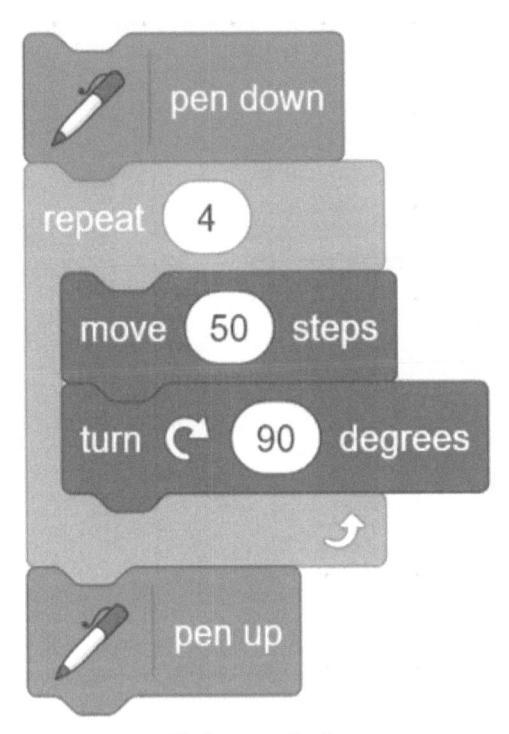

D, Square Code

All of the square code D on the next page has been taken away, placed in the procedure and replaced will a single block with the procedure square name.

Removing the detail from the main program reduces the number of elements we need to examine at any one time, thus reducing our cognitive load.

Once a procedure is created we can mostly ignore how it works and get on with thinking how it can be used or reused.

Procedures can be used to break up longer code

Procedures can be used to break up long sequences of difficult to follow code into shorter, named sections that can be written and understood more easily. See chapter 26 on modularisation and sub goal labelling, for more details.

Adaptable procedures

An adaptable procedure is one that can be changed by adding inputs each time the procedure is called.

These inputs can be text, numbers or Booleans. We call these types of input parameters. On this page we demonstrate text and number parameters for a quiz type question (E & F).

The procedure block has one text or number parameter called 'questions' and one text or

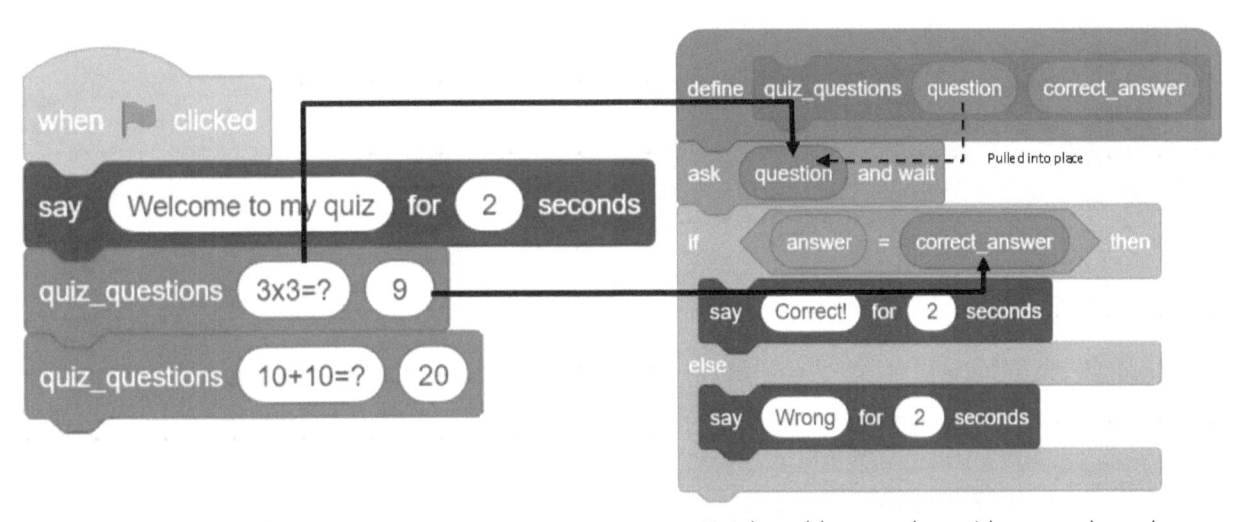

E, Main program

F, Adaptable procedure with text and number input parameters

number parameter called 'correct_answer'. These blocks are then pulled into the places where a question and answer would normally go on a quiz question (dashed arrows).

The blocks that call the procedure in the main program E have spaces to type in the question and answer. Arrows have been drawn to show where these parameters are inputed into the procedure when it is called. Multiple procedure blocks can now use that same adaptable procedure. In our example you can see that the second questions has a different 'question' and 'correct_answer', which will be fed into the procedure when it is its turn to be run.

Nested procedure output from G & H

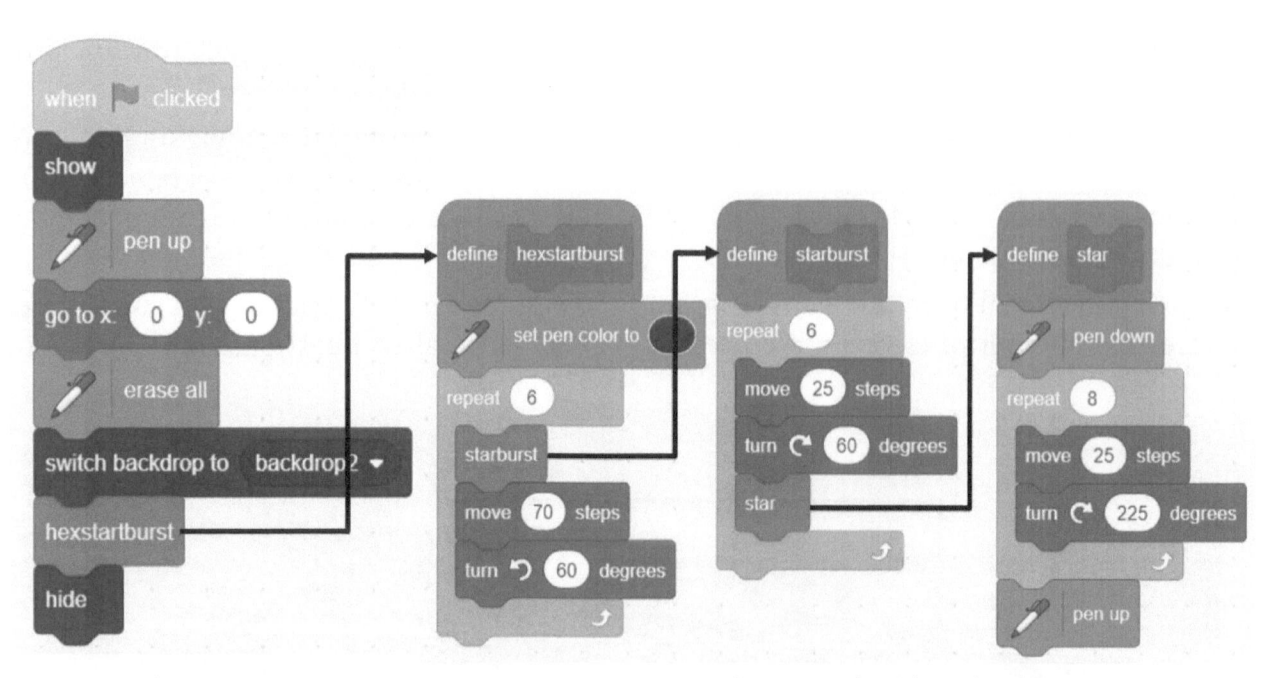

G, Main program

H, Procedures nested inside each other

Nested Procedures

One procedure can be nested inside another procedure, although we need to be careful to avoid calling a procedure inside itself, as it will cause a loop that the program cannot escape from. There are ways to use a procedure that calls itself successfully, but that is outside of the bounds of this book.

In G & H above the star procedure is called inside startburst. The hexstarburst procedure calls the starburst procedure. Finally hexstarburst is called from the main program.

Procedures

Naming a procedure

Parameters

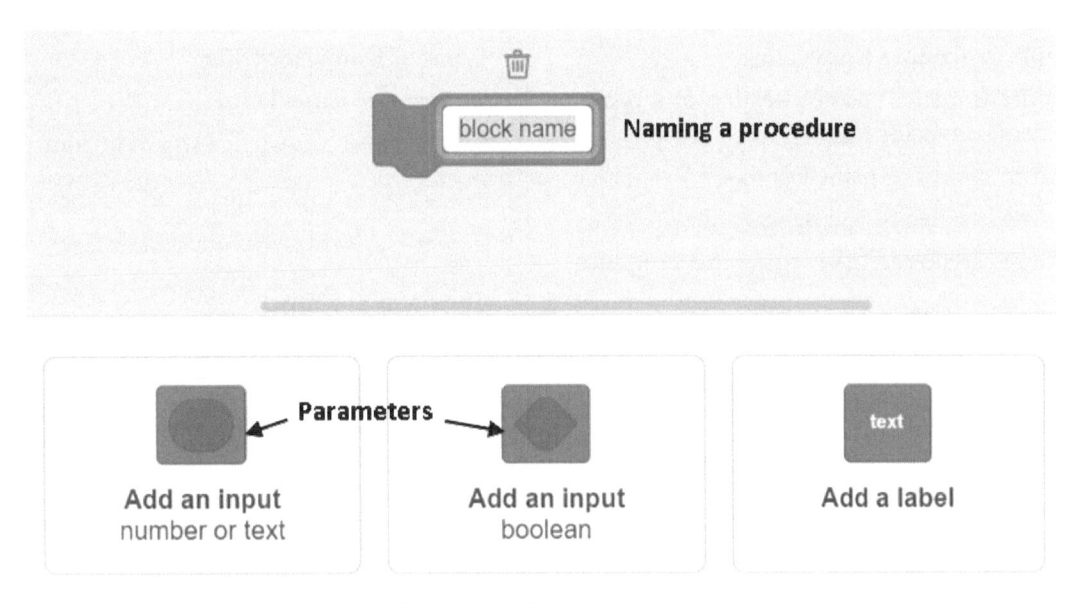

Add an input
number or text

Add an input
boolean

Add a label

Creating a procedure with parameters

Creating a Procedure

Scratch calls these My Blocks, and when you select **Make a block** you are presented with this choice see above.

Click on the parameters to add them into your procedure if you need them. Use the bin icon to delete a part of the procedure or parameter.

Make sure you do not name any procedure or parameter with the same name as any other variable or list name. Scratch will cope with this if you do, but many other programming languages will not.

If you want to change the procedure right click on it and select edit.

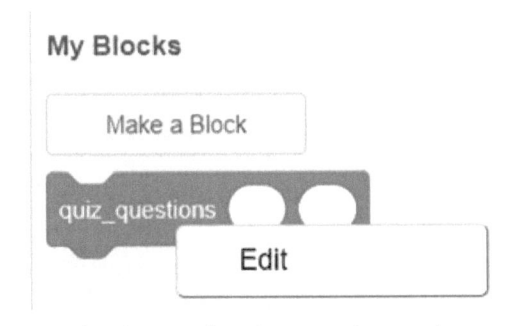

Adapting an already created procedure

Complexity

Based on teaching this, I would estimate the complexity order to be

1. Basic procedures
2. Nested procedures
3. Adaptable procedures

Including Procedures

The UK has a strong tradition of teaching about procedures in primary education. In the past this was mainly using the text-based programming language Logo but with Scratch 2 onwards including procedure blocks it is now much more accessible to all.

Procedures are not mentioned in the UK national curriculum for computing in KS2, but they do simplify complex code and open up new ways to think about programming.

Key Simple Procedure Knowledge

A procedure is a small named section of a program that performs a specific task

A procedure should be named uniquely

A procedure is called or run by its name

A procedure can be run many times in a program

Algorithmic Knowledge

I can name a procedure after the task that the instructions carry out

I can name a procedure using camelCase or under_score to avoid problems creating procedures in text based programming languages

I can name a procedure uniquely to avoid problems with variables or lists in text-based programming languages

Programming Knowledge

I can create a procedure in Scratch from My Blocks

I can create a main program and procedures to call the procedures from within the main program.

I can look for processes I need to use many times and create them as procedures to save time

Types of Knowledge Key

Declarative Knowledge

Static facts or knowledge stored in your memory

Procedural Knowledge

How to perform a specific skill or task

Conditional Knowledge

When to use declarative and procedural knowledge

Further Resources

Frozen – Hour of code Functions

https://www.youtube.com/watch?v=gm3GPfUq0Wg

Beanz – Functions and Procedures

https://kidscodecs.com/functions-and-procedures/

Algorithms

CHAPTER 6

What is an Algorithm?

A set of instructions or rules that solve a problem or lead to a specific outcome.

Chapter Contents

This chapter looks at the relationship between algorithms and programming , and the similarities and differences between both. It examines algorithm writing as a way to plan programming, although design does have its own in-depth coverage in chapter 15. We also make the distinction between formal algorithms that secondary pupils will learn about and everyday algorithms primary pupils might examine.

At the end of the chapter there is a Venn diagram to complete, to see how much you have understood.

Relationship of Algorithms to Programming

Similarities

Algorithms and programming both use

Sequence

Repetition

Conditional selection

Variables

Procedures

Differences

Algorithms are written for another human to understand. Programming is written to run on a digital device.

Algorithms can be written in any way or using any words or symbols, as long as another human can follow it clearly. Programs can only be written in words that a digital device can act on. For example, a human can understand Loop 4 times, Do 4 times or Repeat 4 times, all as a count-controlled loops. The Scratch programming language will only recognise repeat 4 times.

Algorithms can be used to plan any process that benefits from order or rules such as traffic flow or long division in Maths.

Algorithm to Plan Programming

Algorithms are used to plan programming projects. Algorithms are used as they are generally easier to understand than trying to write code.

However with a programming language like Scratch, which is easily read by a human, it can be harder to distinguish between some planning algorithms and code.

Golden Rule

Technically, if planning is written entirely in code language and code syntax it is code not an algorithm. However, it is rarely useful to point this out below KS3.

Scratch Code Planning

Repeat 3
    hide
    wait 1 seconds
    show
    wait 1 seconds

Algorithm Planning

Do 3 times
    hide wizard
    wait 1 sec
    Show wizard
    Wait 1 sec

Formal & Everyday Algorithms

In the wider world algorithms rarely have these formal or everyday labels, but they are useful for children and teachers. A formal algorithm is like a mathematical formula that can be used and studied for its clever design. An everyday algorithm is a much more simple application of rules or sets of instructions such as a food recipe or musical notation. It can be useful, but is unlikely to be studied for its brilliance or cleverness.

Bubble Sort

If you want to find out about a basic formal sorting algorithm studied at KS3 then the BBC bitesize pages have a good, easy to understand description of this algorithm in every day English. https://www.bbc.co.uk/bitesize/guides/z22wwmn/revision/3

Venn Diagram

Why not try and identify which concepts are algorithms, which are programming and which are both by drawing arrows on the diagram below. Answers are on page 56.

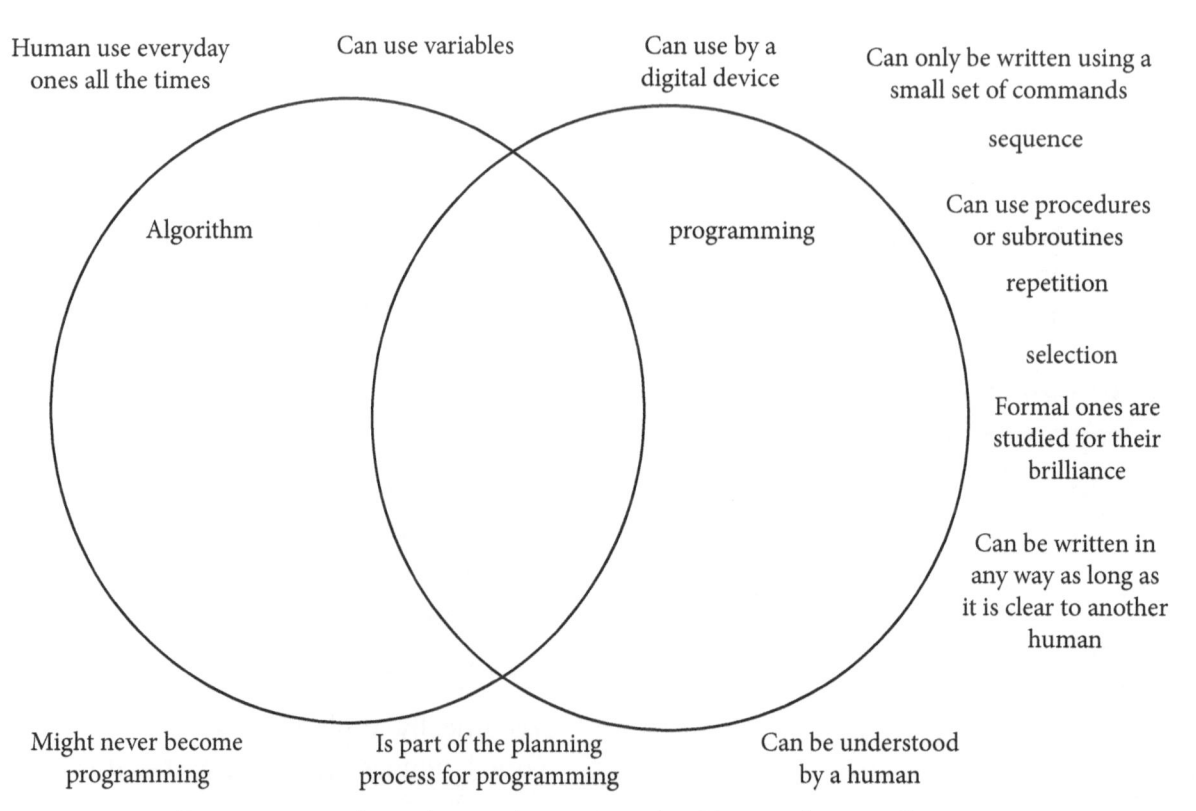

Human use everyday ones all the times

Can use variables

Can use by a digital device

Can only be written using a small set of commands

sequence

Algorithm

programming

Can use procedures or subroutines

repetition

selection

Formal ones are studied for their brilliance

Can be written in any way as long as it is clear to another human

Might never become programming

Is part of the planning process for programming

Can be understood by a human

Draw arrows to show where each statement should go on the venn diagram

Algorithms

Algorithm and Code Knowledge

(Mch of which pupils should already know by end of KS1 in English computing curriculum)

I know that an algorithm is a set of precise instrctions that can be understood by another human

I know that a digital device contains coded instructions to make it do things

I know that digital devices can come in many shapes and sizes

I know that computers are one form of digital device

I know that an algorithm can be used to plan a program on a digital device

I can plan an algorithm that can be turned into code on a digital device

I can debug code that does not do what I want it to do

I can look at code to work out what a program will do when the code is run

Knowledge Key Declarative Knowledge

Static facts or knowledge stored in your memory (what)

Procedural Knowledge

How to perform a specific skill or task (how)

Conditional Knowledge

When to use declarative and procedural knowledge (when & why)

Further Resources

Computer Science in K-12 An A to Z handbook on teaching programming edited by Shuchi Grover Chapter 1 Algorithms by Shuchi Grover

Answer
Venn Diagram

Algorithm

- Human use everyday ones all the times
- Might never become programming
- Can be written in any way as long as it is clear to another human
- Can be understood by a human
- Formal ones are studied for their brilliance

Intersection

- Can use variables
- sequence
- Can use procedures or subroutines
- repetition
- Is part of the planning process for programming
- selection

programming

- Can use by a digital device
- Can only be written using a small set of commands

CHAPTER 7

Decomposition

Define Decomposition
Decomposition is the skill of breaking a complex problem up into smaller manageable chunks and solving these chunks separately.

Two Parts to Decomposition
- Breaking a problem into parts
- Solving these parts

Complexity
The more complex a project the more need for decomposition. The less complex a project the less need for decomposition.

Complex for whom?
Complexity should not be measured by the teacher's understanding but by the pupils. A simple moving character steered and moved by keys might be quite complex for a 7-8-year-old who has just been introduced to Scratch.

Examining Outcomes
Many simple programming projects have lots of separate programming scripts which do different things. A useful initial step in decomposition is running the code and listing all the outcomes. Pupils do not need to

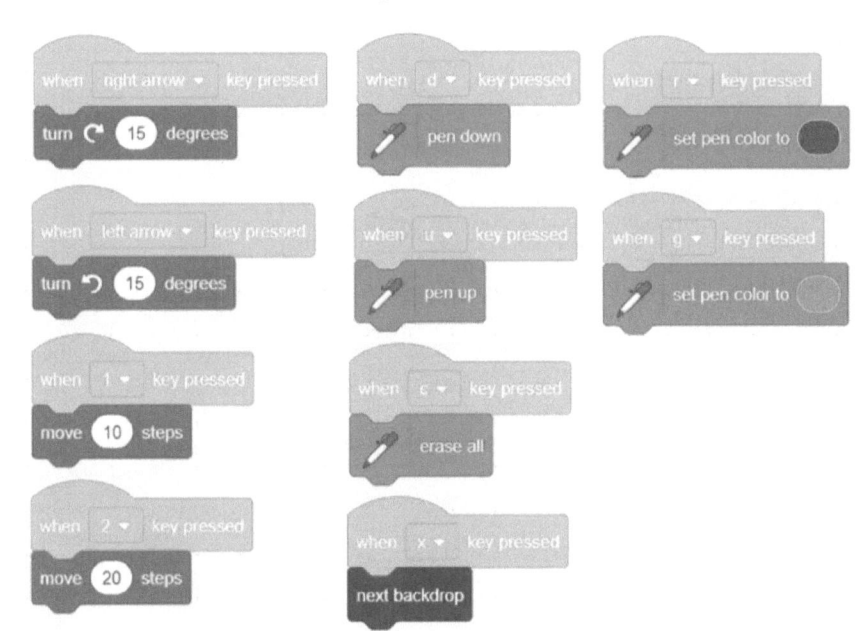

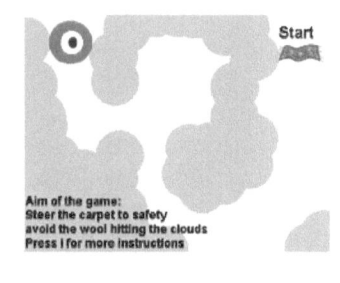

Magic Carpet Game Code and Screen

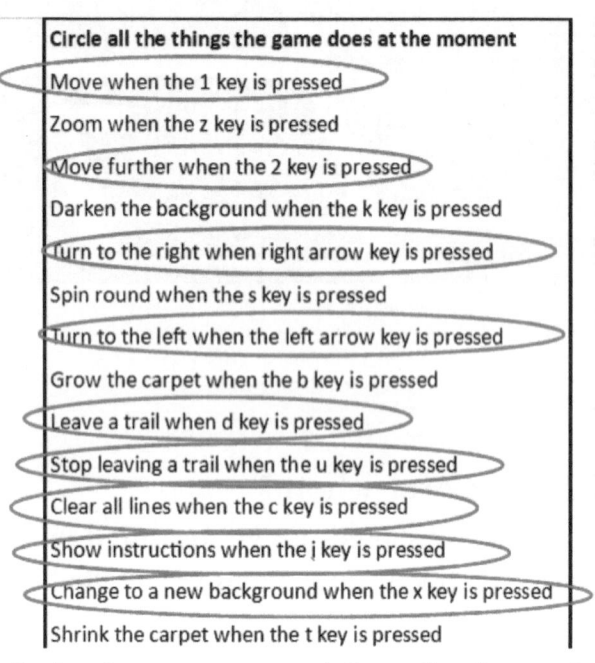

Circle all the things the game does at the moment
- ~~Move when the 1 key is pressed~~
- Zoom when the z key is pressed
- ~~Move further when the 2 key is pressed~~
- Darken the background when the k key is pressed
- ~~Turn to the right when right arrow key is pressed~~
- Spin round when the s key is pressed
- ~~Turn to the left when the left arrow key is pressed~~
- Grow the carpet when the b key is pressed
- ~~Leave a trail when d key is pressed~~
- ~~Stop leaving a trail when the u key is pressed~~
- ~~Clear all lines when the c key is pressed~~
- ~~Show instructions when the i key is pressed~~
- ~~Change to a new background when the x key is pressed~~
- Shrink the carpet when the t key is pressed

Finding the correct commands from a list of true and false ones is a useful early scaffold to help pupils break up a project

examine code at this point, but just list what the code does.

Magic Carpet

In the Magic Carpet example on this and the previous page, year 3 pupils played the game trying to find the instructions that worked and exclude instructions that did not work. This could be done independently, in pairs or with their teacher. Once they had a working list of things that they knew could work they could either investigate how to build these themselves or be shown how these parts could be made. Or, more usually, be shown how some parts work and discover how to adapt these independently.

Two parts to most scripts

Even the simplest scripts have the need for initialisation as well as their main purpose.

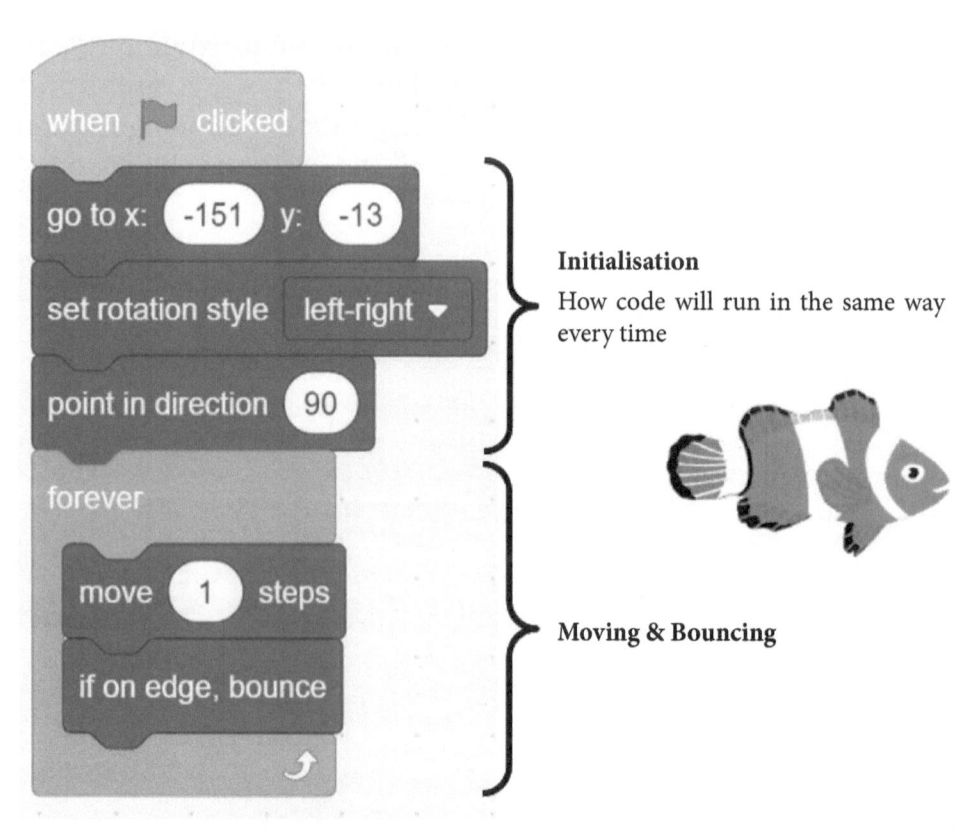

Initialisation
How code will run in the same way every time

Moving & Bouncing

Fish moving code seperated into two parts

In the example fish moving code on the left, the main task is to move and bounce off the edges which it does in the forever loop at the bottom. The top blocks establish the sprites initialisation, where it should start, how it should rotate and in which direction it should face. The initialisation code gives the sprite the same start every time it is run.

By encouraging pupils to separate the main purpose of their code from its initialisation we are growing pupils' decomposition skills.

Multiple Scripts

Because Scratch allows multiple programming scripts to be run at the same time, it is a useful language for novices to decompose projects and solve them in separate code scripts.

The script on the left hand page makes the fish move, and the second script below makes it look like it is swimming by changing costumes. We are decomposing moving and looking like it is swimming into two separate issues, which can be solved in two separate code sections.

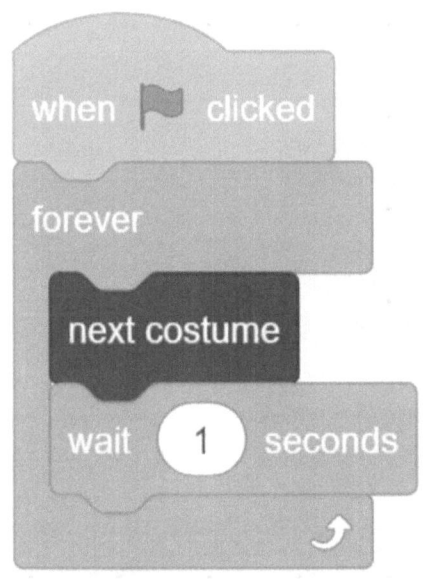

Script to change costume to make fish look like it is moving

Scaffolding Decomposition

An expanded programming planning outline helps pupils to decompose a complex game project into manageable chunks that they can easily code.

When planning Jane Waite advocates four levels of abstraction.

1. Task level
2. Design level (algorithm & objects)
3. Code level
4. Execution or run the code level

Further dividing the task level into two separate levels can really help pupils to decompose complex gaming projects with multiple Scratch scripts.

1. **General task level**, where you say what you want the program to do
2. **Detailed task level**, a list of objects (sprites) and what you would like them to do in detail
3. **Algorithm level**, where each detail from step two is turned into a specific algorithm
4. **Code level**
5. **Execution level**

We can see an ideal version of this below and on the next page and one created by a pupil on page 61.

Expanded Planning Process
General Task Level

Shark swims around, steered by user and eats smaller fish.

Detailed Task Level

A. Shark moves using space key
B. Shark steer right using right arrow
C. Shark steer left using left arrow
D. Shark eats smaller fish

Scratch IT – Teaching Primary Programming with Scratch

Algorithm Level

A,

Loop always
    If space key pressed
        Move

B,

Loop always
    If rt arrow key
        Turn Rt 15 deg

C,

Loop always
    If lt arrow key
        Left 15 degrees

D,

Mouth open costume
Loop always
    If touch small fish
        Mouth closed
        Pause
        Mouth open
        Pause

We would also need planning and code in the smaller fish to respond to being eaten and to move.

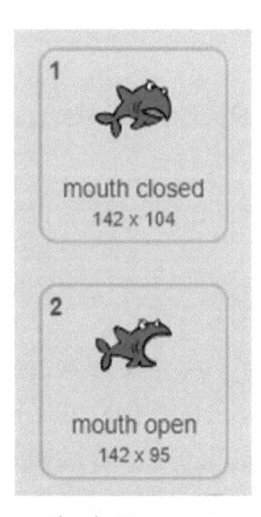

Shark Costumes

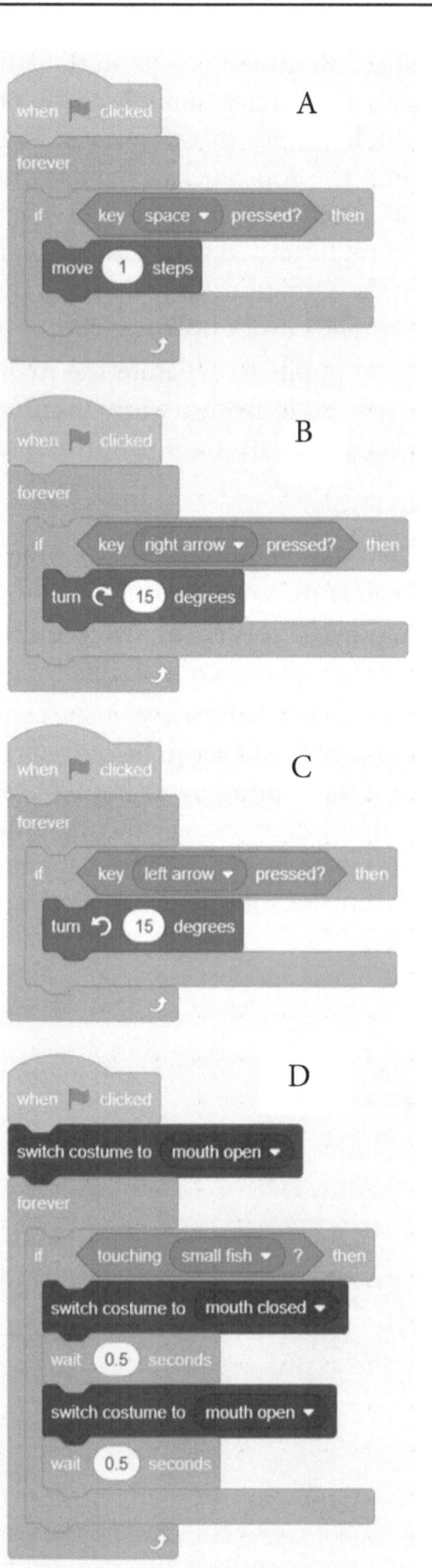

Code Level

Decomposition

Example From 9-10-Year-Old Planning a Game

In this example the pupil has decomposed a detailed task level before turning these into algorithms that were easily turned into code. Different colour circles link the detailed task level and solving it with a planning algorithm.

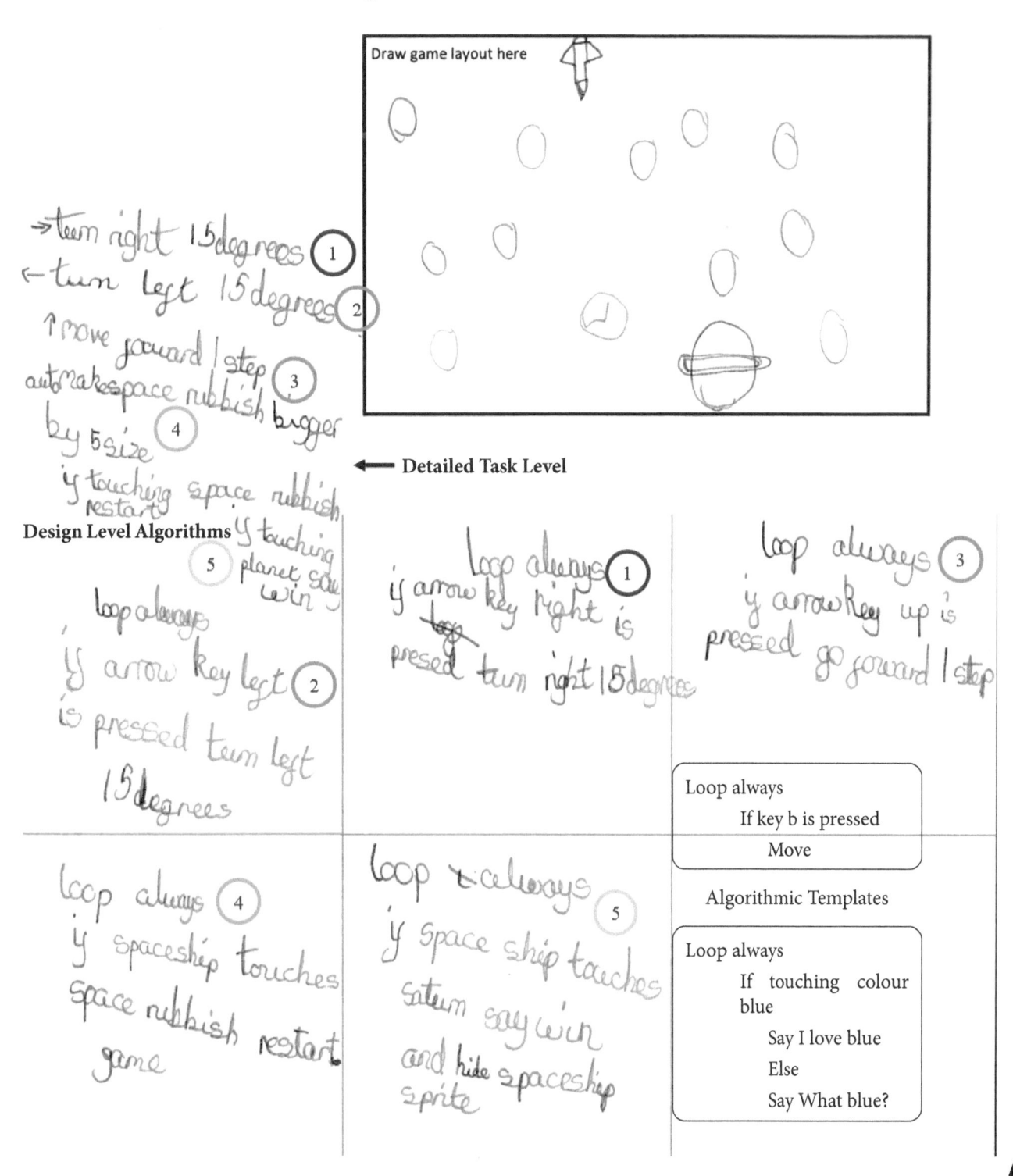

Draw game layout here

Detailed Task Level:

1. → turn right 15 degrees
2. ← turn left 15 degrees
3. ↑ move forward 1 step
4. auto makes space rubbish bigger by 5 size
5. if touching space rubbish restart / if touching planet say win

Design Level Algorithms:

2. loop always
   if arrow key left is pressed turn left 15 degrees

1. loop always
   if arrow key right is pressed turn right 15 degrees

3. loop always
   if arrow key up is pressed go forward 1 step

4. loop always
   if spaceship touches space rubbish restart game

5. loop always
   if space ship touches saturn say win and hide spaceship sprite

Algorithmic Templates

Loop always
    If key b is pressed
        Move

Loop always
    If touching colour blue
        Say I love blue
    Else
        Say What blue?

Detailed Planning Aids
Decomposition

It is far harder for a novice pupil programmer to write meaningful algorithms to convert into code if they have not broken the programming tasks up intothe smallest possible tasks, similar to that shown above.

Whilst this can seem like lots of steps, each step only adds a small layer of increased challenge rather than a large leap. This decomposed scaffolding enables many more pupils to design and create their own independent games.

Useful Code Scaffolds

On the back of this planning sheet useful code blocks with descriptions of what they do were provided. An algorithmic template, as shown above, was also provided. If you look carefully you can see that the loop always were added after a teacher prompt, which were far easier to correct in the planning stage.

Decomposition Knowledge

I know that decomposition is breaking a complex problem up into parts and solving each part seperately

I can break a complex problem like a game up into parts because it is easier to solve each part seperately

---

Knowledge Key

Declarative Knowledge

Static facts or knowledge stored in your memory (what)

Procedural Knowledge

How to perform a specific skill or task (how)

Conditional Knowledge

When to use declarative and procedural knowledge (when & why)

Further Resources

Difficulties with design: The challenges of teaching design in K-5 programming Jane Waite, *, Paul Curzon, William Marsh, Sue Sentence

CSER – The Computer Science Education Research Group

https://www.youtube.com/watch?v=eWSI8xK2upM

PEDAGOGY

CHAPTER 8

Concept before Coding

Code Free Introductions
There are the ways of introducing programming concepts, such as sequence, repetition, selection and variables, in the simplest way possible, helping to reduce cognitive load for novice learners.

Simple Selection
Consider these three examples of conditions that trigger actions outlined at the bottom of the page. Lets outline all the elements that we need to fully understand the examples.

Quiz Example
- That the ask block is a text input for the user of the program
- The answer the user inputs is stored in the answer block
- *Equals means the same as*
- The user's answer (answer block) is checked to see whether it is the same as the correct answer (9)
- That correct is only actioned if the comparative condition is met
- That this condition will only be checked once

Everyday Example
- *The concept of being hungry or not hungry*
- *How to clap hands*
- That clapping hands is only actioned if the user is hungry
- That this condition will only be checked once

Gaming Example
- *Touching the colour red*
- That tens steps is ten pixels on the screen
- That moving 10 steps is only actioned if red is touched

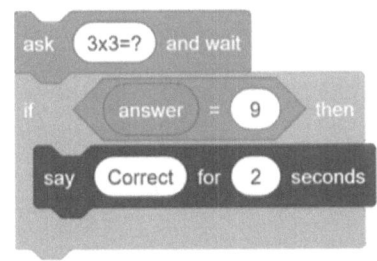

Quiz Example

Everyday Example

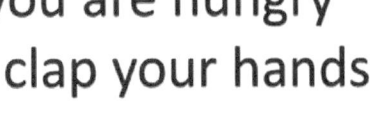

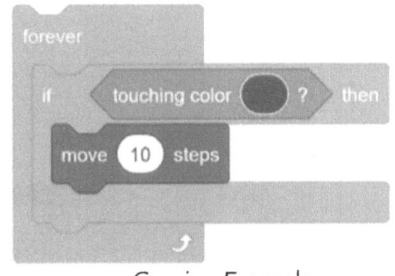

Gaming Example

- That normally this condition is only checked once but that it has been placed in an indefinite loop to check the condition continually
- How indefinite loops work

The elements in *italics* are likely already known.

Everyday Examples

The everyday examples clearly have the least cognitive load, the least new information introduced.

Linking New to Old

Piaget's schema theory identified that *When we can connect something 'old' to something new it helps us better understand the new.* Since each programming concept is new to the learner, it is important to connect with non programming, everyday understanding, of the concept, where it exists, before expanding its use into the programming domain.

Everyday Examples

In the examples below and on the next page, pupils are reminded about sequences in their daily school routines, repetition in dance and procedures through how we might train an animal.

Universal Concepts

When we introduce a new concept, such as repetition or selection, we want pupils to associate these ideas with all programming in any programming language. If we introduce them using the language of a particular programming language such as Scratch, we are tying a universal concept to a specific language. Introducing the concept in a programming neutral form makes it far easier for pupils to transfer the key concepts between different programming languages.[1]

Language Changes

If introducing a key concept before programming in Scratch, we might talk about looping

Everyday sequences

Teacher instructions

- Pack away
- Stack your chairs
- Get your coats
- Line up ready to go

Does the order the children carry out the instructions matter?

Picture by KalvinKalvin

---

[1] Informed and influenced by the work of Michal Armoni
On Teaching Abstraction in Computer Science to Novices Jl. of Computers in Mathematics and Science Teaching (2013) 32(3), 265-284

Everyday repetition

Dance loops

Which parts of the dance are repeated?

Brain Breaks - Action Songs for Children - Happy Dance - Kids Songs by The Learning Station

Everyday procedures

> I have taught my dog to beg, roll over, and shake paw. She does these things when I say beg, roll and shake.

> Can you think of any other procedures that could be taught to the dog?

Sit and stand up are common ones but you might have others

always instead of forever loop or loop 3 times instead of repeat 3. Using language that is similar to code but not the same reinforces the idea that we are working in the algorithmic design level rather than the writing code and running code level. In this algorithmic level we have more flexibility because ideas can be written in language that any other human can understand rather than the rigid set forms of a programming language. It is not always possible to find useful language alternatives but it helps when we can. We discuss this

Roleplay and Write

Roleplay is a very good way to tease out key aspect associated with a key computing concept.

Count Controlled Loop Example

The three slides on this page and the next are part of a series that use roleplay to introduce count controlled loops. In the series of books that accompany this book, there are many sets of slides with explanations on how to use them to help teachers introduce all new programming concepts.

Assessing Understanding

Pupils act out various everyday count-controlled loops before writing their own for their classmates to act out. Formulating their own count controlled loop is important, as it allows teachers to assess who has made progress and support pupils who haven't. Whilst the majority of pupils will write their own, a teacher might scribe for any for whom writing is an issue. The teacher is assessing computing understanding not assessing writing.

Building Depth

In the third slide pupils are then provided with a sequence to convert into a count-controlled loop helping to increasing their understanding of count-controlled loops.

These types of activities then lead into programming using which ever strategy the teacher has chosen.

Flow of Control

During these concept introductory sessions this can also be a great opportunity to introduce the flow of control see chapter 27.

Role Play and Write Examples

On page 70 there are lots of examples of pupils writing everyday algorithms.

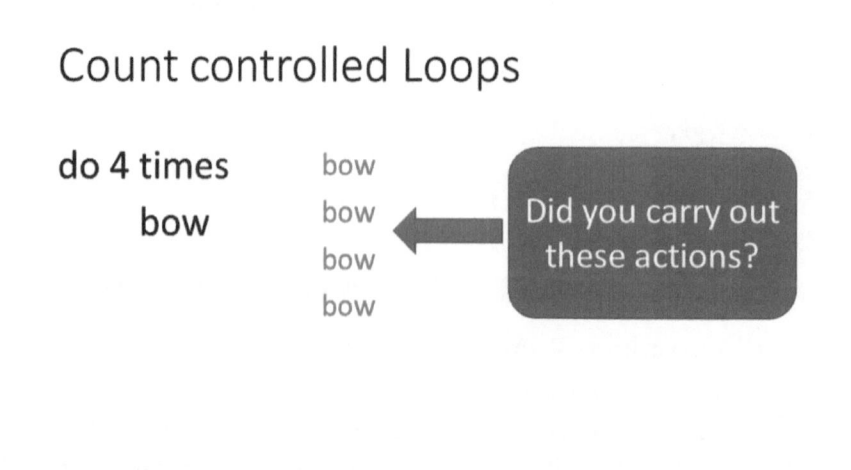

Count controlled Loops

do 4 times
    bow

bow
bow
bow
bow

Did you carry out these actions?

Role playing an algorithm

Count controlled Loops

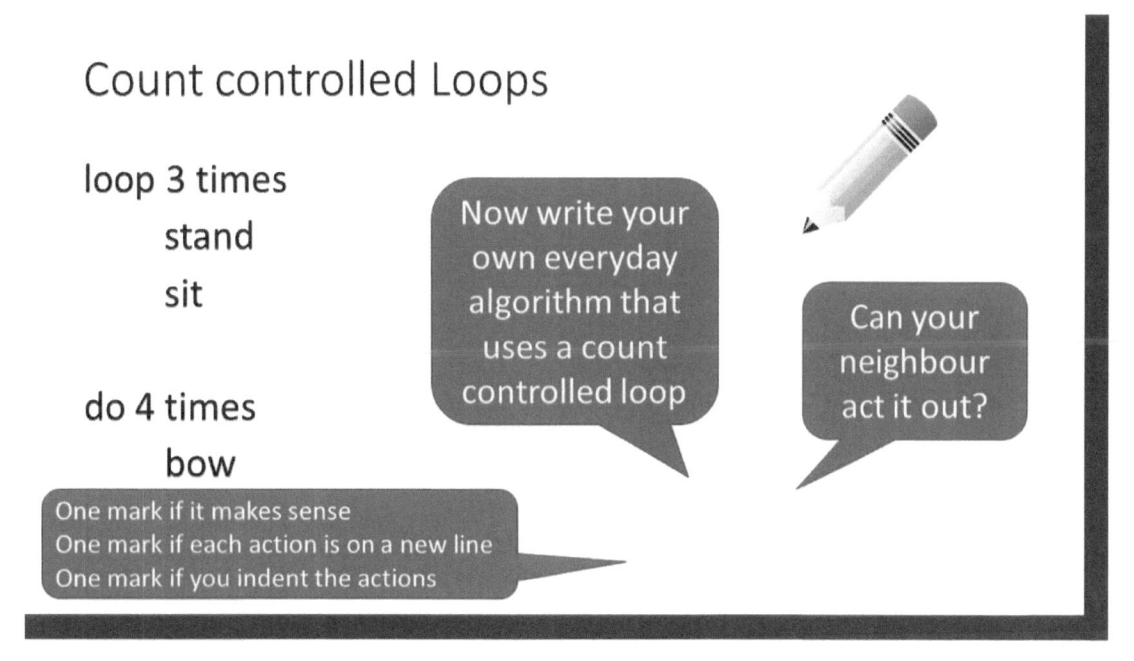

loop 3 times
    stand
    sit

do 4 times
    bow

> Now write your own everyday algorithm that uses a count controlled loop
>
> Can your neighbour act it out?

One mark if it makes sense
One mark if each action is on a new line
One mark if you indent the actions

Writing an algorithm

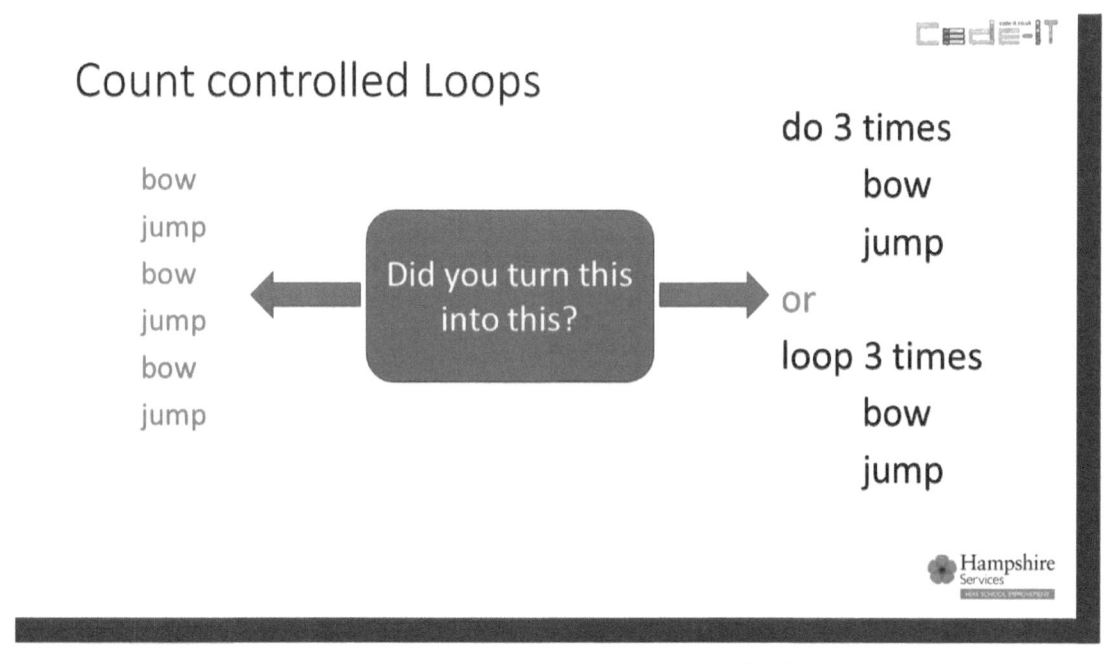

Count controlled Loops

bow
jump
bow
jump
bow
jump

⬅ Did you turn this into this? ➡

do 3 times
    bow
    jump

or

loop 3 times
    bow
    jump

Converting a sequence into a count-controlled loop

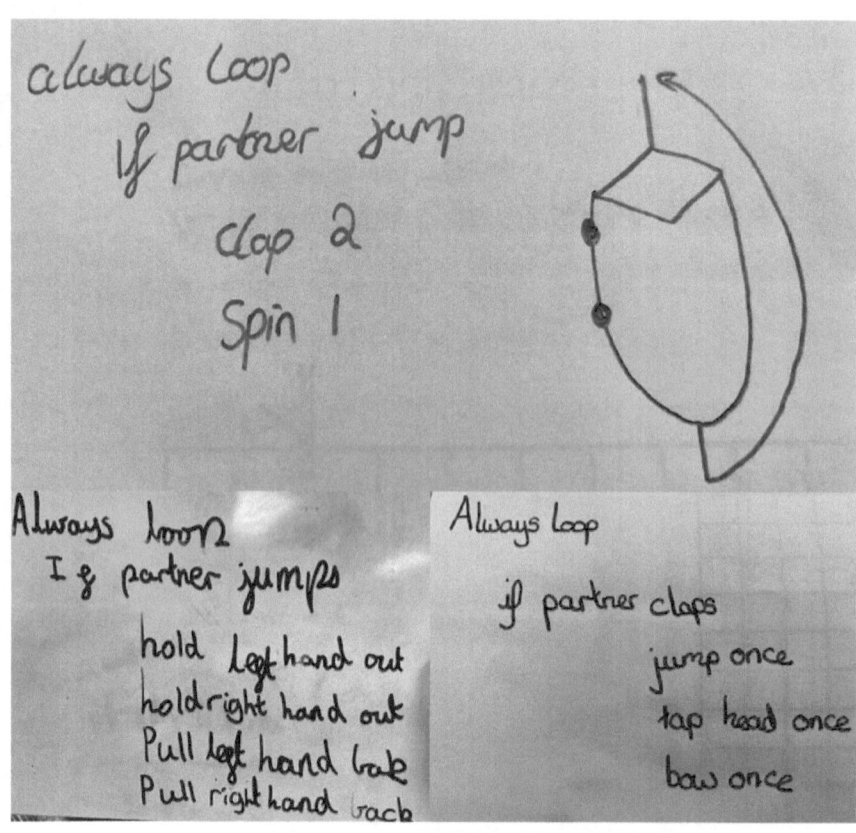

Scratch IT — Teaching Primary Programming with Scratch

Conditional selection within a loop Examples written by 9-10 year olds

Everyday Algorithms

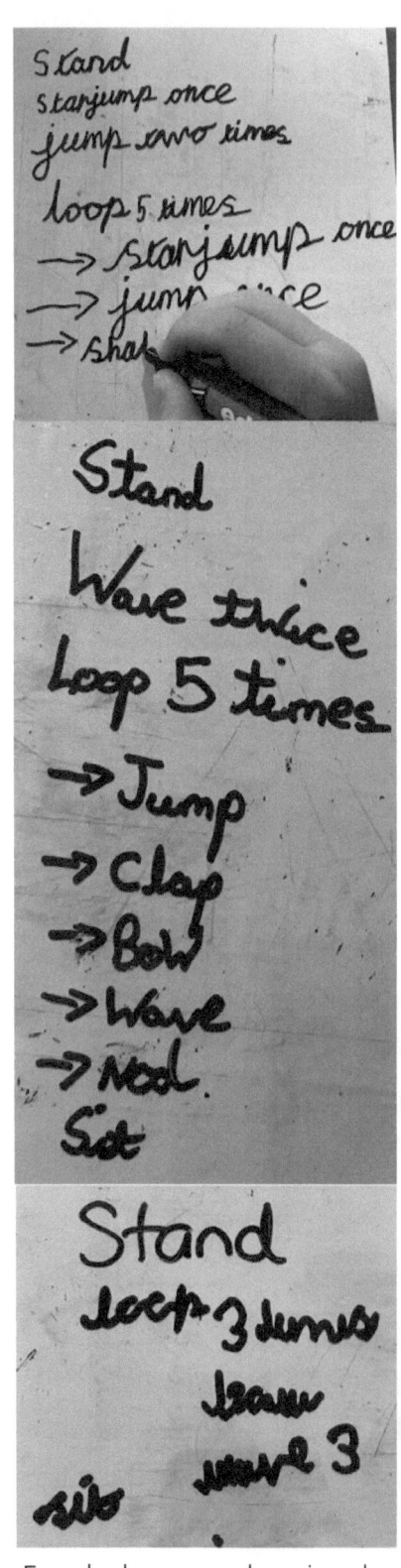

Everyday loop examples written by 8-9 year olds

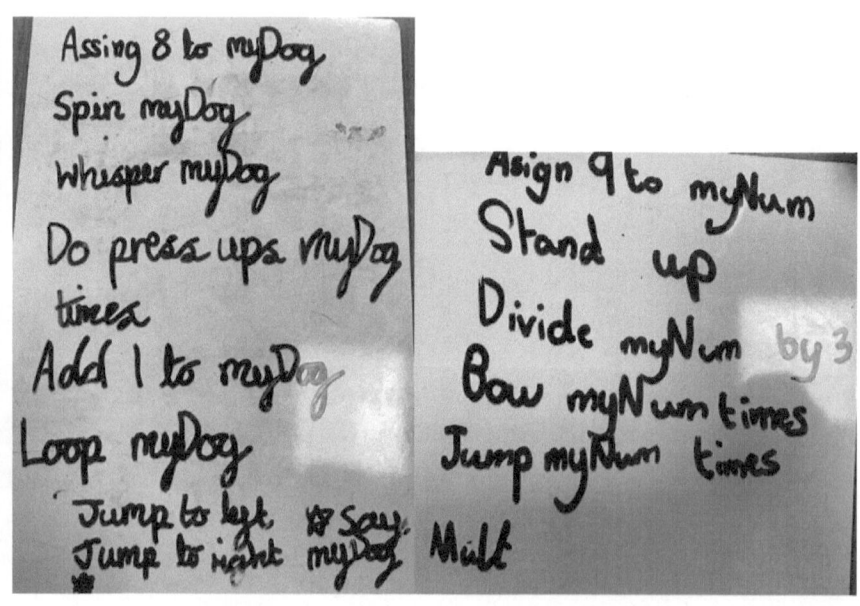

Variable examples written by 10-11 year olds

Story Telling

Grover's research with middle school pupils in the US supported the use of non programming interactives to introduce new programming concepts.

Match Variables

Grover[2] identified the medium of stories as a rich vehicle to connect prior and new learning. For example, when students were introduced to variables they looked as scores during sports matches asking pupils to identify what the values of these scores are at different points in the match. Telling the story of the match using variables, they found that pupils who examined the concept before coding made more progress than those who went straight into code.

Visitors Car Parking Space

The example on the right is from an introduction to variables used with Year 5 and 6 pupils.

Good questioning can help identify if pupils understand

- The difference between the name and the value
- What value was assigned on different days
- What the value is likely to be after office hours

This model can be extended to discuss automatic car parks. What values could a camera be trying to record if we wanted to check who was using the parking and when they were using it? Would more than one variable be needed?

Pupils will come up with a range of useful answers. These can include

- Face recognition
- Number plate
- Make, model & colour of car
- The time of the video

Good Examples

The simpler the better when it comes to everyday examples. Pupils need to be able to concentrate on the fundamentals unhindered by complexity in their early stages of exposure to new concepts.

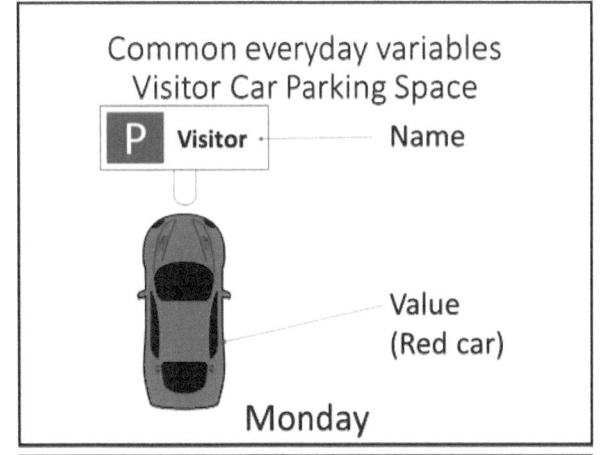

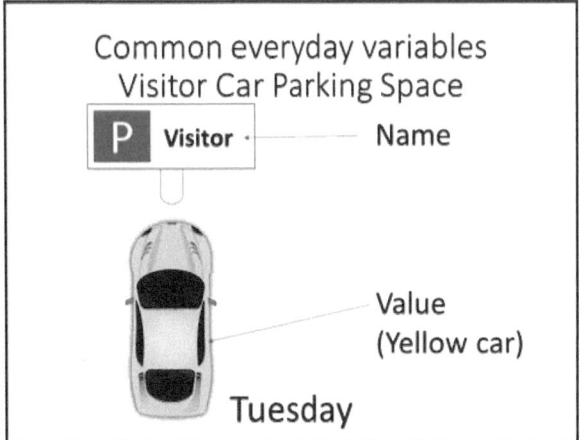

---

[2] Shuchi Grover, Nicholas Jackiw & Patrik Lundh (2019): Concepts before coding: non-programming interactives to advance learning of introductory programming concepts in middle school, Computer Science Education, DOI: 10.1080/08993408.2019.1568955

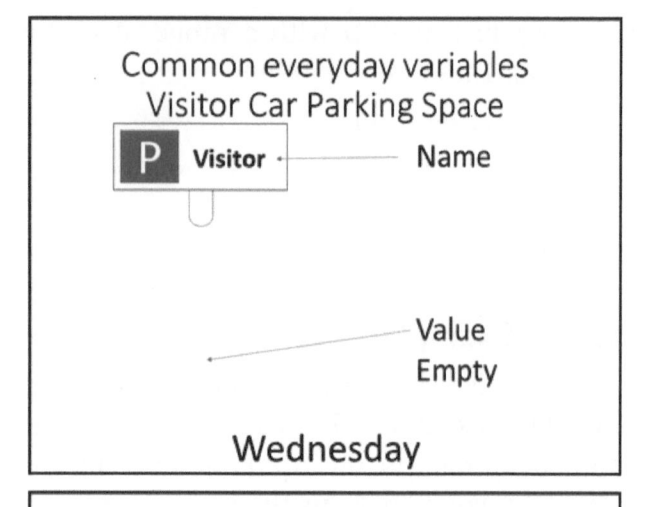

Common everyday variables
Visitor Car Parking Space

[P Visitor] — Name

— Value
Empty

Wednesday

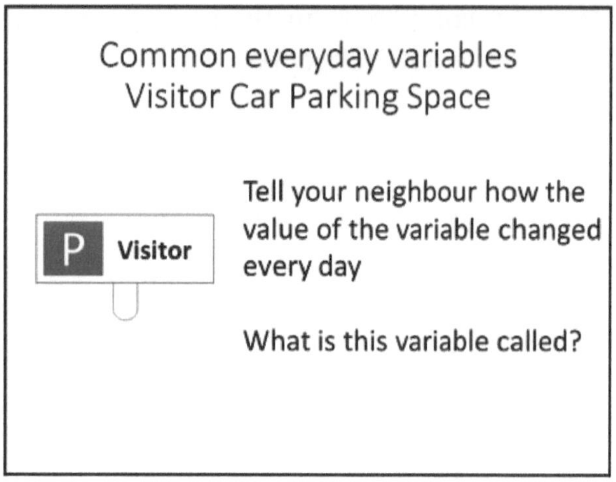

Common everyday variables
Visitor Car Parking Space

[P Visitor]

Tell your neighbour how the value of the variable changed every day

What is this variable called?

Shuchi Grover

An influential learning scientist and computing science and STEM education researcher. Her research is some of the most usable and readable available.

Author of *Computer Science in K-12: An A-to-Z Handbook on Teaching Programming* which is well worth purchasing.

Code Comprehension First Overview

CHAPTER 9

Use Modify Create

Examining quality code first initially derived from the research of Lee[1] and others who advocate a use-modify-create approach. Pupils use programming created by their teacher before modifying it and finally creating something new. The research describes how ownership of the code is gradually conferred on pupils. They have no ownership of the project they use and have partial ownership of the project they modify and full ownership of projects they create.

USE Code	MODIFY Code	CREATE Code
No Ownership	Partial Ownership	Full Ownership

PRIMM

Sentance,[2] working with secondary pupils in 2019, adapts this model to become PRIMM. With this new approach comes a significant new focus on careful code comprehension. Pupils don't just need to use code they need to investigate parts of it guided by careful

Predict	P
Run	R
Investigate	I
Modify	M
Make	M

questions and activities. Sentence also includes prediction before pupils run or investigate code.

Code Comprehension

Taken together these strategies can be described as code comprehension first, in that they advocate reading and understanding code before writing code. Non-specialist teachers who also teach literacy will recognise that pupils' reading development comes at an earlier stage than pupils' writing development, although there is always overlap.

Comprehension Plus

Some are discouraged from using this methodology because the word comprehension has been tarnished for them by experiences of using soulless comprehension books when

---

[1] Lee, Irene & Martin, Fred & Denner, Jill & Coulter, Bob & Allan, Walter & Erickson, Jeri & Malyn-Smith, Joyce & Werner, Linda. (2011). Computational thinking for youth in practice. ACM Inroads. 2. 32-37. 10.1145/1929887.1929902.

[2] Sue Sentance, Jane Waite & Maria Kallia (2019) Teaching computer programming with PRIMM: a sociocultural perspective, Computer Science Education, 29:2-3, 136-176, DOI: 10.1080/08993408.2019.1608781

teaching literacy. However, a better analogy would be like completing a comprehension exercise where you could read the text and watch the video, the later stages give you a chance to adapt the text and watch how your changes affect the characters and plotlines. Finally you get to write your own story using some of the methods, vocabulary and plot devices you have learnt about.

Prior Knowledge

Most pupils need a basic knowledge of the programming environment to be successful in code comprehension projects: How sprites can have many costumes, how the stage can have many backdrops. How sprites can be hidden or shown, etc. This type of knowledge is assumed in many of the predict, investigate and modify challenges.

Hands Off

Code comprehension projects really make pupils think deeply about the code but there is less opportunity to have direct hands-on time manipulating code and learning the basics of sprite creation and deletion.

Many stages of code comprehension benefit from pupils discussion facilitated by paired work which, whilst useful for so many reasons, also reduces the direct hands-on time each individual has with the programming environment.

Limitations

Even simple predictions, investigations and modifications are quite difficult without essential programming environment background knowledge and simple code manipulation skills.

Initial Strategy

For these reasons I would suggest that code comprehension not be your initial starting strategy when introducing younger pupils to block-based programming. If you are looking for useful initial strategies I suggest

Guided Discovery	Chapter 17
I build you build	Chapter 18

However, it doesn't take long for pupils to grasp the basics of your chosen programming environment and once they have, code comprehension is a must to develop deep thinking and pupil agency.

Following Chapters

If you primarily bought this book to improve your teaching of computing through exposure to new pedagogue then I suggest the following chapters on the aspects of code comprehension will help.

Code Comprehension Prediction
Chapter 10

Code Comprehension Run & Investigate
Chapter 11

Code Comprehension Modify
Chapter 12

Code Comprehension Create-Make
Chapter 13

If you are interested in adapting or making your own resources then in addition I suggest the chapter on

Code Comprehension Adaptations
Chapter 14

Code Comprehension Prediction

CHAPTER 10

Predict

Prediction encourages pupils to think about the wider purpose of the code.

In this aspect of code comprehension, pupils are given a paper or picture copy of the code on a digital device and asked to predict what they think it will do when the code is run.

They will need to read the code in the order it is likely to run in and predict meaning from it. If the examined code is a long project, they will need to break it into sections and work out what each section does before piecing them together to gain an overall prediction of the code's purpose. In these cases prediction uses a pupil's decomposition skills.

Programming Concepts in Prediction

Pupils will need to be able to interpret correctly how the code uses any specialist programming concepts encountered such as repetition, selection, procedures or variable use, which makes it important that pupils are not asked to predict using these concepts if they have not been taught how these work first.

Clues

Scratch is a very visual programming language and pupils will need to be provided with other pictorial or written clues to help them, such as costumes or backdrops.

If variables are included, then readouts of what values are assigned at different stages of the code should also be included.

Forms of Prediction

Prediction might involve a written prediction, a drawn prediction if the programming output included lines, pictures or graphics, or an oral prediction.

Reluctant Readers

Some pupils will be reluctant to read code because their general reading ability is poor. An adult or a learning partner could read the code for them whilst pointing to the blocks. They could take it in turns to read a line of blocks with their partner. If the code is a long script it could be cut up into sections so reluctant readers only see and read a small part at a time. It must be easy to assemble these sections in the right order, if there is a

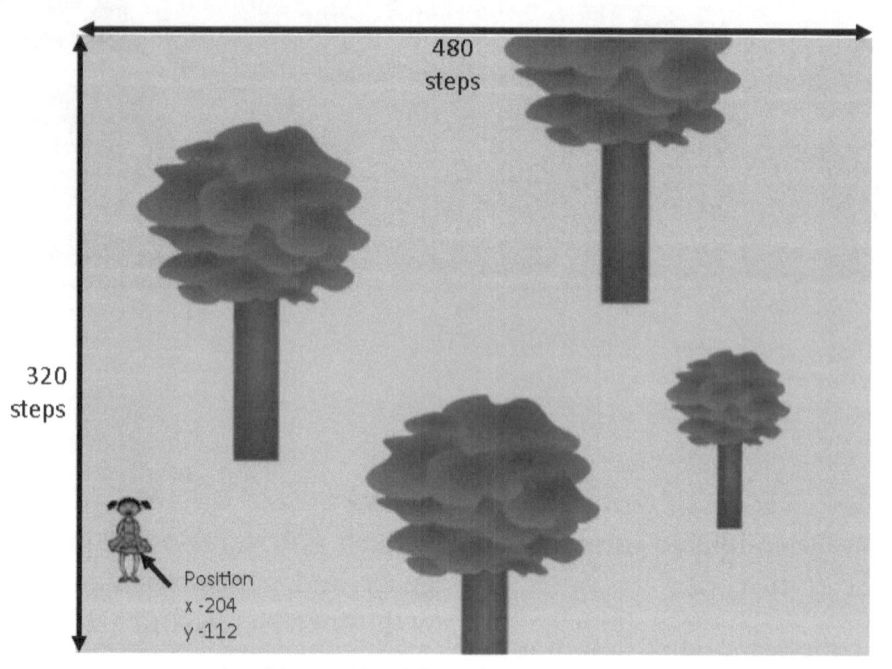

Scratch IT — Teaching Primary Programming with Scratch

Example additional backdrop clue provided alongside code

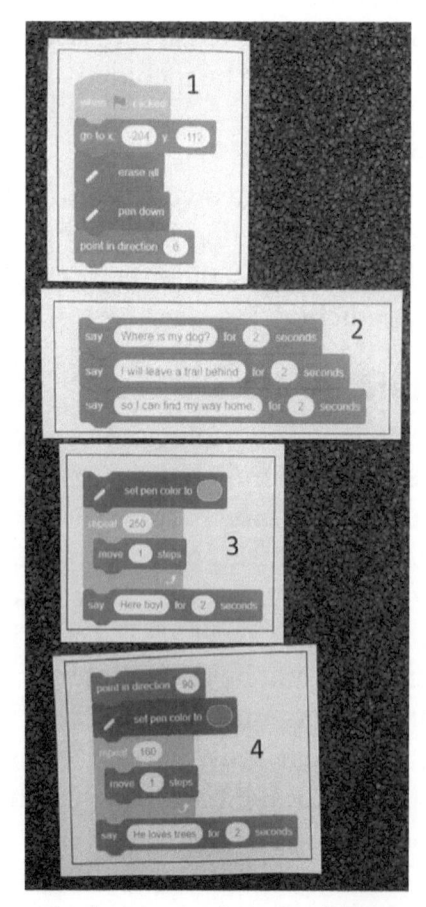

Predicting a section of code at a time to help reluctant readers

right order, as shown on the left. Otherwise a strategy designed to reduce cognitive load could inadvertently increase it.

Predicting Success

A prediction doesn't have to be fully correct to be a success. The aim of a prediction is to ensure pupils look deeply at code and try to decipher what it will do. Even a partial prediction of the whole or a correct prediction of a part will further pupil understanding. When pupils run the code, in later aspects of code comprehension, you often hear a sigh as pupils see what the code really did. Their partial understanding formed whilst predicting is being made more complete.

Classroom Organisation

Pupils can read and predict code on their own, although they miss out on the opportunity to discuss the code provided by working with a learning partner or small group. Teachers could work with the whole class, reading a section of code with everyone before each pupil writes a prediction on a whiteboard or paper. This can be useful to exemplify the process but will hinder the fastest finishers whilst they wait for the rest of the class and may not provide enough thinking time for all who need it.

I recommend similar-ability pairs, with most pairs working independently but with the teacher supporting pairs that struggle.

Examples

In this next section we will outline some example block-based predictions. You can find many more in context in the schemes of work that go with this book.

Context & Prior Learning

In the code example, shown below and on the next two pages, Year 4 pupils (8-9 years old) have just been introduced to the concept of repetition and specifically count controlled loops. They have roleplayed and written simple count-controlled loop everyday algorithms (see chapter 8 on concept before code). They had explored how different costumes work the year before.

The only other unknown apart from the count-controlled loop in a code context is the inclusion of an x and y block and pupils can either be instructed to ignore this block if they have not learnt about coordinates first or told that it just sends the sprite to a certain place on the stage/screen.

Questions to Encourage Code Reading

This example also included a few questions to encourage pupils to read the code carefully and engage with the main count-controlled loop concept before making predictions. For example *'Circle the count-controlled loops which repeat the most?'* These can be delivered by the teacher in a group or whole-class context or provided printed with the code.

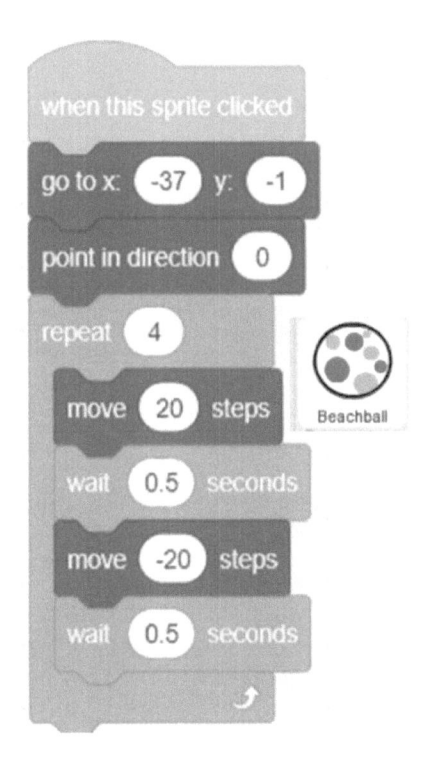

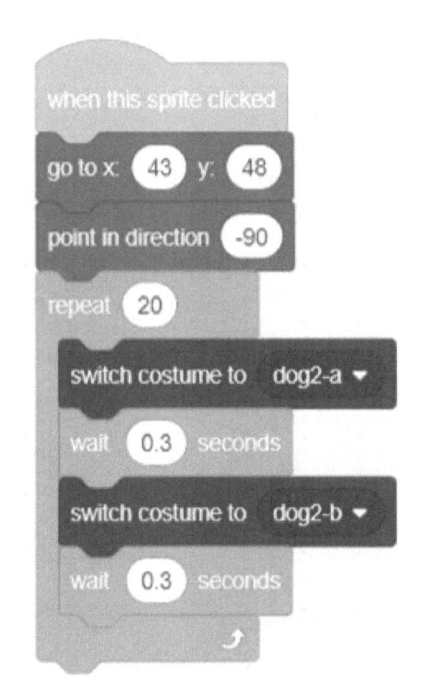

2 out of 5 toy giveaway code samples for pupils to predict the outcome

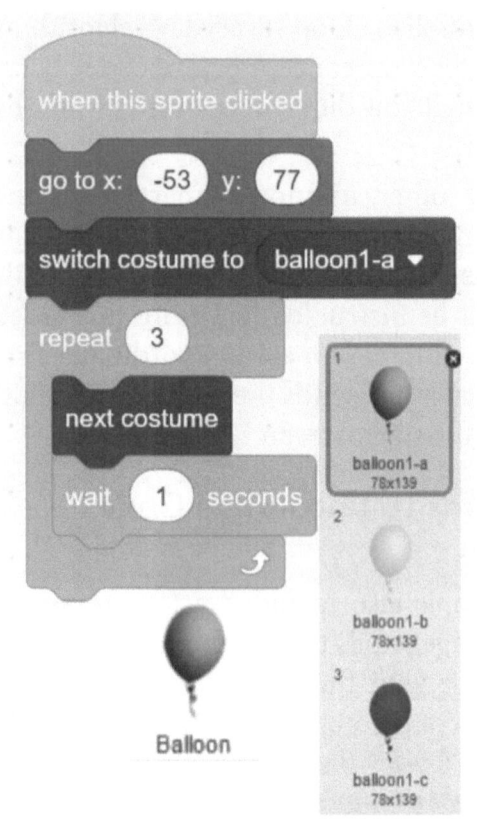

Scratch IT — Teaching Primary Programming with Scratch

Remaining 3 out of 5 toy giveaway code samples for pupils to predict the outcome

Pupil Prediction Examples

Pupils **A** is not really clear that a prediction is a summary of what will happen when the code is run and has decided to write out the code in order. Teachers can ask questions like *'What do you think the beachball will do when the code is run?'* or *'What will the beachball do when the code is run?'* to help pupils realise that a summary is needed.

Pupils **B** has many partially correct predictions. Despite not getting many fully correct there is evidence of code reading and understanding. In the beach ball they correctly predict movement and are only incorrect about its direction. The language used suggests that they have some understanding of what the loop does: *'go back and forth'*, *'keeps changing direction'*, *'it keeps changing character'*.

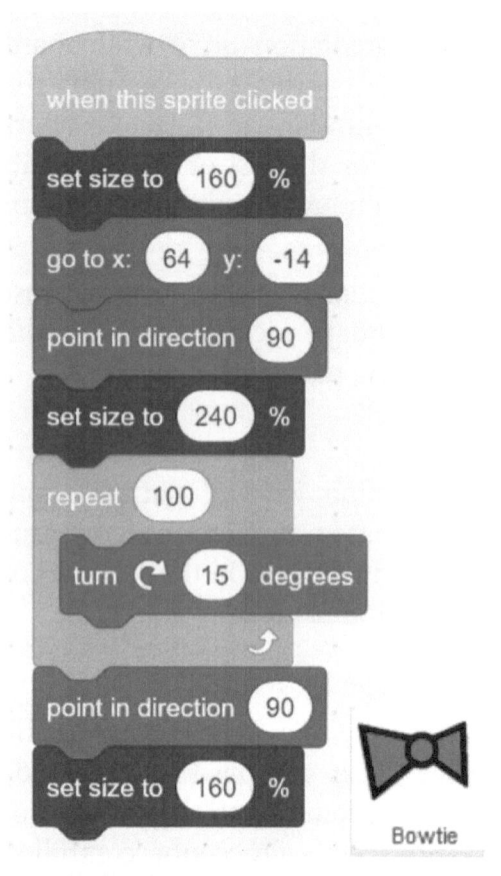

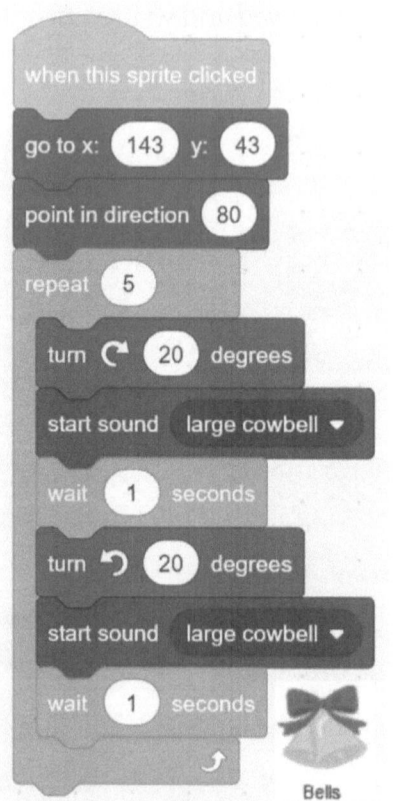

Code Comprehension Prediction

	Beachball	Balloon	Bowtie	Bells	Dog
A	When this sprite is clicked go to x:-37 y:-1 point in direction 0	When this sprite clicked go to x:9 y:775 switch costume to	When this sprite clicked set size 160 % go to	When this sprite	When this sprite
B	Go back and forth and wait ✗	It keeps changing direction ✗ ✗	It keeps changing sizes ✗	It keeps on changing music ✓	It keeps on changing character ✗
C	bounce	change colour	spin around	jingle	move legs
D	Side to side	change colour	~~GB~~ Get Big + small + spin	Ring	~~Walk~~ Walk ~~move~~ change

Toy Give Away Pupil Prediction in Year 4

Pupil C has correctly predicted what all the sprites will do, although they have missed out on the bow tie getting larger and smaller.

Pupil D has predicted correctly all sprites actions and has also included the bow tie change of size.

Drawing a Prediction

These examples are on the next page provided by Year 5 pupils (9-10 year olds) who have just been introduced to the idea of simple procedures. There were seven questions that encouraged them to read the code first. They were then asked to draw what the code would output on the screen.

Programming outcome

When this algorithm is converted into code and run it draws the pattern shown called code outcome on the next page.

Prediction Errors

The majority got most of the questions and the first part of the prediction correct. Triangles were correctly identified and the number of triangles was often predicted correctly, indicating that their introduction to count-controlled loops was remembered. The spiral pattern was the most missed element.

Matching Code to Code Summary

Another useful prediction method is to ask pupils to match the code to the code summary. This requires no writing, which reduces cognitive load.

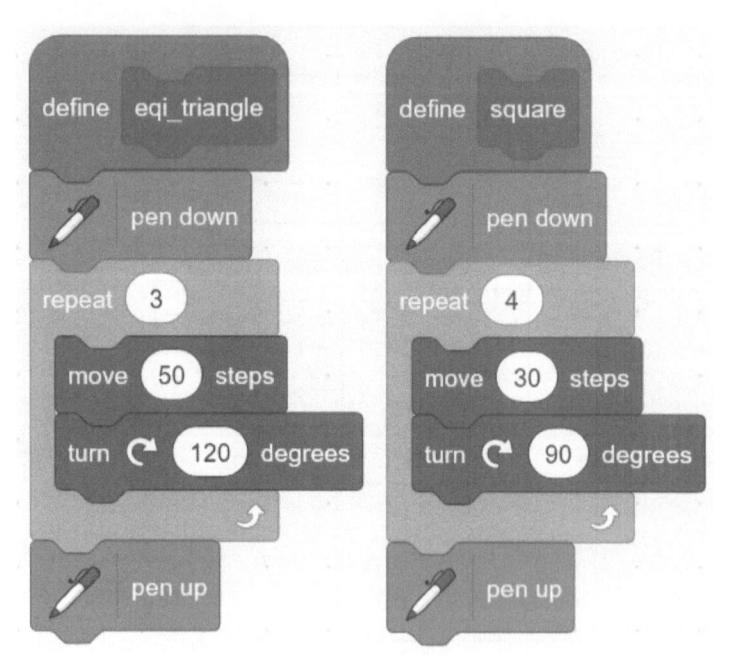

Scratch IT – Teaching Primary Programming with Scratch

Procedures

```
define eqi_triangle
    pen down
    repeat 3
        move 50 steps
        turn ↻ 120 degrees
    pen up
```

```
define square
    pen down
    repeat 4
        move 30 steps
        turn ↻ 90 degrees
    pen up
```

Code outcome

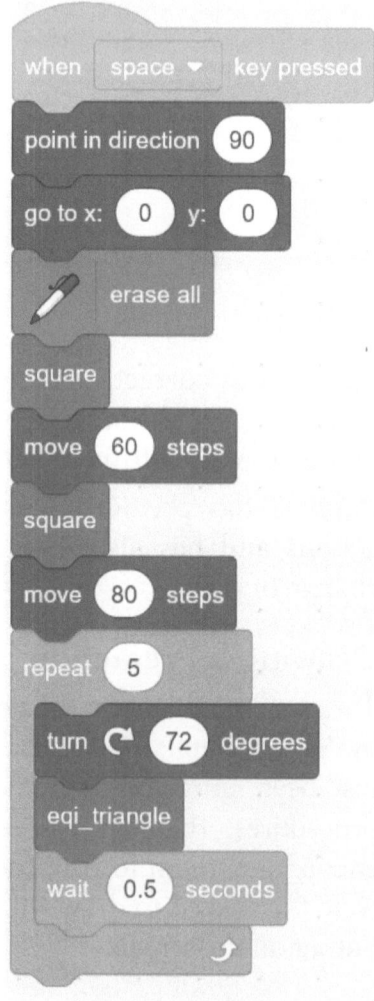

Year 5 Pupil Predictions

Main program that calls the procedures

```
when space key pressed
point in direction 90
go to x: 0 y: 0
erase all
square
move 60 steps
square
move 80 steps
repeat 5
    turn ↻ 72 degrees
    eqi_triangle
    wait 0.5 seconds
```

80

In the example on the right, pupils have to match code with conditions to the summary on the left. Many pupils would struggle to write descriptions that accurately distinguished between very similar code examples. This is especially true of the first three code examples.

Teachers can also provide a correct match, which pupils can examine first as a simpler way in to the task as shown by the arrow.

Predicting the Flow of Control

Predicting can also involve thinking about the flow of control which you can look at in more detail in **Flow of Control** chapter 27.

Summary

Code prediction is a really useful tool that helps pupils to think about the bigger purpose of the code. However, my classroom observations at primary school level suggest that this stage can be excluded with minimal overall effect on pupils overall comprehension and ability to create quality code. However, my statement has no research basis and the classroom practitioner always needs to be open to the fact that they are missing something important which might come to light through further rigorous research.

Match the code on the right to the correct summary on the left by drawing lines. One has been done for you

Summary
Asks a question and gives **different** answers if your answer is the **same** or **different** to the answer in the condition
Asks a question **over and over again** until you type in the answer in the condition
Asks a question and gives different answers if the number you type in is **same as, less than or greater than** the number in the condition
Asks a question and says something if your answer is the **same** as the answer in the condition
Says something until Scratch **senses a noise greater than 50**

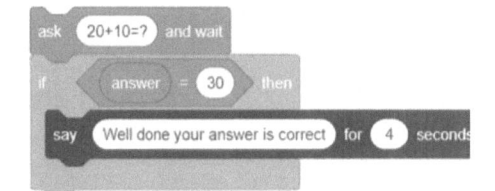

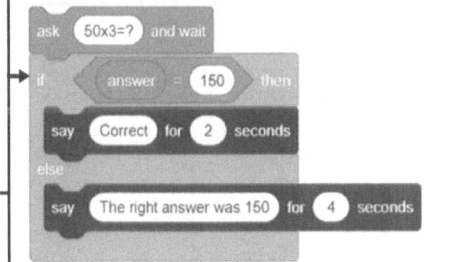

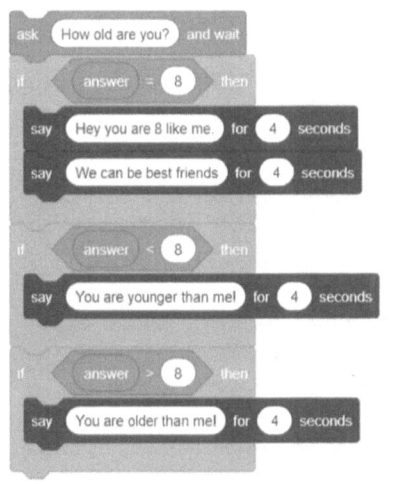

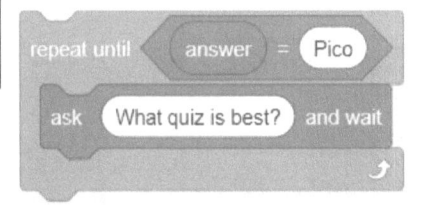

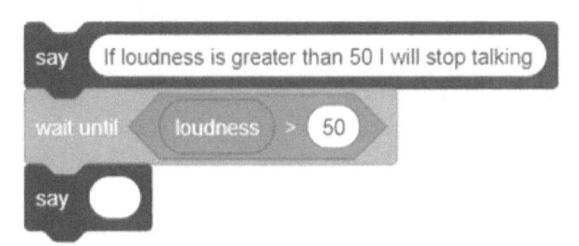

Sue Sentance,

Developed the influential **PRIMM** strategy **predict, run, investigate, modify, make.**

She is now chief learning officer at the Raspberry Pi Foundation.

The correct matches

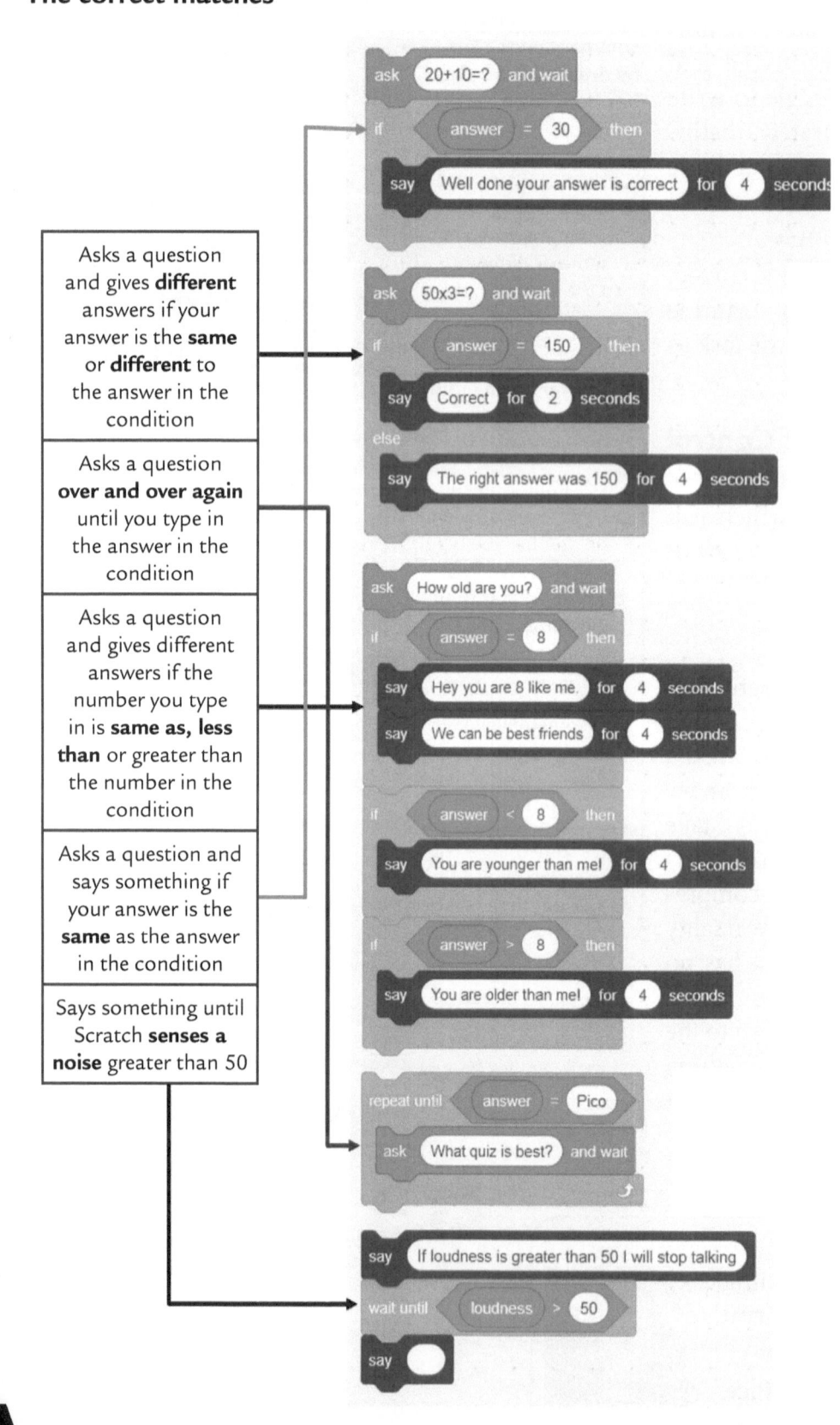

Description	Scratch blocks
Asks a question and gives **different** answers if your answer is the **same** or **different** to the answer in the condition	ask 20+10=? and wait if answer = 30 then say Well done your answer is correct for 4 seconds

Asks a question **over and over again** until you type in the answer in the condition	ask 50x3=? and wait
	if answer = 150 then
	  say Correct for 2 seconds
	else
	  say The right answer was 150 for 4 seconds

Asks a question and gives different answers if the number you type in is **same as, less than** or greater than the number in the condition	ask How old are you? and wait
	if answer = 8 then
	  say Hey you are 8 like me. for 4 seconds
	  say We can be best friends for 4 seconds
	if answer < 8 then
	  say You are younger than me! for 4 seconds
	if answer > 8 then
	  say You are older than me! for 4 seconds

Asks a question and says something if your answer is the **same** as the answer in the condition	repeat until answer = Pico ask What quiz is best? and wait
Says something until Scratch **senses a noise** greater than 50	say If loudness is greater than 50 I will stop talking wait until loudness > 50 say

Code Comprehension Run & Investigate

CHAPTER 11

Run, Investigate, Use

Run and investigate are the second and third stages of **PRIMM**, Use is the first stage of **Use-modify-create** (see code comprehension overview, chapter 9). Essentially, both posit the idea of pupils exploring pre-prepared code first.

Formal or Informal Code Examination

When first trying to use-modify-create, I took use literally and asked pupils to use the code without any stipulation, question or instruction. My best programmers and those of my pupils who are good at asking question got something out of the exercise, but the vast majority of pupils made no attempt to read the code carefully or define their own questions. It wasn't until approaching using code through the prism of PRIMM that I realised that using code need to be much more run and investigate guided by the teacher. Most pupils won't investigate the code carefully without teacher input and guidance.

The Aim

The aim of run and investigate is to examine code carefully, to see how it works. To know what it does and how it does it. As teachers we have to ask ourselves: how do we know that pupils have really done this if we have not guided them through the things we know are important? That is why this chapter is much more about Run and Investigate code rather than just using code.

Whole Class, Groups, Pairs, Individuals

There are lots of ways you can run and investigate code with pupils. Working with the whole class at the same time will help everyone to understand the process clearly, but will frustrate faster or slower workers and limit discussion to teacher-designated times. Providing written questions that pupils can progress through at their own pace overcomes these limitations. Whilst some pupils will work admirably working on their own, the vast majority of pupils will benefit from the discussion that comes from working with a partner of similar ability.

Good Questions

Superior written question for younger pupils:
- Are written as simply as possible using the least complex language ,
- Don't contain duplication of question type within the same module unless there is an important difference in each example studied,

- Force pupils to examine the key aspects of the program,
- Can be answered by the pupil using as little writing as possible,
- Gradually increase in difficulty,
- Contain reminders of technical words or phrase meanings when these need to be used,
- Link to key programming concepts introduced,
- Revise previously taught concepts aiding retrival practice

Example Questions and Answers

2. How many **condition switches-between-action** blocks are there?

   3 (1 mark)

3. What condition switches **between** the forward and reversing backdrops?

   space key pressed (1 mark)

Pupil-Marked Teacher-Checked

Self-marking allows pupils to check their work before they proceed and acts as a filter.

Those who get most of the questions right and can see where they went wrong can proceed without teacher intervention.

Those who got most questions wrong or don't understand where they went wrong can seek teacher support.

Macro or Micro

Macro questions focus on the wider purpose of the program or section of the program. Micro questions focus on smaller parts of the code. Looking at the example below, a macro question might ask the pupil to *describe in their own words what this code section does?* A micro question might ask *what stops the sprite from moving and pointing towards the mouse-pointer?*

Predicting using PRIMM is a form of macro question. However, it is different to macro **run-investigate** type questions in that the pupil can run the code to aid their understanding.

Code Reading and Code Running

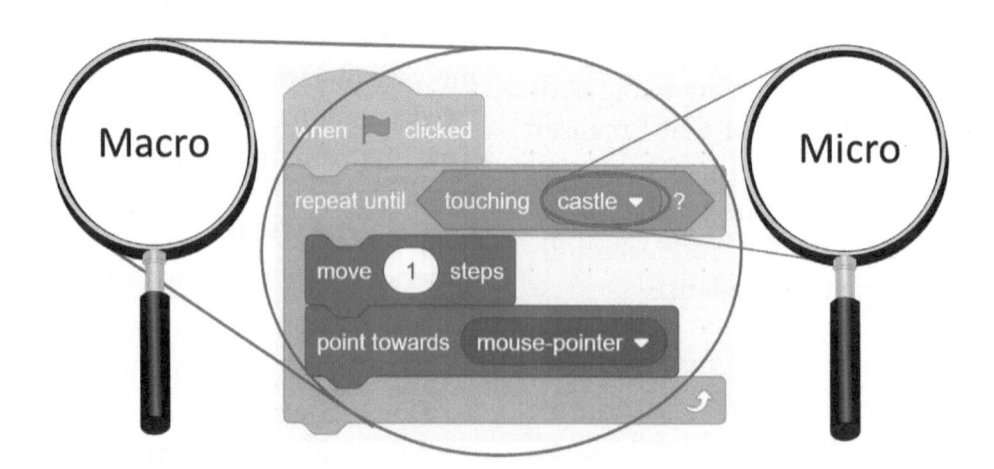

Both of these questions from the last section could be answered purely by observing the program running without looking at the code. However, this can take a long time. In this example it might take a lot of gameplay until you finally accidentally touch the castle and observe that your sprite stopped moving. Something else might have been happening at the same time your sprite stopped, and you could draw the wrong conclusion as to why it stopped. It is the combination of observing the code in action and being able to read the code which makes run and investigation so useful.

An analogy taken from book comprehension is being able to read a portion of Shakespeare and also having access to a quality video of it being acted out.

Cognitive Overload

But wouldn't these two sources of information code and running code, provided at the same time, increase the pupils' cognitive load and make it harder to comprehend?

Observing pupils using, reading and investigating code, they tend to focus on one aspect at a time, running the code separately and then reading parts of it. In fact many pupils put the code into full-screen mode when executing it and observing its effects, which might be due to the fact that they don't want to be distracted by the code or simply that they can see more in full-screen mode.

It would be interesting to research if enforcing full-screen mode during code running and testing makes any difference to pupils learning.

Literal, Inferential, Evaluative

Literal

Literal questions have answers that are directly stated in the text. Examples using the code example on the right might include.

What curved starting block is used in this example? How many steps does the sprite travel in every repeat?

Inferential

Inferential questions require the answerer to infer meaning from the context or put together multiple pieces of information to infer meaning. Examples using the code example above might include:

What stops the sprite moving and pointing towards the mouse-pointer? Summarise what this section of code does when it is run. Can the user predict accurately how many loops will be executed before the loop is stopped? Explain your answer. Loops are either definite in that they have a known number of repeats or indefinite in that the number of repeats are unknown. What type of loop is used here?

Evaluative

Evaluative questions require the user to formulate a response based on their own opinion. Examples using the code example might include:

Is this the most effective way to end movement and steering in a game? Explain your reasoning.

Literal questions are always easier for students to answer than inferential and evaluative questions and as such often dominate code comprehension investigation in the early stages. Their main purpose is to force the pupil to read the code carefully.

Evaluative questions tell you the most about a pupil's code comprehension but take longer for pupils to answer and will cause the most support issues. It is perfectly possible to exclude all evaluative questions from primary programming and still meet the original aim of examining code carefully, to see how it works. However, as pupils progress in understanding, these questions become more useful.[1]

Revisiting Learning

We know that revisiting previous learning can trigger memories that make it easier to build new learning. Asking a question that focusses on prior learning can be a way to achieve this. *Inside the loop (on the previous page) what is the second instruction in the sequence?* The current focus is not on sequences as these were learnt about in the last module, but a sequence question will trigger previous learning memories.

Paper or Digital?

Questions can be asked and answers collected using a variety of different media. Traditional paper has its charms and makes it easier to show others, who are less technically minded, what has been achieved.

Questions can be displayed on a screen and answered directly on screen through typing or writing if the screen is touch-sensitive. Teachers have used code comprehension materials via management systems such as Google Classroom, Office 365 or Seesaw effectively.

With a little more work, teachers could record the question so that pupils could hear as well as read the question.

Platforms like Seesaw also provide ways for users to record their answer audibly and provide an oral rather than written input, widening the appeal of this methodology for younger, less confident readers.

Simple Procedures Example

On the right we have two simple procedures or sub programs at the top, and below that we have a main program that calls those procedures at certain times, calls, means, triggers, or, starts, the procedures. So the square block will call the define square procedure as shown by the arrow.

Questions

Here are six questions that require pupils to run the program and read the code carefully to answer.

1. How many times in the main program (starts when space key is pressed) is the square procedure called or used?
2. What shapes do the two procedures draw?
3. When the square procedure is run. how many times will it move 30 forward?
4. How many times in the main program is the eqi_triangle procedure used?
5. Which shape would have the longest perimeter?
6. If we removed the loop from the square procedure, what would the square procedure draw?

Question Commentary

Questions 1 and 4 help pupils to realise that procedures can be called multiple times. Making them an eloquent way to write code.

Questions 3 and 4 are revision questions that links back to count-controlled loops.

Question 5 is essentially a maths question. However, maths shape understanding is essential for this type of programming.

---

[1] The block model research by Carsten Schulte may also be a useful way of thinking about questions in PRIMM. Matthew Wimpenny-Smith and I discuss it in this video. https://youtu.be/aWwfBJTCns8

Code Comprehension Run & Investigate

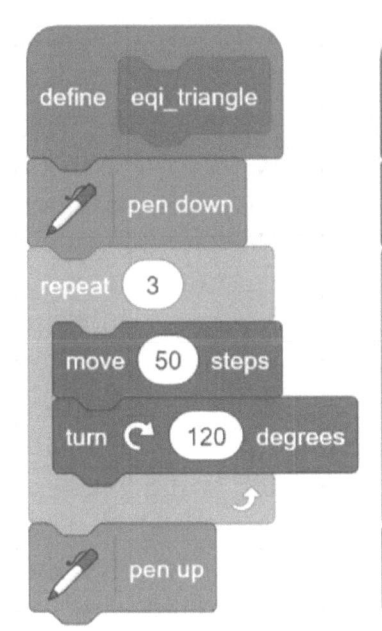

Procedures

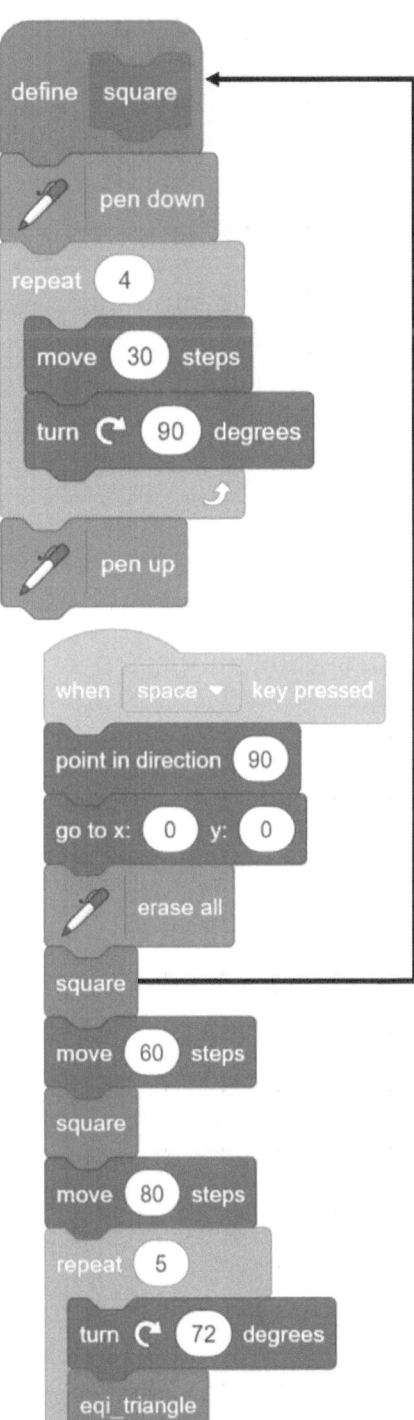

define eqi_triangle
- pen down
- repeat 3
  - move 50 steps
  - turn ↻ 120 degrees
- pen up

define square
- pen down
- repeat 4
  - move 30 steps
  - turn ↻ 90 degrees
- pen up

Main Program

when space key pressed
- point in direction 90
- go to x: 0 y: 0
- erase all
- square
- move 60 steps
- square
- move 80 steps
- repeat 5
  - turn ↻ 72 degrees
  - eqi_triangle
  - wait 0.5 seconds

Question 6 can be answered as a prediction or by removing the loop or both. It spans the gap between code comprehension sections, between using code and modifying it.

Adaptable Procedures Example

In the example below, pupils examined a game written using adaptable procedures. They had time to play the game before spending time answering these questions about how it works. Although the example is from a Year 5 pupil, the complexity of work is more applicable to secondary pupils ages 11 years old plus.

Example Code

You can find the game code on the Scratch website at

https://scratch.mit.edu/projects/333233360/

It is too complex to print here.

Question Commentary

Question 6 is a question about initialisation. Pupils are asked to identify blocks that are used for initialisation purposes. Questions like this are very useful ways of exemplifying what pupils should be doing when they write their own code.

Question 9 asks pupils to explain what they think the code does in their own words. These types of questions are the hardest to self-mark, as there is often a degree of difference in the answer modelled and the answer provided by the pupil. This pupil has navigated this difficulty successfully and interpreted the answer given successfully, but not all pupils will, especially when they are new to code comprehension techniques.

6, Name three blocks that are initialisation (designed to set the program back to how it looked and ran when it was first run). *go to x:-210 y:141, Switch backdrop to a backdrop & RESET Timer.*

7, Which procedures are not inside loops in the main programs? *end-level & endgame.*

8, In level 1 how many procedures are inside a loop until ScratchCat touches the **open_orange** sprite? *HINT Repeat until is a loop.* *4.*

9, The restart procedure has a complex condition. Explain in your own words how you think it works. *Is it touches the orange or any rows it will go back to the start.*

10, Look at the move_right adaptable procedure. What will the speed of x be when the right arrow key is pressed in level 1, level 2 and level 3? *HINT Look at the procedure and the blocks that run the procedure in the main program.* *Level 1 = 2 Level 2 = 1.75 Level 3 = 1.5*

11, Look at the **gravity** adaptable procedure and the blocks that run it in the main program. In which level does the ScratchCat fall fastest? *Level 1*

> **The correct answer provided to question 9**
>
> Any indications that OR means that any of the conditions can send the cat back to the start. (1 mark)

Questions 10 and 11 involve pupils having to examine multiple sections of code linked by procedures and common purpose. It would be appropriate to assign higher marks to these types of questions, as they are far more complex than earlier questions.

Other Ways to Indicate Comprehension

Both the examples on this page and the last are aimed at upper KS2 or KS3 pupils from about 9 years old who have covered more basic programming concepts previously. See chapter 21 on Block-Based Programming Progression for more information. However, less confident writers can show comprehension by circling, underlining or other forms of answering. Multiple choice questions can also be used to reduce the amount of writing. However, these methods will only take you so far and often include printing larger questions.

If the real issue is that pupils can't read the code, then block-based programming may not be appropriate for these pupils until their reading improves. Programming is nearly always an exercise in reading both on and off the screen.

Summary

Investigate and run the code is an important part of PRIMM which encourages pupils to really examine and learn from quality examples.

Where this stage has been removed from PRIMM a significant number of pupils have struggled to create quality code, which has led me to conclude that it is a vital part in the process.

Code Comprehension Modify

CHAPTER 12

Modify

Modify code is the second task in use-modify-create and the fourth task in PRIMM.

Three Main Aims

It has three main aims. Firstly it continues the work of investigating aspects of code. Secondly it provides a bridge between passive code investigation and fully active code creation, a half way stage where programming novices can experience some aspects of code creation in a more supported manner. Thirdly it increases the ownership of the code example, as some aspects have now been changed by the pupil.

Code Comprehension

All the advice about good code comprehension questions outlined in the previous chapter apply to code modification questions.

Recording Modifications?

Additionally, teachers have to decide whether the changes in the code are enough or require a description of the changes?

Pro Not Recording

- The process is shortened providing more time for code creation
- As long as the code sample the pupil changes is saved then evidence of work is preserved
- The amount of writing is reduced, which makes the process more enjoyable for less confident or less quick writers

Pro Recording

- Answers recorded can be more easily checked by pupils to see if they are correct or not
- The act of summarising the changes made forces the pupil to engage at a deeper depth with what they have modified.
- If they have worked in pairs, how does the teacher know that both pupils understood the changes made?
- Written answers checked and marked by the pupil are much less time-consuming for teachers, assessment purposes.

Recording Options

If teachers decide that recording modifications is desirable, then what are their options?

Tick list

A tick list is a simple way for a pupil to record that they have completed a modify challenge. However, it provides no record of what was done to modify the code and there is no way for a pupil to self mark it.

Describe Changes

This is more useful to the teacher, as it can be marked or self-marked if the teacher provides a marking rubric or modelled answers.

Copy the Screen

Pupils can use screen capture software to copy and annotate their modification.

Classroom Observations

Including a requirement to record modifications and mark them has led to many pupils giving the activity a higher status and spending more effort on it. For these reasons I recommend recording changes. If pupil's writing is very slow, screen capture and annotation provide an alternative process.

Code Modification Examples

Helicopter Example

Below, we see examples of code provided to modify a module designed to teach pupils about infinite indefinite loops.

View Code Online

You may wish to view this project inside Scratch and you can access it here.

https://scratch.mit.edu/projects/316961043/

Pupil Answers

These answers on the right were produced by Year 5 pupils (9-10 years old) working in pairs although each pupil recorded their answers separately.

Question Commentary

Questions 1-3 directly relate to indefinite loops where pupils have to make changes within a forever loop to effect change to the game.

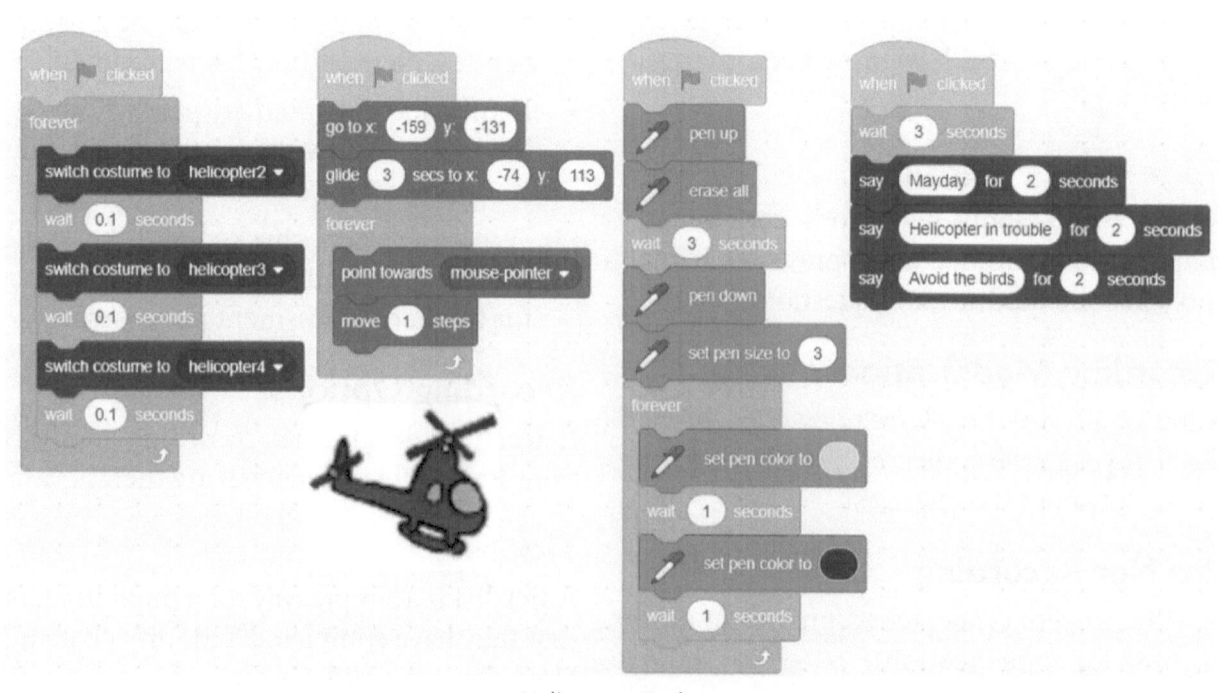

Helicopter Code

Code Comprehension Modify

A

Helicopter Sprite Questions

1, Can you make the rotor on the helicopter run slower? What did you change?

I changed on the switch costume 0.5 to 3sec ✓

2, Can you make the helicopter move faster? What did you change?

I changed the amount of steps ✓

3, Can you make the smoke trail change colour quicker? What did you change?

I change the amount of seconds inbetween ✓

4, Can you make the smoke trail wider? What did you change?

I changed the pen size ✓

5, Can you make the smoke trail start earlier? What did you change?

After the clear block I changed the wait block. ✓

B

Helicopter Sprite Questions

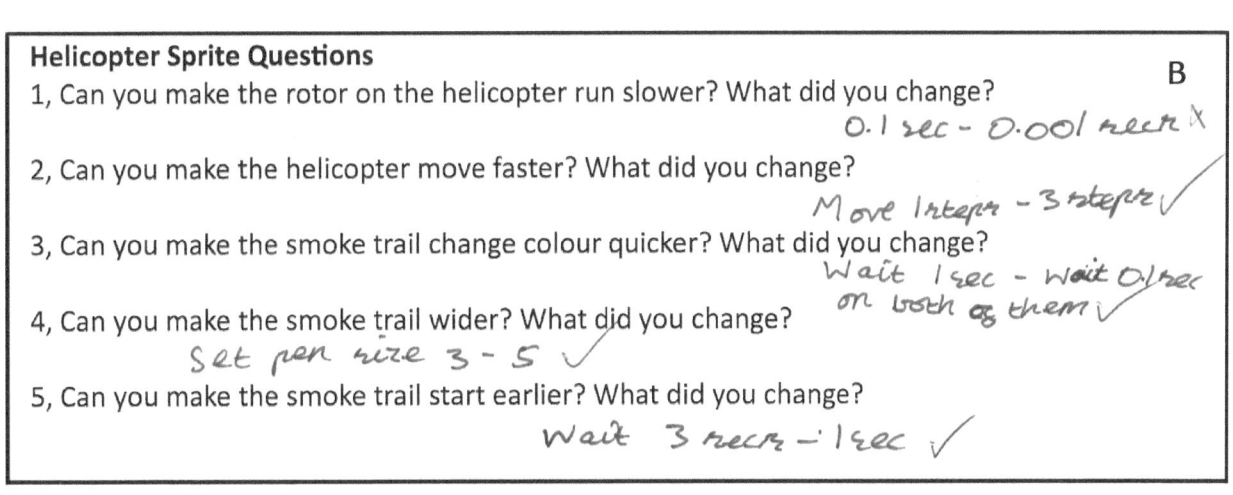

1, Can you make the rotor on the helicopter run slower? What did you change?

0.1 sec - 0.001 sec ✗

2, Can you make the helicopter move faster? What did you change?

Move 1step - 3 steps ✓

3, Can you make the smoke trail change colour quicker? What did you change?

Wait 1 sec - Wait 0.1 sec on both of them ✓

4, Can you make the smoke trail wider? What did you change?

Set pen size 3 - 5 ✓

5, Can you make the smoke trail start earlier? What did you change?

Wait 3 secs - 1 sec ✓

Two pupils modify code answers

Provided Answers

1. Increase the wait time of all three blocks above 0.1 seconds. (1 mark)
2. Increase move to more than 1 step (1 mark)
3. Reduce wait 1 second to less than 1 second (1 mark)
4. Set pen size to greater than 3 (1 mark)
5. Reduce wait 3 seconds to less than 3 or remove the block. (1 mark)

Questions 4 & 5 are about the smoke trail created using pen blocks. These are included to encourage pupils to explore this mechanism in case they wish to adapt and use it in their own game creation later, another consideration for both investigate and modify questions.

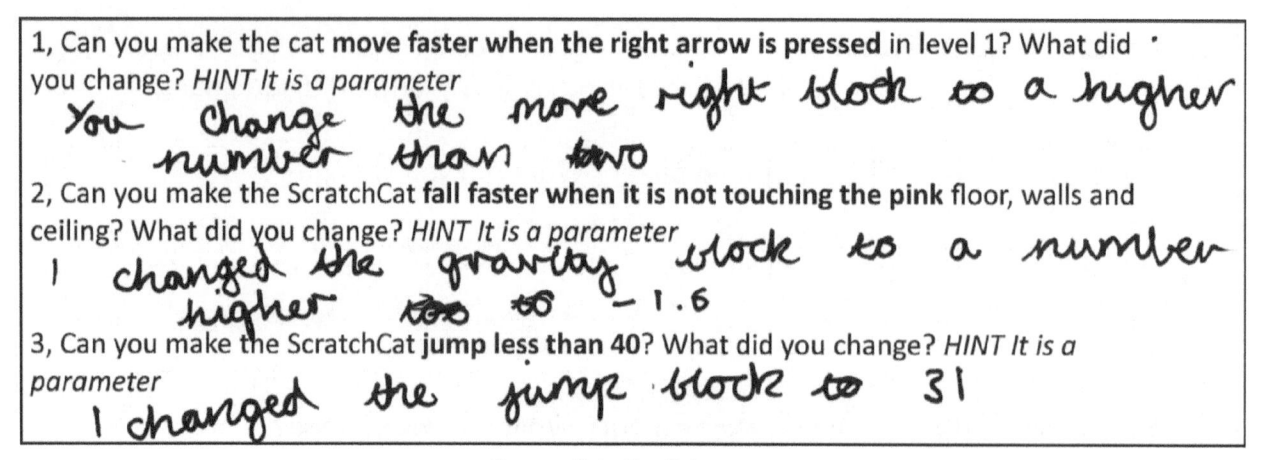

> 1, Can you make the cat **move faster when the right arrow is pressed** in level 1? What did you change? HINT It is a parameter
>
> *You change the move right block to a higher number than two*
>
> 2, Can you make the ScratchCat **fall faster when it is not touching the pink floor, walls and ceiling?** What did you change? HINT It is a parameter
>
> *I changed the gravity block to a number higher too to -1.6*
>
> 3, Can you make the ScratchCat **jump less than 40**? What did you change? HINT It is a parameter
>
> *I changed the jump block to 31*

Orange Run Pupil Answers

Orange Run

In this next example pupils are modifying game code to learn more about adaptable procedures. Whilst the example is from a Year 6 (10-11 years old) pupil, work of this complexity is more typical in secondary (11-14 years).

Full Code

The code is too complex to print in full here, but you can access it all online at

https://scratch.mit.edu/projects/333233360/

Question Commentary

All three questions focus on how parameters change the programming that they are used in. This links back to the overall module aim, which was to introduce and model how procedure parameters are used in gaming.

All three questions include a hint to focus pupils on modifying parameters. This was added because pupils were spending lots of time trying to modify the code without changing the parameters. Whilst there are always multiple ways to achieve the goal in programming and finding alternate methods is valuable, it was detracting from the main lesson objective and significantly increasing the time needed to modify the code.

Focussing pupils on the most important part of the question using bold text was another attempt to increase the number of hints.

A question focussed on alternate methods to accomplish the same goal would be a useful bridge between modification and making.

In question 2 the pupils' answer is wrong, although she has identified the correct parameter to change. A partial mark might be appropriate.

> **Provided Answers**
> 1. Change move_right (2) to a higher number in level 1 (1 mark)
> 2. Change gravity (-2) to a lower negative number such as –3 (1 mark)
> 3. Change jump (40) to a lower number such as jump (30) (1 mark)

Pupils Enjoy Modifying Projects

When questioned, even pupils who were not interested in playing or creating games enjoyed modifying the game code.

Modify is a Step to Create

It can be tempting to stop after the modify sections. Pupils have been challenged, they

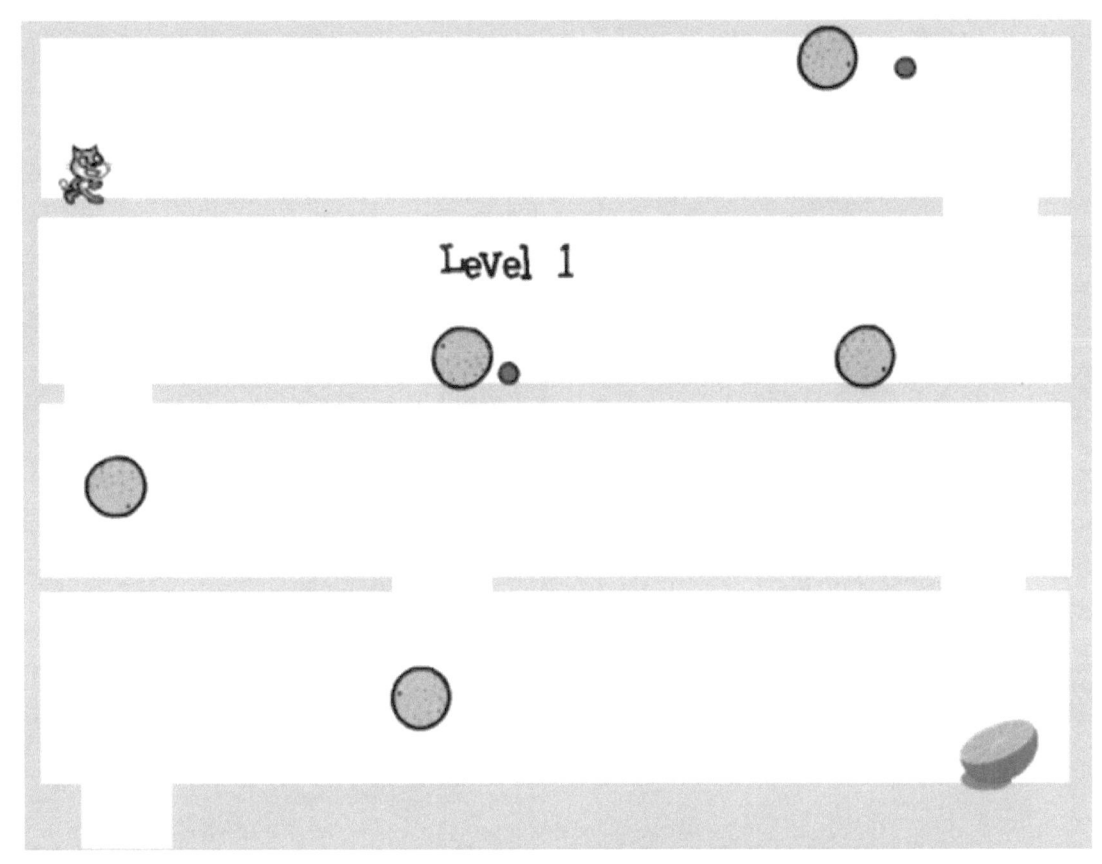

Orange Run 1st Level Screen

have had to think deeply and code comprehension has been increased.

I think it is important to constantly have pupil agency in the forefront. Full agency is only achieved when pupils can create their own programming using the concepts and understanding modelled through predict, investigate and modify. For that to become a reality pupils must make the jump from modify to create.

With that end in mind I will often reduce the number of modify challenges for those who are struggling to complete work in the time allocated. I do this by crossing out or reducing the number of questions so that pupils always have time for create. I rarely do this to start with as I have been proved wrong by individuals working harder than I expected on too many occasions. Making time for create is important.

Can We Leave Out Modify?

As a test I left out the modify section of one module with Year 4 pupils. When they got to create they really struggled, and many pupils created very little. Modify is an important scaffolding step to creation.

Investigate and Modify Working Methods

One Screen or Two

When pupils are working on investigate or modify, they mostly work in pairs. I purposely make them only use one computer. This forces them to talk to their partner increasing discussion.

Main program

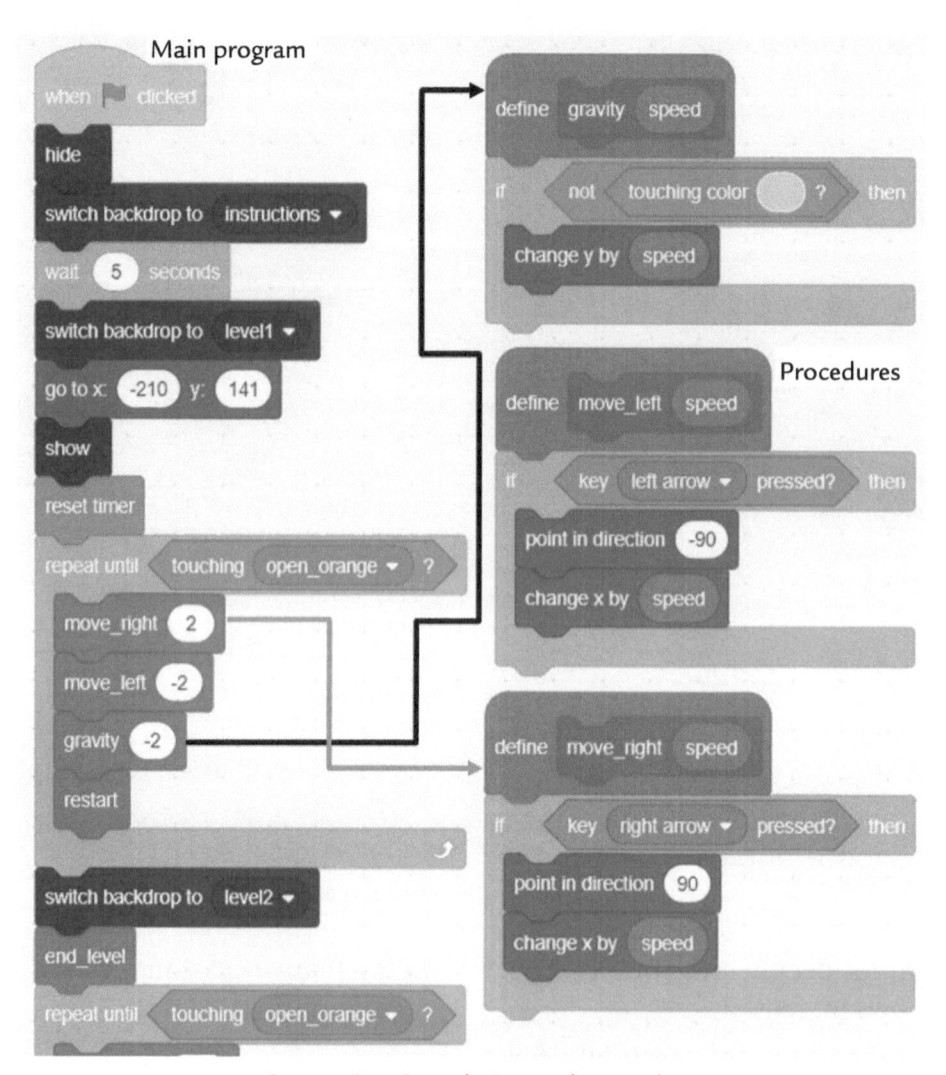

```
when [flag] clicked
hide
switch backdrop to instructions
wait 5 seconds
switch backdrop to level1
go to x: -210 y: 141
show
reset timer
repeat until <touching open_orange?>
    move_right 2
    move_left -2
    gravity -2
    restart
switch backdrop to level2
end_level
repeat until <touching open_orange?>
```

Procedures

```
define gravity speed
if <not <touching color [ ]?>> then
    change y by speed

define move_left speed
if <key left arrow pressed?> then
    point in direction -90
    change x by speed

define move_right speed
if <key right arrow pressed?> then
    point in direction 90
    change x by speed
```

Orange Run Scratch Cat Code Sample

I insist on only one pupil being allowed to touch the keyboard and mouse. When they move on to a new question that pupil changes. This avoids arguments and makes sure that both pupils get equal access.[1]

If they are working in pairs I also insist that they stay at the same speed as their partner.

---

[1] Influence by paired programming research which you can read more about in chapter 20.

Code Comprehension Create

CHAPTER 13

Hardest Transition

Sentance, in her research into code comprehension strategies using PRIMM with secondary pupils, identified the transition from modify to create as one of the hardest steps that pupils make.[1] Other educators who have used code comprehension resources have also echoed her observation.

Taking the lessons from her research and teacher observations into account, I recommend making the transition from modify to create a more gradual one.

Progression in Creative Projects

When first designing creative projects I was motivated by the constructionists, and so I built as much choice into projects as I could. I observed that many pupils would often go straight past a project choice that would have built on their understanding to attempt things that sounded exciting or fun, often to detriment of their progress in learning.

I realised that I have a far better understanding of progression in programming than my pupils have. Armed with this knowledge, I group create challenges by complexity, instructing pupils to choose one or more

Toys in the Toy Giveaway Project with space to add more sprites on the table

easier projects first before progressing to harder ones. This has definitely improved my pupils' creative output. In the most complex sections I still try and keep an open-ended choice that links to the concept taught for those who are inspired.

Create Within the Exemplar Project First

Some pupils find it hard to create new code when they start a blank copy of their programming environment. All their handy

---

[1] Sue Sentance, Jane Waite & Maria Kallia (2019) Teaching computer programming with PRIMM: a sociocultural perspective, Computer Science Education, 29:2-3, 136-176, DOI: 10.1080/08993408.2019.1608781

examples are now closed, and for many this hinders their flow of learning.

Trying to find creative projects they can first accomplish within the exemplar project has really helped. In the Toy Giveaway Project, illustrated on the previous page, pupils were asked to either add a new toy (sprite) to the table or create a costume animation. The only stipulation being that they must use a count-controlled loop. Creating within the existing programming environment has led every child in most classes to complete one or more of these opening challenges.

If you are working online, you can also instruct your pupils to keep their earlier work open in a separate browser tab, whilst working in a new tab on their creative project.

I think this is similar to having your workings to hand in maths or key words in literacy. Being able to quickly refer to examples you investigated and modified really helps.

When pupils ask me if they should create a new project or adapt the existing one, I give them the choice and, if they are not sure, steer them towards creating within the exemplar. Many choose to continue to create even the harder challenges within the exemplar project.

Modify More or Easy Creation First

Of course it might be argued that easy creations within an existing project are more the domain of the modify stage. In Scratch, if it involves adding a new sprite or building new sections of code within an existing project rather than adding a few blocks to or changing existing code then I classify it as create.

Transition from Other Methodologies to Code Comprehension

Some pupils treat the freedom to choose in the create or make section as an excuse to ignore the challenges and do their own thing. Very rarely has this been a higher order project, and if it is they can proceed with my blessing. Checking in on pupils and asking them what challenges they have chosen is a nice way to find out more about them and their preferences and check they are on task.

Enough Time

It is very important that every pupil gets enough time to create a project. Trun-cating other sections of PRIMM process for SEN pupils and slower finishers enables that.

Working Solo

Whilst I love listening to the fantastic programming talk, that comes from paired work in the earlier stages of PRIMM, it is so important that pupils' knowledge and understanding is tested in the best way possible, by having to create their own project. For this reason I aways insist that pupils create on their own.

I have also found that some pupils will sit back and let their partner lead in all things if they know that they don't have to create on their own. Knowing that you will have to design and create code makes it important to be a full partner in all of the earlier PRIMM stages.

Create easier choice (Choose one or more of these ideas first)

1. Look for another toy sprite to add to the table. Decide what the toy is going to do. Adapt one of the ideas from **toygiveaway** such as moving up-down, rotating, changing costumes, playing a sound etc to program the toy to do something when clicked on.

2. Find two character that have multiple costumes (not all sprites have multiple costumes). Animate them to look like they are moving for a short period of time using a count controlled loops.

Create harder choice (Choose one or more of these ideas second)

1. Make your own scene with sprites that do something when they are clicked. You must use count controlled loops as part of each sprites programming.

2. Make a sprite move around the screen using multiple count controlled loops, the move steps and the point in direction blocks.

3. Make your own program that uses count controlled loops.

Toy Give Away Creative Challenges Illustrating Easier Projects Within The Exemplar Project First

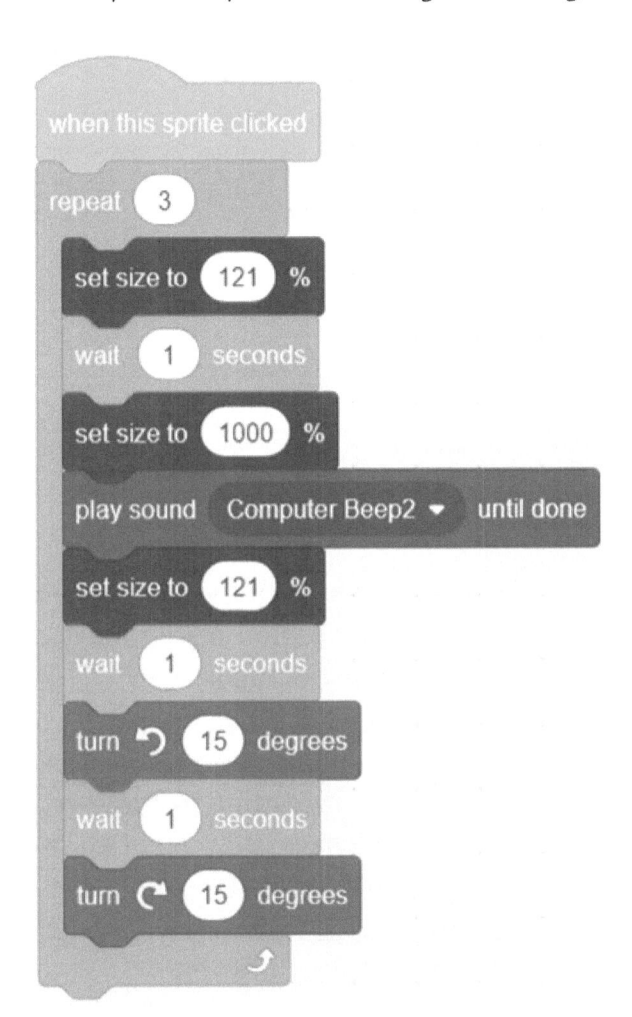

Two Examples Of Pupils Creative Projects Created By Year 4 Pupils Toy give away

FIRST CREATIONS (Do Either Option 1 or Option 2)

1. Create new code to say the 5x tables and add it into the menu as option 5

2. Create your own mathematical procedure and add it into the menu as option 5
Ideas for maths procedures
- *Subtract a number from another number*
- *Divide a number by another number*
- *Find perimeter of square by inputting distance of one side*

LONGER PROJECTS (Do Either Option 3 or Option 4)

3. Create a class countdown timer from 30 to 0.
Prepare three different effects to show when the timer counts within
30-20 seconds
20-10 seconds
10-0 seconds
Additionally provide teacher controls so that the length of the timer can be changed

4. Design and create your own project that uses variables to do mathematical operations

Ada Lovelace Creative Challenges Illustrating Easier Projects
Within The Exemplar Project First and Space to Plan

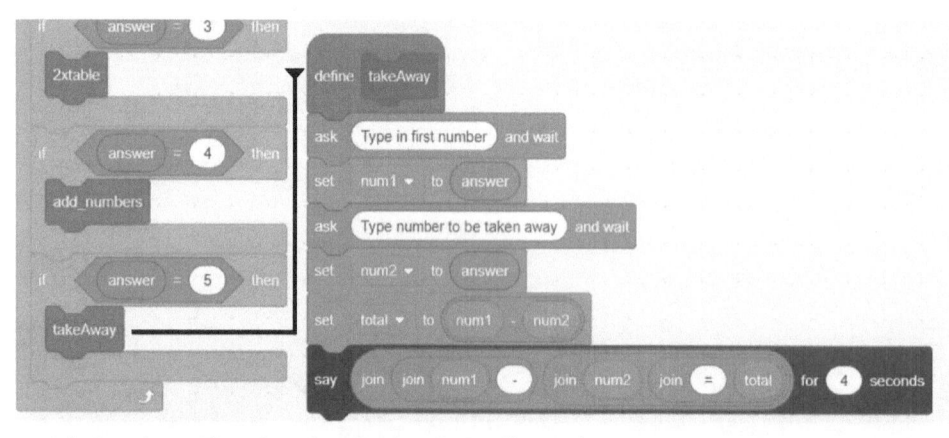

Ada Lovelace, First Creation Option 2, Pupils Work From Year 6 (10-11-years-old)

Conclusion

I recommend

- Starting with simple programming projects first before progression to more complex projects,
- Always allowing time for the create phase in every project for every child,
- Including design in the create phase, especially where the project is greater than one simple script,
- Modelling design in the create phase (see code comprehension further adaptations for an example of this),
- Including create challenges that can be created within the exemplar code example first before proceeding to more complex create challenges that involve creating from a blank canvas,
- Insisting pupils work on their own on the make part of PRIMM.

Code Comprehension Adaptations

CHAPTER 14

Adaptations

Because code comprehension strategies often start from the code rather than from a plan they can be weak in exemplifying programming planning examples and methods.

Algorithm Parsons, Investigate, Modify, Create

An adaptation that helps to overcome this lack of design limitation is one where pupils are given an algorithm for a section of code and provided with the already selected blocks. They then use the algorithm to help them construct the code. Once the code or part of the code is built and checked then the other stages of code comprehension can continue, although prediction is not possible as pupils have already worked with the code.

Context

In this gaming example on the next page five scripts have to be built from the algorithms in green provided. They all use condition starts action within an indefinite loop, a concept which was introduced away from the computer see chapter 8 concept before coding.

Points to Note

Note how some code blocks shown on next page have been pre-attached to further reduce cognitive load. Also note how the language of each algorithm is slightly different from Scratch code to signify that this is part of the design phase. See chapter 15 on design.

Other Algorithmic Forms

We could also start with other forms of algorithm such as a flow chart. These make good sense but don't mirror the indentations of block based code as these algorithms do. However, in the absence of good research evidence, the author supposes that it would be good for pupils to be exposed to different algorithmic planning forms.

Benefits and Limitations

There isn't enough research into using Parsons problems with block-based programming languages to know how effective this strategy is in developing understanding, but we do know that Parsons problems of many different shades are a useful tool in text-based programming with older students.

Younger pupils often like the hands on code-construction-first introduction to code comprehension that Parsons problems can accomplish.

Algorithms

Start on green flag
Loop always
   If touching light grey
      Stop everything

Start on green flag
Go x219 y153
Point down
Loop always
   Move 1 step
   Bounce if hit sides

Start on green flag
Loop always
   If left arrow key pressed
      Turn left 15 degrees

Start on green flag
Loop always
   If touching Fish1 sprite
      Say Beetle wins for seconds
      End everything

Start on green flag
Loop always
   If right arrow key touched
      Turn right 15 degrees

There is always a fine line between the benefit of what can be accomplished and the time it takes to accomplish it. Although each of these algorithms is easy to complete on their own, the presence of five of them in this example and a lot of code blocks may be too much for some younger or slower readers.

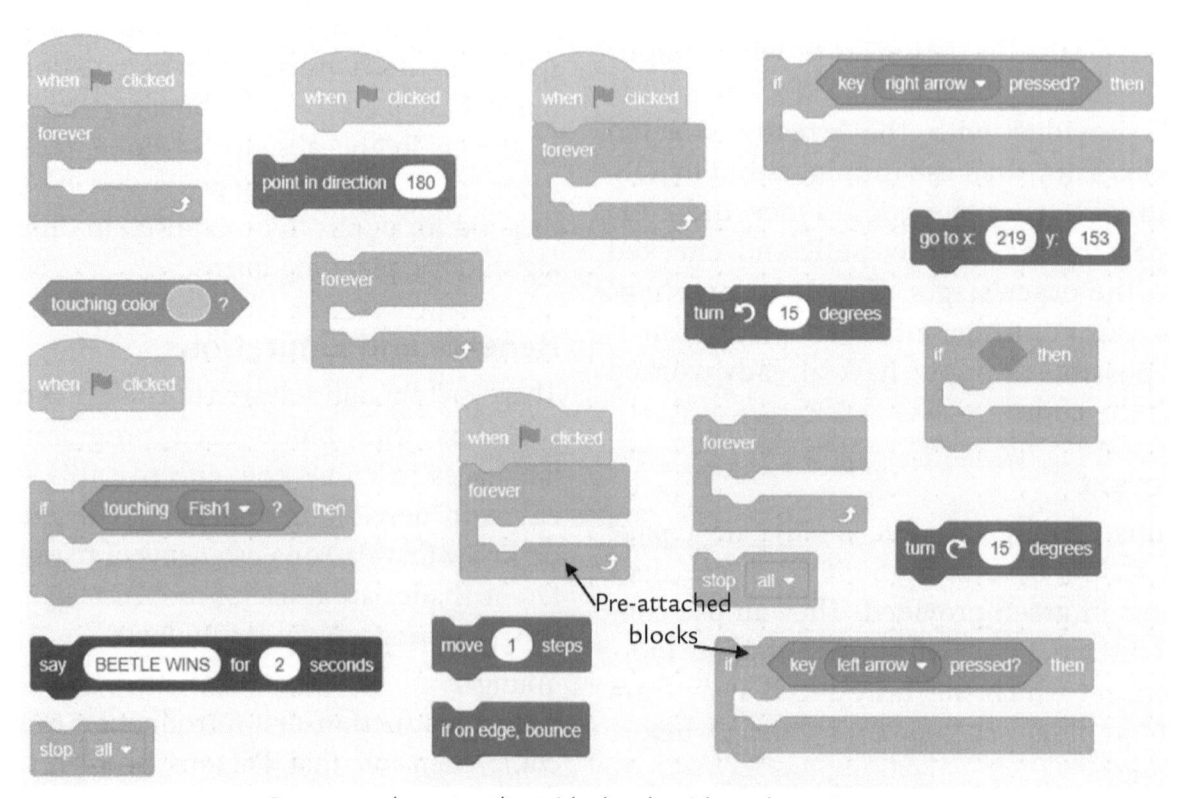

Parsons code to use alongside the algorithms shown in green

Code Comprehension Adaptations

We should also reflect that one of the reasons for developing code comprehension strategies such as PRIMM was to avoid excessive code copying.

Whilst blocks are not the same as text based coding we might be creating the same type of rote task.

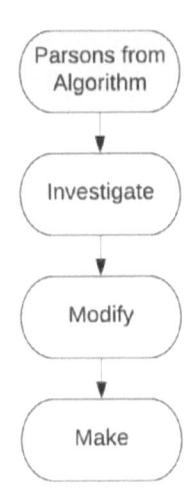

How parsons from algorithm might fit into the PRIMM process

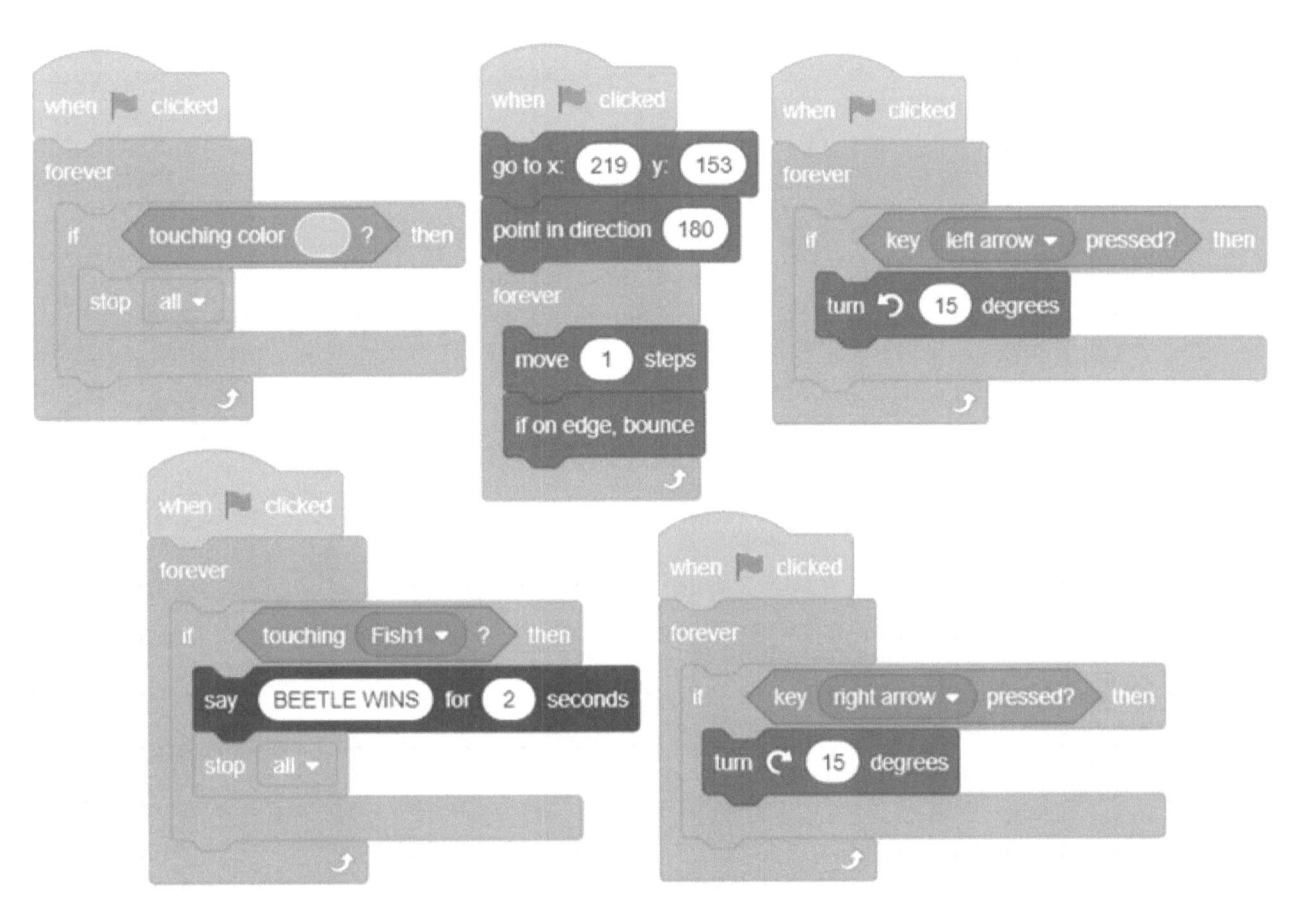

Pupils can either check their completed code using an answer sheet like this or continue their code comprehension using a prebuilt correct version

Prediction Using an Algorithm

Another useful adaptation designed to increase the exposure to planning exemplars is to replace the code in a prediction with an algorithm. The example on the right shows two procedures used in a main program design.

Questions First

This example also included some questions designed to encourage pupils to read the algorithm carefully first before they were asked to predict its outcome.

Prediction

Pupils were instructed to:

Think about what the instructions do in the main program algorithm starting at the top and working through to the bottom. Explain them one by one to your partner. Now draw what you think the program will look like after it has been converted into code and run.

Conclusion

Whilst there might be benefit in demonstrating programming planning using an algorithm, I suspect that this might be offset by the extra complexity of a complex text based algorithm. One more thing for researchers to look at in block based programming.

Procedure
define eqi_triangle procedure
Start drawing pen down
loop 3 times
   Move 50 forward
   Turn right 120 degrees
Stop drawing pen up

Procedure
define square procedure
Start drawing pen down
loop 4 times
   Move 30 forward
   Turn right 90 degrees
stop drawing pen up

Main program
Start
Point right
Return character to centre with x and y command
Clear all previously drawn lines
square procedure
Move forward 60
square procedure
Move forward 80
Do 5 times
   Turn right 72 degrees
   eqi_triangle procedure

Predict from Algorithm
↓
Investigate
↓
Modify
↓
Make

How predict from an algorithm might fit into the PRIMM process

Code Comprehension Adaptations

How view design exemplar might fit into the PRIMM process

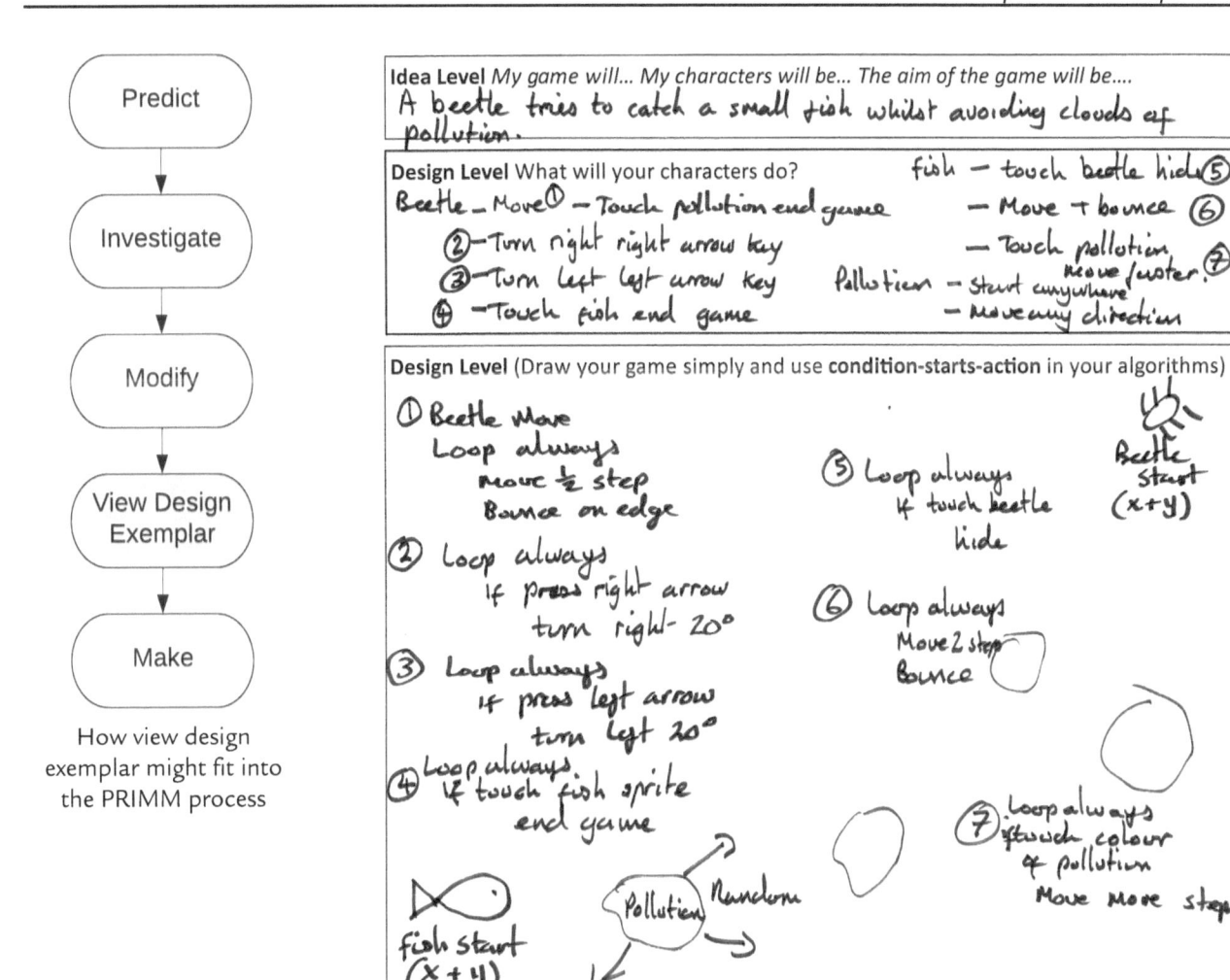

Planning Exemplar

Design Exemplar before Plan and Create

This adaptation continues the theme of adaptations that help pupils to see that there is a planning structure to programming projects.

During one code-comprehension gaming project, once pupils reached the create stage they were encouraged to design their own game before programming. It quickly became obvious that even with a clear design planner they were struggling to plan a game, as they didn't know what this type of planning might look like.

I quickly created a planning exemplar for the project they had used and modified and provided it as a design exemplar.

Exposure to this exemplar definitely had the desired effect in improving the designs created after it was introduced.

Design in Programming

CHAPTER 15

Lack of Design

In the English primary national curriculum for Computing it says

'*design, write and debug programs that accomplish specific goals*'

Waite, researching programming in primary education in the UK found a marked lack of design in primary programming practice.

Not Popular

Planning is not always popular with pupils. Many can see it as a restriction of their hands-on creative tinkering coding time. Research by Waite showed that planning improves programming and enables pupils to discuss their work with others more clearly.

Four Levels of Abstraction

Waite,[1] adapting the work of Armoni,[2] suggests four levels of programming development, four levels of abstraction:

- Ideas level
- Design level
- Code level
- Run the code or execute the code level

Ideas level

Here the programmer summarises what they want the program to do and who and what it is for.

Design level

On the design level the programmer converts the idea into a detailed plan. It includes an **algorithm**, step by step instructions that another human can read explaining how their idea can be made to work using algorithmic constructs such as sequence, repetition, selection, etc. It could also include other information such as **initialisation**, how the project will operate in the same way each time, a list of the **objects** that will appear in the project. It might also include **appearance** design showing how the project will look. If programming is combined with electronics such as the Micro:bit or Crumble, then **structural** design such as a wiring diagrams would also be important.

---

[1] Waite, J. L Curzon, P, Marsh, W, Sentence, S, & Hadwen-Bennett, A, (2018) Abstraction in action: K-5 teachers' uses of levels of abstraction, particularly the design level, in teaching programming. International Journbal of Computer Science Education in Schools, 2(1), 14-40

[2] Armoni, M. (2013) On teaching abstraction in computing science to novices. Journal of computers in mathematics and science teaching, 32(3), 265-284

Code Level

Here the programmer converts the idea and design into code using their chosen programming language.

Execute the Code Level

At the run the code level the programmer observes how the code acts when run on a specific digital device and fixes any bugs that occur.

Linear, Cyclical or Decomposed?

Whilst there is a natural flow from idea to design to code to testing the code which at times can make the planning process seem a purely linear one, in reality it is often far from linear. Often a new method or additional idea identified whilst creating or testing code can result in significant change being made to the idea and or design level. These changes make the process much more cyclical rather than just linear.

Linear to Cyclical Example

A pupil has planned a game. They have spent time thinking about their overall idea, who the game is for and how the user will win. They have drawn a picture to show the first

Jane Waite,
Influential computing science researcher at Queen Mary College, University of London
Author of a primary design toolkit for programming which should be out soon.

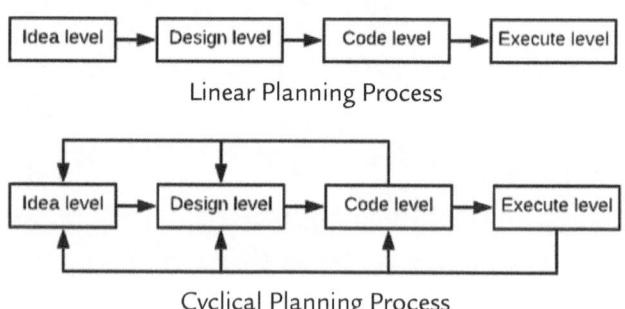

Linear Planning Process

Cyclical Planning Process

level of the game and indicate where sprites will start (initialisation) and where they will encounter obstacles. They have written short algorithms to show how the main sprite will move and steer and end the game. When they start to convert their plan into code they discover an exciting way to send the sprite back to the start rather than ending the game. This would lead to major changes to the idea level as how the game will be won has significantly altered. Some of the algorithms in the design level are now no longer needed.

Adapt the Plan or Not?

Although many pupils will be tempted to avoid adapting their idea and design levels after a big change it can really help the overall project if they do. What other elements of the plan will need to be changed after such a significant adaptation? Even a few minutes identifying parts that are no longer needed, what might need to be added and what might need to be changed is useful. However, teachers need to balance the usefulness of adapting the plan against any possible break in creative concentration. Some less confident writers may also avoid coming up with changes as they know it might lead to more writing. A useful compromise with these pupils is get them to talk about What is obsolete, What needs to be added and what needs to change with the teacher scribing. Informing pupils that struggle that you will scribe for them if they need to make changes often leads to them being much happier to take part fully in the design process.

Decomposed Modular Planning

Some projects, such as game planning, can really benefit from a decomposed planning process as shown in the flow diagram below. Pupils write an idea and part of the design level. They decide on all the objects and initialisation, but only write algorithms to solve a part of the planning. They then convert the algorithms that they have made into code and test them. Pupils then return to the design level to think about another part of their program and write an algorithm to solve it.

Ideas Level

Young pupils might express their ideas level verbally.

This is an example of a 7-year-old expressing their ideas level orally to their teacher before coding in Scratch

'I want to make a zoo. When you click on the animals, they make their noises and say their names.'

A good follow-up question would be: are you making that for other children in the class or for younger/older children? This would start pupils thinking about audience in their ideas level.

An ideas level might include a simple diagram which pupils use as an aid to verbalise their idea or to support a written description.

The ideas levels shown on the next page were created by 9 to 10-year olds as part of their planning to create a game.

Ideas Level Diagrams

Everyday Language

An ideas level doesn't use programming language or refer to programming concepts such as selection, procedures or variables. It should be easily understood by anyone who reads it.

Modelling an Ideas Level

A teacher-modelled ideas level might show more information than is strictly necessary to help students think about how they might convert an idea into a detailed design. This is

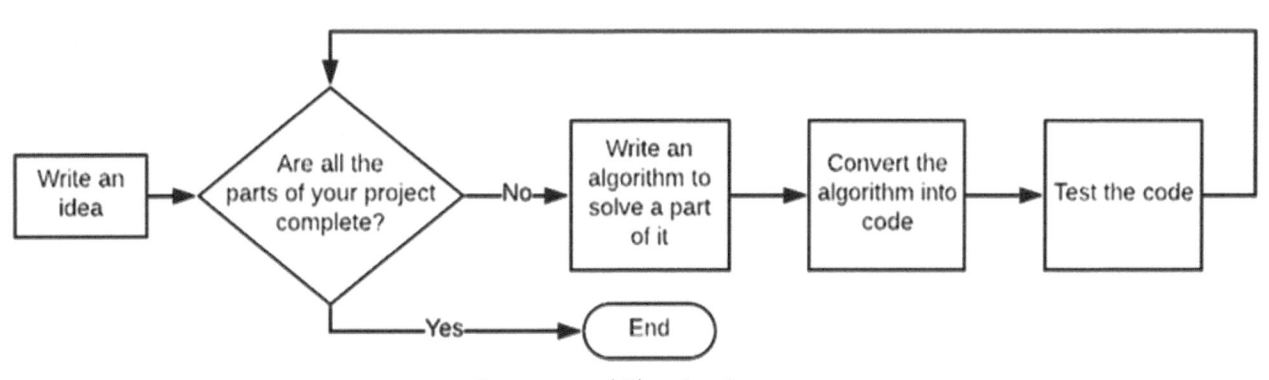

Decomposed Planning Process

> **Idea Level** *My game will... My characters will be... The aim of the game will be....*
> the penguin and the crocodile. The aim is the penguin has to catch the crocodile.

> **Idea Level** *My game will... My characters will be... The aim of the game will be....*
> The aim of the game is to get to the learning habbits without touching the pieces of work. My characters will be ellie the ant and a school person

> **Idea Level** *My game will... My characters will be... The aim of the game will be....*
> the aim of the game is to cross the road without hitting the car. Spider and car.

Ideas Levels 9-10 Year Olds Planning for a Game

> To make a programme that records your steps. other a day.

Ideas Level for 9-10 Year Old Planning a Utility Program

an idea modelled with a class of 10 to 11-year olds before they planned and wrote their own money and time conversion programs.

Modelled Ideas Level

Write a program that turns miles into kilometres by asking the user to input a number of miles and then dividing their answer by 0.621371192 and showing the result. This program is going on the school website maths section to help other students convert miles to kilometres.

Idea Provided by Someone Else

It is common for professional programmers to be asked to write a program by someone else. They might be provided with a detailed design brief or they may get nothing more than a short idea. If the idea is unclear then pupils may need to spend some time unpicking it. Pupils can use principles adapted from Polya[3] to help them such as

- Do they understand all the words used in the idea?
- What do they think the outcome might look like or display?
- Can they draw a picture to help them understand the idea?
- Do they think there is enough information to create something?
- What information might be missing?
- Can they explain the idea out loud to a classmate or a teacher?

Sometimes a person commissioning a program has little experience of programming. They just want an application to solve their problem or meet their needs. It is the programmer's job to discuss their needs with them and then come up with a detailed plan.

Teachers can model this process with older pupils by either writing a number of slightly ambiguous programming ideas and providing more information when asked, or asking other pupils to provide ideas that their class can choose from and time to ask more questions from the idea author.

Design Level Characters or Objects

Before pupils convert their idea into an algorithm it can be worth listing the characters or objects in the plan and asking what each one of these will do. Or if the program is likely to

---

[3] Polya, G. (1945) How to solve it. Princeton University Press, Princetown

Design in Programming

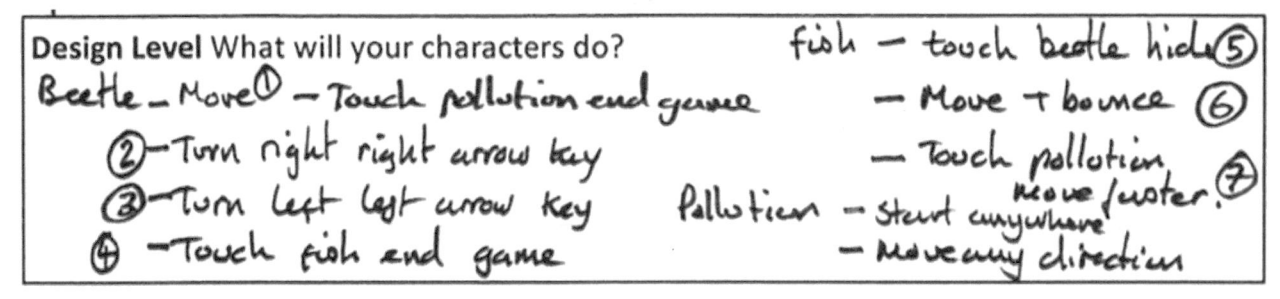

> **Design Level** What will your characters do?
> Beetle — Move ① — Touch pollution end game
> ② — Turn right right arrow key
> ③ — Turn left left arrow key
> ④ — Touch fish end game
>
> fish — touch beetle hide ⑤
> — Move + bounce ⑥
> — Touch pollution move /water ⑦
> Pollution — Start anywhere
> — Move any direction

What Will Characters Do in a Game? Teacher Modelled

be a single object or character what it will do at each stage in the program.

Above is a modelled example of this created by a teacher for a game design.

Algorithm

Probably the most crucial and difficult element in planning programming is turning an idea into an algorithm. If pupils have not seen a variety of algorithms modelled before then their ability to construct one will be severely limited.

Pupils need to understand that an algorithm is written for another human to understand and that there is no formal language of algorithms but that students need to be precise and avoid ambiguity.

An algorithm is not planning in code

Pupils need to know that writing an algorithm is not the same as writing in code. Code is limited by the expressions that a digital device will recognise and act on.

In Scratch a count-controlled loop can only be written as above.

However, a human can express a count-controlled loop in many ways, do this four times, loop four times, repeat 4 lots, etc. A human can use any language or

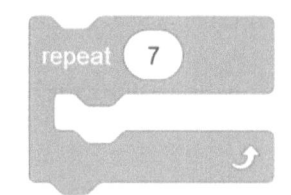

repeat 7

Count-conrolled loop in Scratch

symbols that another human would interpret as a count-controlled loop, including a flow diagram.

Non-Scratch Language

Armoni,[4] working with novice programmers, recommends that when teachers model or teach aspects of the algorithm in the design level they use language that is similar but not exactly the same as the language of the chosen programming environment. A teacher using Scratch might refer to a continuous, indefinite or always loop rather than a forever loop. When referencing a count-controlled loop, they might speak of looping so many times or doing so many times rather than repeating so many times. If talking about a sprite in the design level, they might refer to a character. This helps to underline for the student that they are in the planning stage rather than any other level. It also benefits students in that programming constructs are learnt about and explored in a manner that is programming

---

[4] On Teaching Abstraction in Computer Science to Novices Michal Armoni (2013) Jl. of Computers in Mathematics and Science Teaching

language agnostic that aids the transfer of universal constructs such as repetition or selection from one programming language to another.

Algorithmic Grammar

Algorithms can use simple grammar such as new concepts on a new line or indentations to show which aspects are inside a loop or are started by a condition. These make more complex algorithms easier to read and comprehend but are an optional extra.

Examples

In both the examples on this page pupils have chosen to use non-programming language to write algorithms that use an indefinite loops some of the time. The pupil designing at the bottom has also used a lot more code language. I don't advise asking

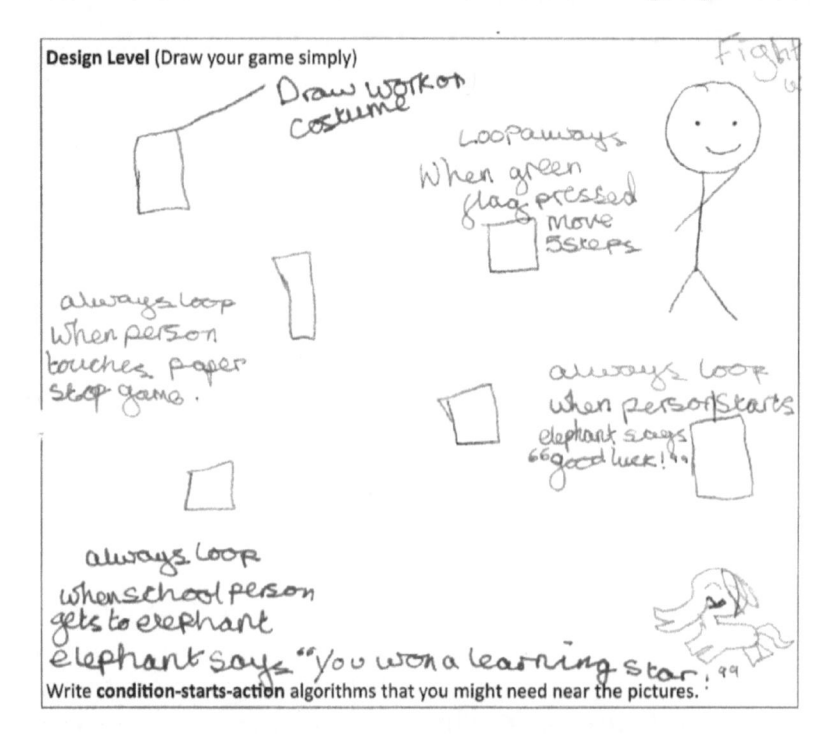

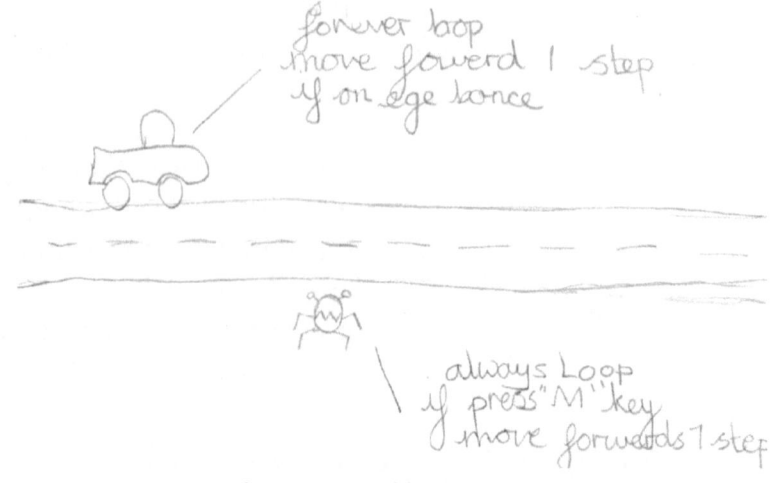

Design Levels 9-10 Year Olds Planning for a Game

younger pupils to change their design when they use code language but I do believe modelling planning that uses non Scratch language helps to separate algorithm from code.

Neither pupil has chosen to indent to show what is inside a loop or actioned by a condition but all their algorithms are readable which is the most important thing.

Algorithmic Errors

The top design has a couple of algorithms that will be difficult to convert into code without some change. Circling these and either asking pupil to explain what they want it to do or just giving them warning that it will need some adaptation in the code level will help them prepare for adaptations when converting these into code.

For written algorithms, algorithmic grammar and conventions are useful and should be modelled and encouraged, as they aid clarity, reduce error and make it easier to convert algorithm into code.

Flowchart Algorithms

Some programming projects (especially those with a single flow of control), where

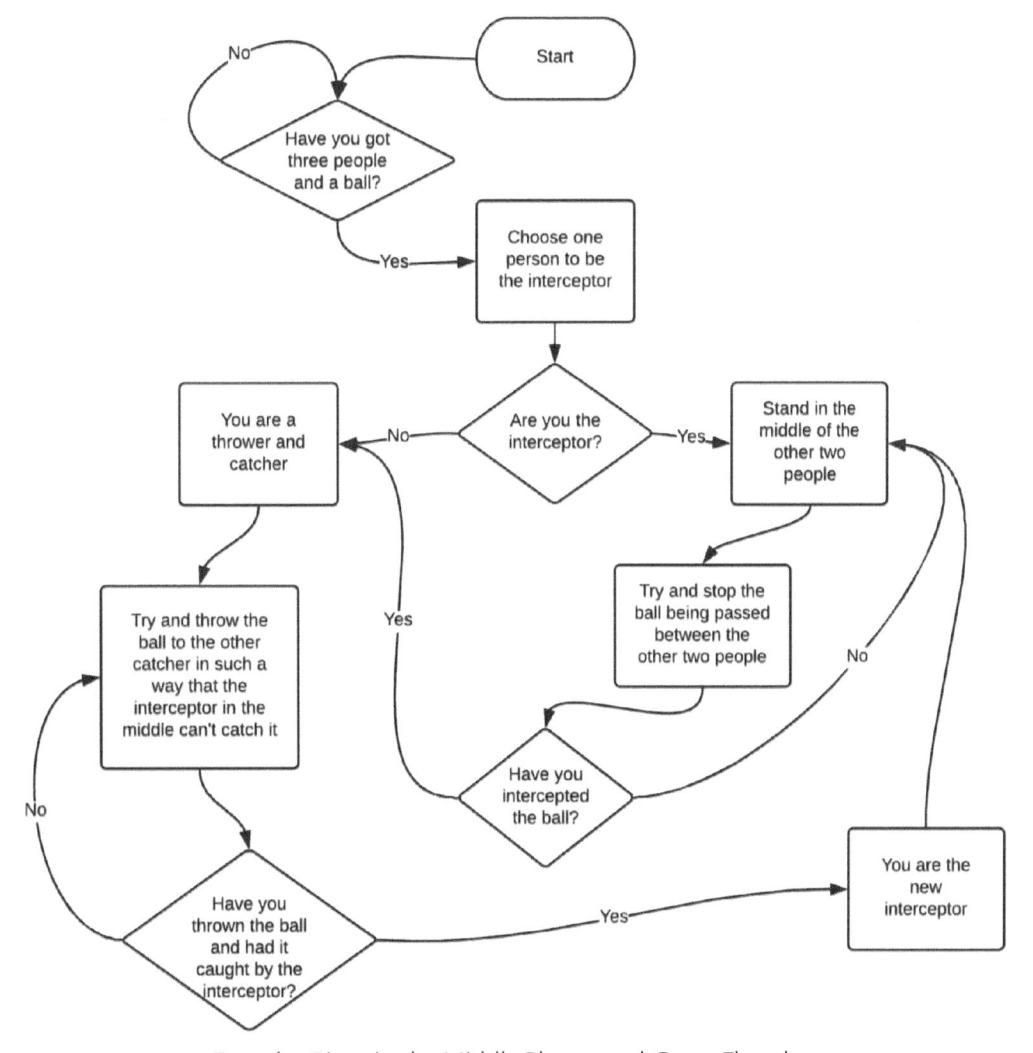

Everyday Piggy in the Middle Playground Game Flowchart

the program progression is linear, benefit from being planned using flow chart topography. Whilst these are rarely used in industry, they can be useful for novice programmers to think through aspects of decision making. Educators working with younger pupils have to weigh up the benefits of simplifying the flow of control versus the extra time needed to introduce the new shapes and what they mean.

Everyday Flow Charts Reading before Writing

If teachers decide to use flow charts, students always benefit from being given exemplar projects and questions that require them to read and interpret flow-chart algorithms before writing their own.

In the example on the previous page, pupils are given an everyday flow chart without being told what game it plays. They then work in a small group to determine what it does before playing the game.

In the second half of the lesson they are provided with a bugged version of the same flow chart and access to the good version is removed: they then need to debug this. Although this lesson works really well, I have yet to find real success in getting primary pupils to take the next step and write their own flow charts to plan programming.

Comparing Algorithmic Forms

In the examples on the below we can directly compare two popular forms of algorithm. A flow chart alongside a purely textual algorithm.

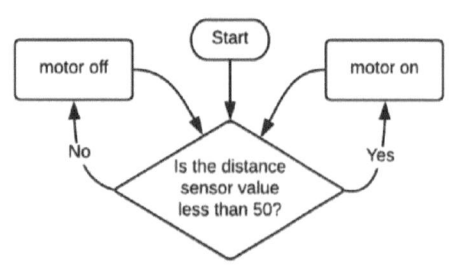

Flowchart Algorithm to Design a Lego Wedo Sensor & Fan

Loop always
    If distance sensor detects less than 50 mm away
        Turn motor on
    Else
        Turn motor off

Text Based Algorithm to design A lego wedo sensor & fan

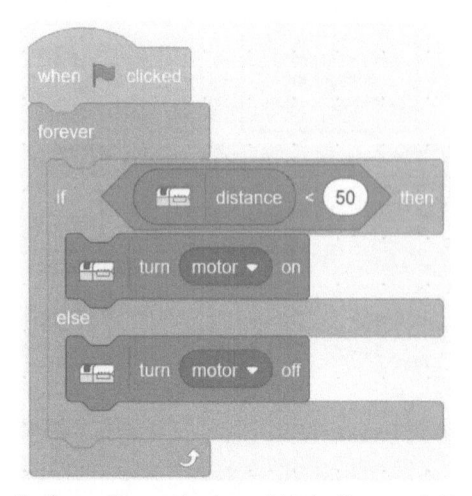

Code to Control a Lego Wedo Sensor & Fan

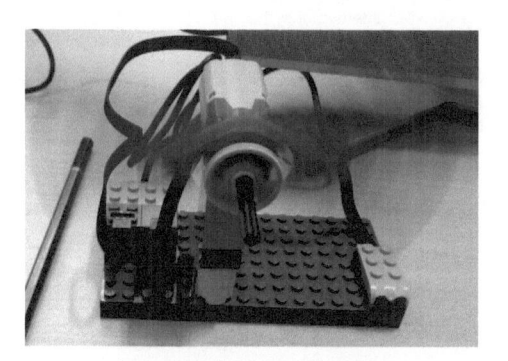

Lego Wedo Sensor & Fan

Both have their strengths and weaknesses when used for planning block based programming.

The flow chart arrows encourage you to answer the questions and continue round the loop more than once. This gives you a better sense of the types of branches that selection in a loop can create.

The text-based algorithm, with the indents to show what aspects are triggered when the condition is met or not met, is much closer in structure to the code. Which might be the reason in has been a useful early step into algorithm writing for primary pupils.

However, as programs become more complex the text-based version becomes much harder to read. Imagine trying to turn the piggy in the middle flowchart into a text based algorithm!

In This Scheme

In this scheme of work that accompanies this book there are no plans to use flow chart algorithms at the moment but I will continue to experiment with the format.

(You might also be interested in chapter 27 on the flow of control which, whilst not a flow chart, has some similarities with it.)

Design Knowledge

I know that an algorithm is a set of precise instructions that can be understood by another human

I know that an algorithm can be used to plan a program on a digital device

I know the four levels of design. Idea, design, code and run code

I can write an idea for a program that can be turned into a detailed design that includes algorithms.

I can plan algorithms that can be turned into code on a digital device

Chapter 16

Faded Example

Faded Example

A faded example seeks to exemplify a method to solve a class of problem.

In a faded example pupils first encounter a fully solved and documented problem which they can study and learn from.

Secondly, they encounter a partially solved problem which they have to complete, using the knowledge they gained from studying the completed model.

Finally they have an example devoid of any scaffolding to solve using the methods they have learnt from the previous examples.

Pupils get to see how the problem was solved in detail to help them solve similar problems.

Similar to Code Comprehension?

Teachers can be forgiven for thinking that this is similar to code comprehension strategies, but there are fundamental differences.

A faded example could include all the reasoning, planning and notes that went into the project. It is not just about examining the finished code. It is about the project in total.

Faded examples provide a very good context in which to exemplify the four levels of abstraction planning process (see design chapter 15).

A faded example could be similar to code comprehension, in that it might also allow pupils to run the code as well as inspecting the planning and the code.

A faded example could contain written or oral questions to make sure the pupil examined the first example carefully.

A faded example could contain a self-marking sheet with the answers to the part-completed examples, so pupils can check their progress independently.

Live Build

If the example was short enough to keep pupils' concentration, the teacher might model the first example to help the pupils see how an expert tackles it.

Changing a variable within a loop

In the example on the next page the teacher wants to exemplify the use of a loop to change the value of a variable.

John Sweller,
1946- Formulated the influential theory of **cognitive load** and its influence on instructional design.
Suggested **faded examples** as a way of reducing cognitive load.

First Example

Task Level
Slowly grow the sprite over a short period of time using a variable inside a count controlled loop.

Design Level
Objects
Main Character, size variable

Initialisation
Set the size of the main character to 0 so it can't be seen.
Set the size variable to 0

Algorithm
Assign 0 to the size variable
Use size variable to set the size to 0
Loop 100 times
    Set the size to the size variable
    Add 1 to the size variable
    Pause to slow growth down

Code Level

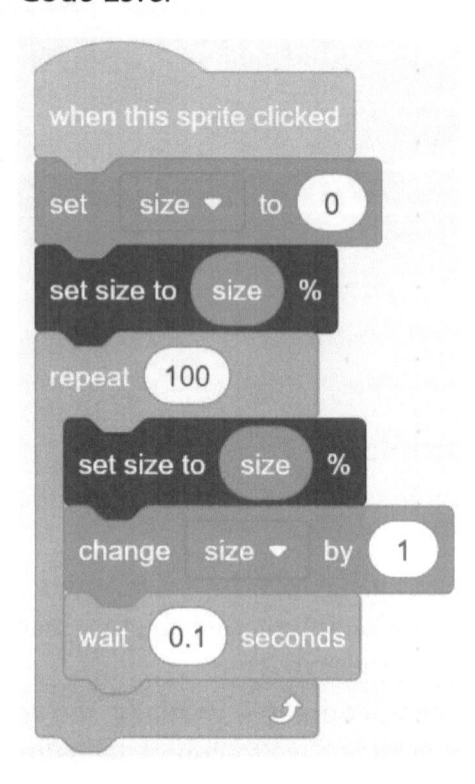

```
when this sprite clicked
set [size ▼] to (0)
set size to (size) %
repeat (100)
    set size to (size) %
    change [size ▼] by (1)
    wait (0.1) seconds
```

Notes
- The initial value of the variable is set outside the loop
- The variable is then used for some purpose inside the loop. In this case to change the size of the sprite.
- The variable is then changed using a mathematical operation (add)

Second Example

Task Level
Move the sprite across the screen slowly during a short period of time using a variable inside a count controlled loop.

Design Level
Objects
Main Character, _____ variable

Initialisation

Go to x and y so the program always starts in the same place.

Algorithm

Go to middle using x and y

Assign ____ to the ____ variable

Loop ____ times

      Set x to the ____ variable

      Add ____ to the ____ variable

Code Level

In the second example pupils use their knowledge of the pattern found in the first example and the part completed clues in the second example to complete the blank spaces in the planning and assemble the Parsons problem blocks. They might also be asked where in the code they have set the value of the variable outside the loop, used the value inside the loop and changed the value using a mathematical operation inside the loop to check their understanding of the method.

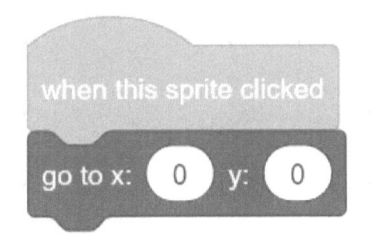

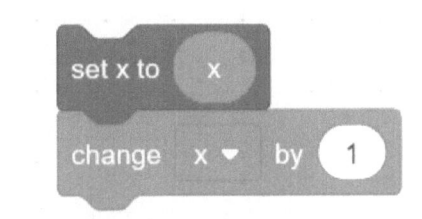

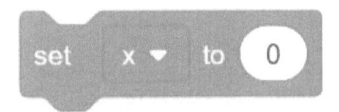

Third Example

Complete the following example using a variable that is changed within a loop. The task level has been done for you. Complete the design level, code level and execution level. In the code level use comments to show where you have

- Set the initial value of the variable outside the loop,
- Used the variable for a purpose inside the loop,
- Changed the variable value using a mathematical operation inside the loop.

Task Level

Make a program that counts from 1 to 10, where the sprite says the number using a count-controlled loop and a variable called count.

Design Level

    Objects

    Initialisation

    Algorithm

Code Level
Only Three Stages?

There is no reason why this example might not be exemplified in more than three stages. This could be a more gradual fading of examples or a fourth stage where pupils create all the processes including the task level.

Completed Second and Third Example

Completed second and third example follow. You can view the code provided to pupils at https://scratch.mit.edu/projects/366297573/

Completed Second Example

Task Level

Move the sprite across the screen slowly during a short period of time.

Design Level

Objects

Main Character, x variable

Initialisation

Go to x and y so the program always starts in the same place.

Algorithm

Go to middle using x and y
Assign 0 to the x variable
Loop 120 times
    Set x to the x variable
    Add 1 to the x variable

Code Level

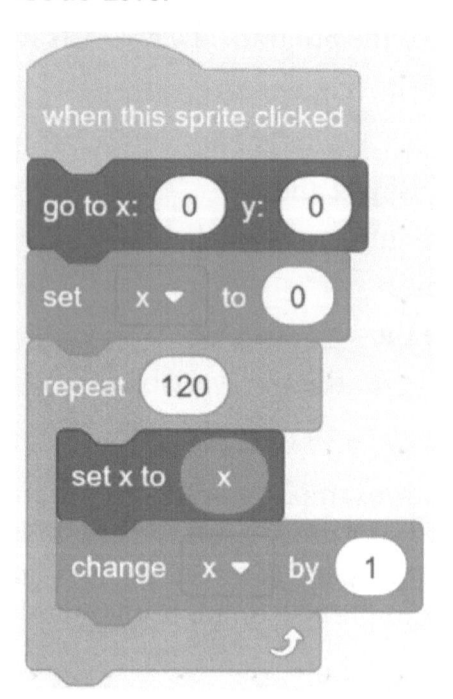

```
when this sprite clicked
go to x: 0 y: 0
set x ▼ to 0
repeat 120
    set x to x
    change x ▼ by 1
```

Completed Third Example

Task Level

Make a program that counts from 1 to 10, where the sprite says the number using a count-controlled loop and a variable called count.

Design Level

Objects

Main character, count variable

Initialisation

Variation A

Assign 1 to the count variable

Variation B

Assign 0 to the count variable

Algorithm

Variation A

Assign 1 to the count variable

Loop 10 times

    Say count variable for 1 second

    Add 1 to the count variable

Variation B

Assign 0 to the count variable

Loop 10 times

    Add 1 to the count variable

    Say count variable for 1 second

Note

Note how variation B changes the value of the variable before using it in the say command, so it has to start with a lower number assigned to the variable before the loop.

Code Level

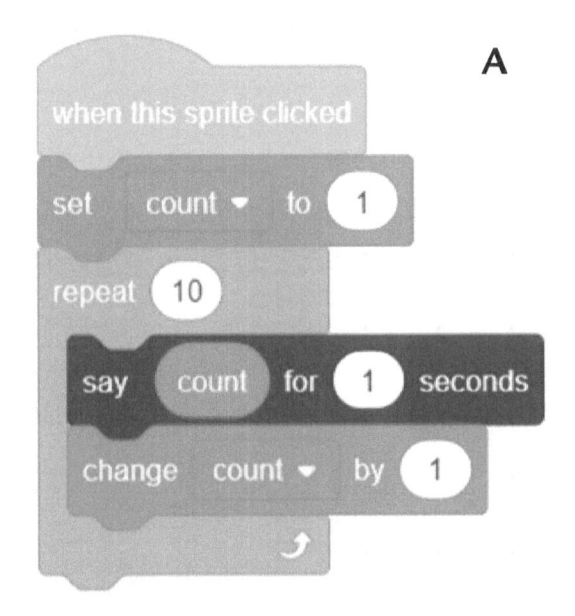

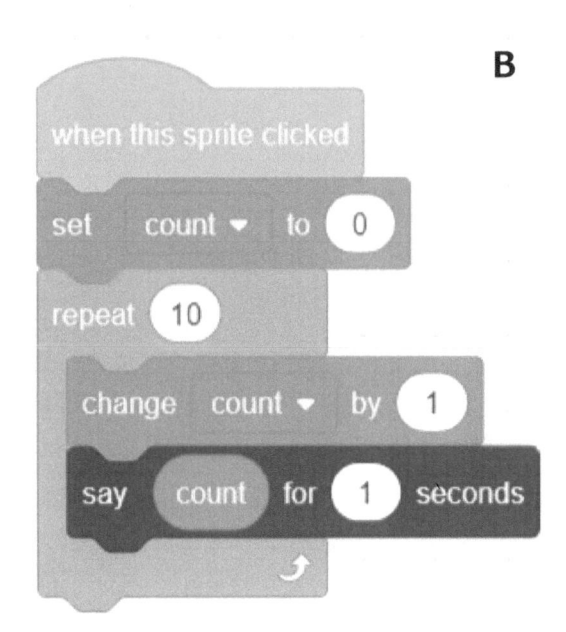

A

B

In Conclusion

Faded examples can be a very useful addition to a teacher's learning methodologies, especially when the concept being introduced goes beyond those classified as basic or combines elements of multiple concepts as the example does, combining variables and count-controlled loops.

The final fade might be to ask pupils to come up with their own creative idea that uses the concept.

Chapter 17: Constructionism

Discovery Learning

Discovery and constructionism are different ways to describe a similar process where pupils are expected to discover the fundamental principles of programming through exploration.

Unassisted Discovery Learning

Originally discovery learning was advocated that involved no teacher intervention, but this was discounted as it placed too high a cognitive load on younger pupils leading to little or no retention of learning.

Typical Guided Discovery

Includes the following aspects

- Low teacher guidance,
- Minimal teacher explanations,
- Emphasis on multiple ways to solve problems,
- Using hands-on material rather than just learning about a topic,
- Little or no repetition of learning opportunities,
- No memorisation of facts,
- Learners taking charge of their learning.

Constructionism

In computing the main advocate of discovery learning was Papert, who wrote and spoke extensively about it. Papert influenced many, including Resnick, who leads the MIT learning laboratory responsible for Scratch.

Positives

Pupils who have taken part in discovery learning are often more positive about the learning and more likely to engage in self-learning.

There are always multiple ways to find solutions to programming problems. Encouraging diversity of solution is an important part of programming.

Programming is not just about intellectual concepts, it is also rooted in how to use these concepts to make artefacts that do things. Because of this, programming is very hands-on which lends itself to exploring materials rather than just learning about them.

Negatives

Pupils take longer to discover concepts through discovery learning than through instruction.

Seymour Papert, 1928-2016
Developed **Constructionism** after being influenced by the work of Piaget on Constructivism. His **Mindstorms** educational computing book in 1980 remains influential.

It is possible to learn misconceptions through discovery learning which then need to be unlearnt.

Teachers need to be highly skilled in the subject material to guide pupils with the least amount of intervention whilst steering pupils away from misconceptions.

We know from the work of Ebbinghaus that revisiting concepts or revising materials is an important part of increasing retention of concepts over longer periods of time this is often lacking in constructionism as pupils rarely wish to go over perviously explored material.

To make good progress, pupils need to be motivated to explore things themselves. There are some topics where the majority of a class can be inspired to explore. There are other concepts that might be harder and potentially less exciting, making it harder to motivate all pupils to explore independently. In these cases only those who are self-motivated make good progress.

As a Filter

Sometimes discovery learning techniques are used as a filter to discover who has an interest in programming by excluding those who are less self-motivated to learn independently. This is seen as a way of helping pupils to determine if programming is something they wish to continue in the future. Whilst this might be a useful aspect of a short taster module, it is a very poor principle on which to build a progressive universal curriculum.

Constructionism's Influence

Whilst pure constructionist programming curricula are rare, it is fair to say that this philosophy has had a wide spread influence on other programming teaching methods.

In code comprehension strategies there is a make or create section where pupil use their understanding to make something meaningful using programming. The importance of this aspect was definitely influenced by constructionism.

Many strategies also emphasise tinkering, often described a playful exploration, as an important aspect of programming. There is a definite connection between tinkering and discovery learning.

Constructionism influence can also be seen in how many educational research papers cite constructionism or refer to their methodology as constructionist.

Discovery Learning Example

In this example pupils are learning about coordinates.

Minimal Instruction

The teacher starts by dragging out common blocks that reference x and y and showing pupils where they can open a stage backdrop that illustrates a coordinate grid. The teacher also shows pupils how they can view the x and y coordinates of their sprites through ticking the show x and show y tick boxes. The teacher has briefly drawn pupils attention to the coordinate work they have done in maths.

Constructionism

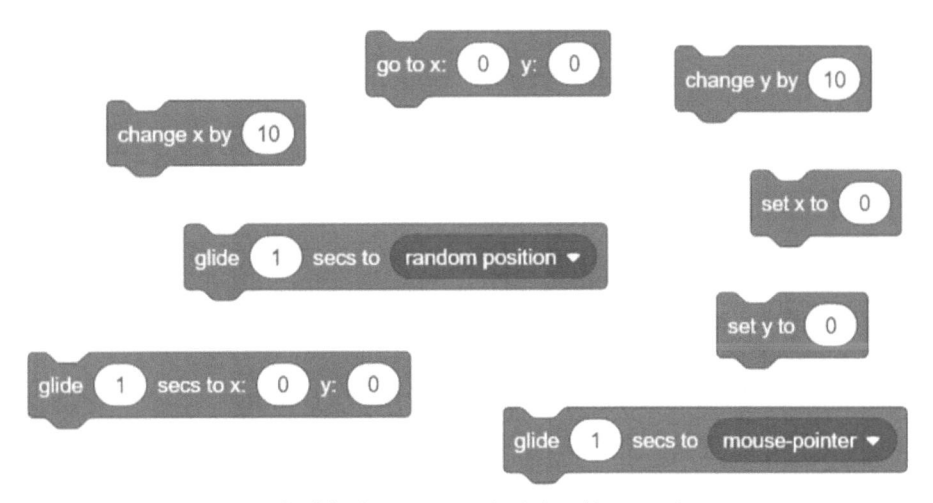

X and Y blocks as part of minimal instructions

Tinkering Time

Pupils are then asked to explore how they can use these coordinate blocks to control the sprite or stage? At the end of the time they are asked to explain their findings with a response partner, small group or the whole class.

Next Steps

Typically at this point some pupils will have already decided things that they want to explore further linked to the main theme of coordinates, in which case the teacher would encourage them to continue.

Other pupils may have reached the end of their interest, in which case the teacher will reignite interest by minimal intervention. These might include:

- Showing pupils how lines might be drawn by linking coordinates with pen blocks,
- Encouraging pupils to experiment with loops and glide to x and y blocks,
- Showing pupils how x or y could be changed by the use of a variable inside a loop.

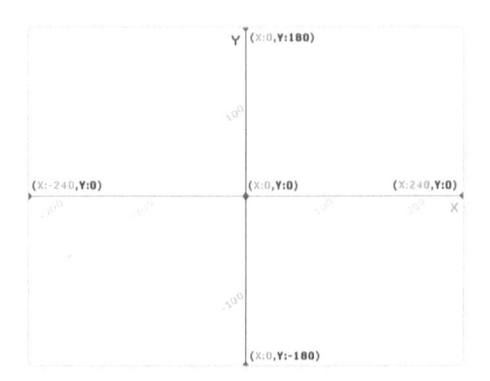

X and Y Backdrop Grid

Show X and Show Y Tick Boxes

An expert teacher would know which ones of these are more or less useful or appropriate to their pupils prior computing learning and previous maths skills.

Body Syntonic

If pupils are struggling with a concept or as an alternative start with younger pupils, the teacher may explore coordinates away from a computer using chalk on the playground or masking tape on the floor, with pupils acting out the role of sprites. Physically manifesting an abstract concept can help pupils to gain essential understanding which they can transfer into programming.

Influence

Whilst this author doesn't recommend a purely discovery learning, constructivist approach, all programming learning should include elements of learning by making that involve pupil choice.

CHAPTER 18

I Build You Build

I Build You Build
I build you build, sometimes called copy code, is an approach where the teacher shows pupils how to build a particular section of code with explanation before pupils copy it.

Value
It has value when pupils are totally new to the programming environment and are unskilled in the basics such as:
- Where to find a block of code,
- How to delete a code block,
- How to connect particularly tricky parts of code which fit inside each other,
- How to find your way around the extras of your chosen programming environment such as sprite and backdrop creation.

Limitations
As a strategy to encourage pupils to think about programming concepts such as repetition, selection or variable use, it is much less useful. It is too easy for a pupil to copy code without any real understanding of how the code works or how it can be adapted. There is also little opportunity for meaningful formative assessment other than the speed it takes pupils to create code or identifying any pupil who is unable to copy.

Adaptations
A useful adaptation is I build, you build something slightly different. This can increase the creative challenge slightly.

Verdict
Use when pupils are new to your chosen programming environment and when introducing a new aspect of that environment, such as creating complex conditions or how to create procedures using build a block.

Examples
In these examples pupils are introduced to a few concepts using I build you build. The examples are void of context to illustrate the concept but you can find other examples in context in the curriculum books. I build you built is rarely used on its own as it is illustrated here.

`< touching ( ) and score < 1 >`

A complex condition that pupils will benefit from seeing created

Keyboard Inputs

Curved starting blocks

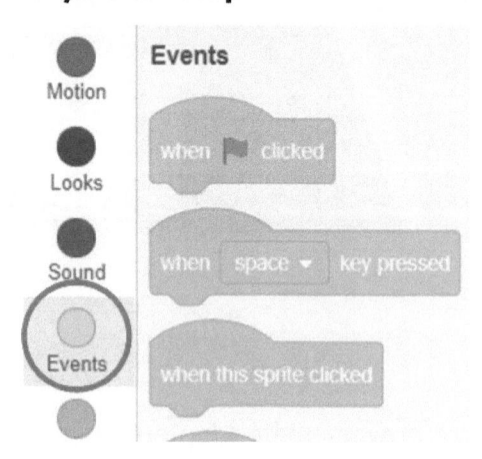

Motion Blocks

First click on events to find some curved starting blocks.

Drag out a **when space key is pressed** block into the scripts area of your sprite. It is the second block in the events section. Now you drag out five of these blocks and experiment to see what happens when you left click on the little triangle.

Give pupils time to try this.

Gather pupils back and left click on the triangle menu yourself. Demonstrate how to use the scroll bar to find an option at the bottom of the list. Ask them to tell their partner what they think the options are.

Say well done if they noticed that these are all keys on the keyboard. These blocks allow us to program the computer to act when a key is pressed on the keyboard. We call these keyboard **inputs** because they **put-in** instructions into the computer/program.

Explain that this keyboard input block is useless without an instruction.

Navigate to the motion blocks and slowly drag out a move 10 steps block into the scripts area.

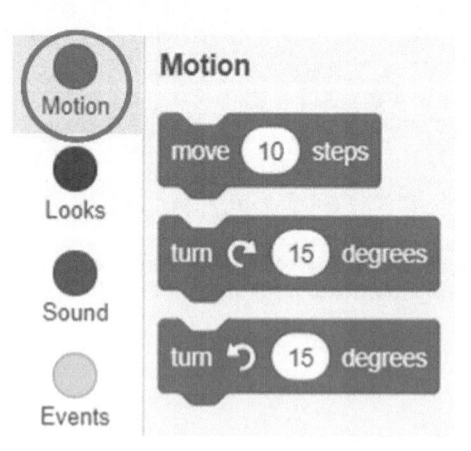

It is important to drag slowly as pupils will make simple location snapping errors if they are not careful when snapping blocks together. Placing blocks in the wrong places. Explain that each step is one dot or pixel on the screen. This block moves the sprite 10 dots on the screen. The Scratch screen has 480 pixels or dots from side to side and 360 dots or pixels from top to bottom.

Hold the move 10 steps block close to the keyboard input block until a shadow appears. Explain that this is the snap to shadow that shows you where the code will be connected once you let go of the mouse or trackpad left button.

Demonstrate how this block is run when you click the 1 key on the keyboard. Overemphasise pressing the button, so that pupils really connect the keyboard button with the action.

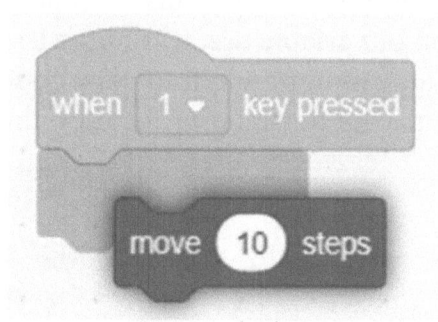

Snap to shadow

I Build You Build

Now give pupils time to recreate this in the scripts area of their chosen sprites.

As pupils finish, challenge them to make another starting block move 20 steps and another 30 steps.

As pupils create these ask if they can make it move backwards 10 steps only using these same two blocks.

Gather pupils back and demonstrate the following.

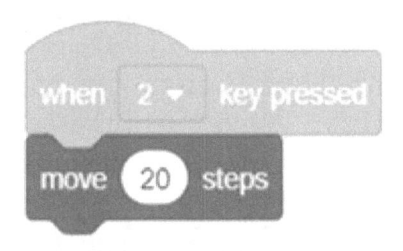

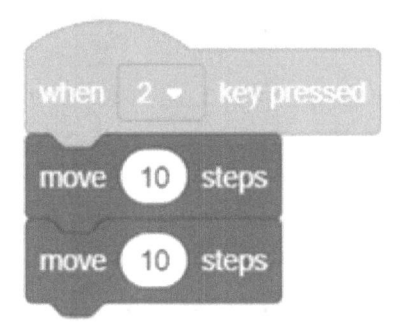

Different ways of producing the same result

Drag the code out as shown above and ask who created the top method by typing a new number into the white circle area and who added another block as shown by the second example.

Explain that there are often lots of ways of doing the same thing in programming. Both methods are correct and do what we want them to do. The top method is slightly more elegant, as it uses less code. You might want to make the link to a well-crafted sentence that says the same thing using fewer words.

Building Complex Conditions

In this example, pupils have used Scratch for a while, but now benefit from seeing a complex condition built.

We can build complex conditions using multiple AND, OR & NOT Boolean operations. In this example we are using AND to link two conditions that must be met.

AND Boolean Operative

First drag out an AND block as shown, from the operators.

Navigate to sensing and find the touching colour block. Note the American spelling of colour without the U.

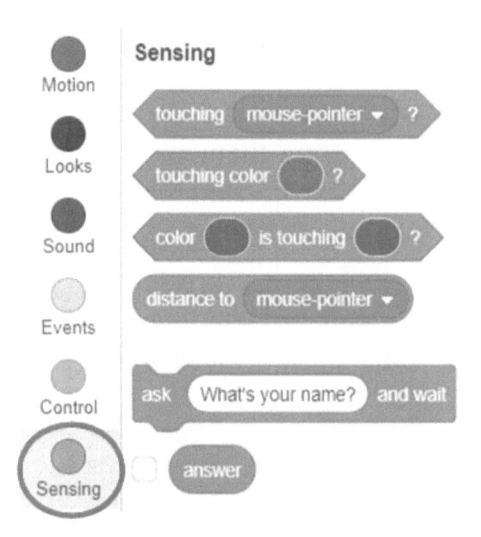

It is the left-hand side part of the block that we use to place it within another block like the AND block. Hover touching colour over both and spaces. Point out that the spaces in

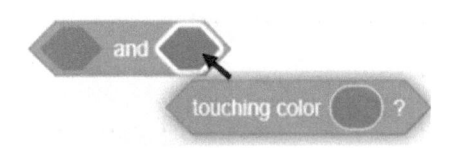

Demonstrating the Connection

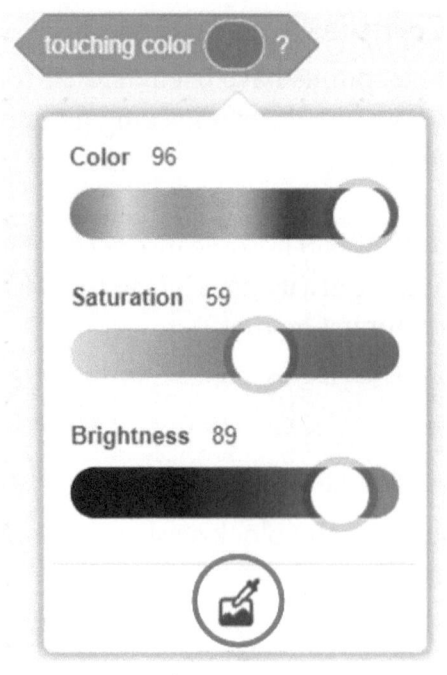

Building Complex Conditions

Colour Dropper

Magnifying circle

the AND block lights up highlighted with a white outline when it is lined up correctly.

You might wish to remind pupils how to change the colour using the colour dropper that you can find at the bottom of the colour choice option as shown above.

Click the dropper button circled above and move the cursor over the stage area. A magnifying circle will appear. Move this until the centre dot is over the colour of your choice then left click. This colour will now become the selected colour to be touched.

The second condition we are going to demonstrate is more complex, and we will build it separately before adding it in opposite our touching colour condition.

Drag out a less than block from the operators blocks. From variables create a score variable for all sprites and drag out a score block and place it in the left hand side of the less than block. Change the value on the right hand side of the less than block to 1. This now reads score is less than 1. Then pick up the block by the less than sign and line up the left hand side of the block with the empty AND side as shown above. Take your time and warn pupils that if they don't line things up carefully the conditions will jump out and move into the wrong places.

Finally, when placing this completed condition inside another block they need to hold the completed block by the central AND.

Now instruct pupils to go and drag out and create a multiple condition similar to the one shown before going back to their independent projects.

What makes a good I build you build demonstration?

The two examples above will have given you a flavour of I build you build, but what factors should be taken into account when creating your own?

Brevity

Pupils' attention span and the amount they can retain are limited by their age and their experience of the chosen programming environment. In the first example with Scratch novices, only a small amount was demonstrated before pupils had to copy or adapt it. In the second demonstration with pupils who had used Scratch for some time, more could be demonstrated before they replicated it.

Blocks Dragged Slowly

Both groups benefit from code being dragged slowly into place. Many errors are caused by pupils dragging code quickly into the wrong place. Code dragged slowly is also easier to follow.

Extra Information

Not all information is obvious. The explanation of how the colour chooser works is a good example of this. Pupils will easily discover how to change the colour using the mixing sliders shown above (colour, saturation, brightness), but less obvious effects like the colour chooser can easily be missed.

Preparation Beforehand

Trying this out beforehand identifies small issues that may be lost by just following a guide such as this or the curriculum examples that go with it.

Thinking Like A Novice

It is hard to unlearn what you know, but trying to put yourself in the novice learners' place helps you see how complex some aspects can seem. At the very least it can help you break things up into smaller segments.

CHAPTER 19

Parsons Problems

Parsons Defined
Parsons problems are a method of simplifying programming problems into larger sections that need to be correctly ordered.

Text Origins
Originally designed to be used with text-based programming problems, there are many ways these can be adapted to use with blocks.

Ordering Algorithms
Although these were originally designed to be used with code, one adaptation is to correctly order an algorithmic plan rather than the code it would build.

In the shape drawing Parsons algorithm below left pupils are asked to cut out the sections of the algorithm, identify what each section is going to do before arranging them in the order that will draw the shape.

They can then convert the algorithmic plan into code, be shown the correctly built code or view the correct solution as an algorithm.

Simple Ordering Code
In this version on the next page, pupils are given the full algorithmic plan, and all the code is contained within the sprite but the blocks are unconnected which they have to assemble correctly.

Start drawing pen down	A key starts
	Erase lines
	Blue pen
	Pen size 1
Pen up stop drawing	Loop 4 times
	Move 40 steps forward
	Pause 1 second
	Turn right 90
	Pause 1 second

Shape Drawing Parsons Algorithm

| B key starts |
| Erase lines |
| purple pen |
| Pen size 1 |
| Start drawing pen down |
| Loop 6 times |
| Move 45 steps forward |
| Pause half second |
| Turn left 60 |
| Pause half second |
| Pen up stop drawing |

Simple Ordering Code Algorithmic Plan

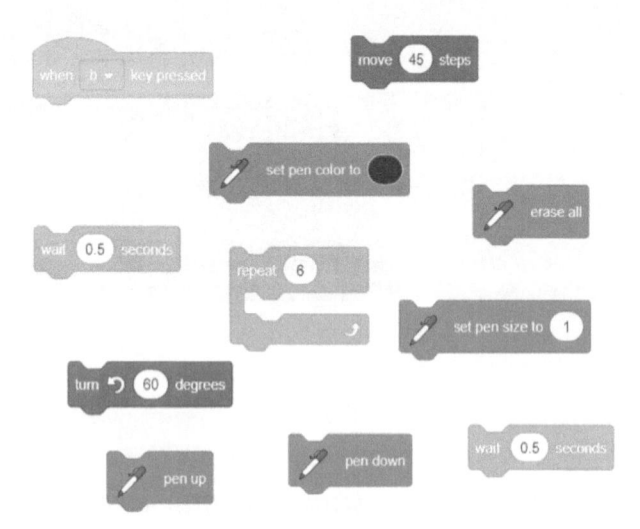

Scratch IT — Teaching Primary Programming with Scratch

Simple Ordering Code Blocks that need to assembled

This version is useful when pupils still need practice to connect blocks carefully and is often used with SEN[1] pupils.

Adapting Difficulty

The simple ordering code method can be made easier by connecting parts of the code in a similar way to the ordering algorithm on the last page as shown at the bottom in code. Pupils can still use the algorithm plan to help them identify the correct order.

Extra Blocks

Simple ordering code can be made harder by disconnecting all the blocks and adding a few

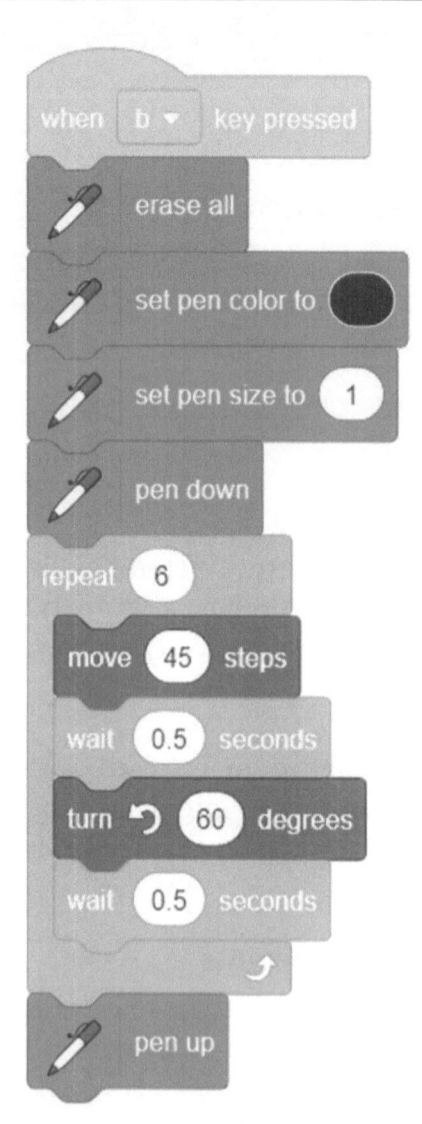

Simple Ordering Code

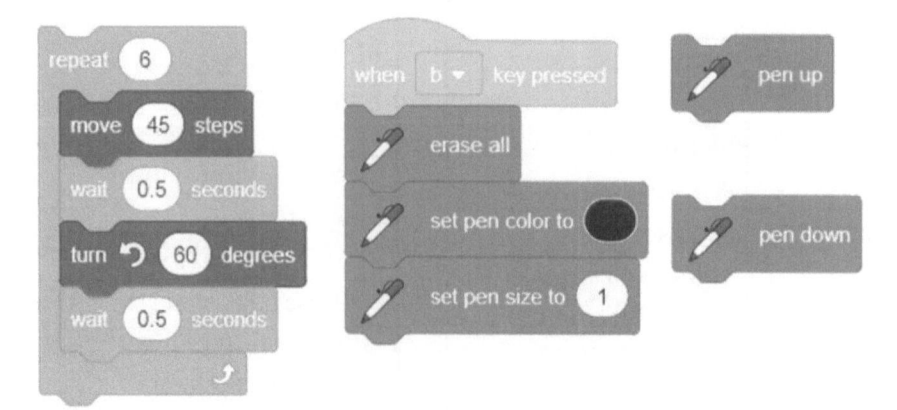

Adapting Difficulty Making Parsons Problems Easier

[1] Special educational needs

extra blocks that are not needed into the task. These are called distractors which increases cognitive load for novice learners quite a lot.[1]

Parsons problems can be made even more complex by removing the planning algorithm. Pupils are asked to assemble the code without any instructions, although you might provide a picture of the final outcome or tell pupils what the overall purpose of the code is.

Part Assembled Code

If you use part-assembled code, it is worth breaking the code into sections that go together so pupils can think deeply about what each section does before ordering it. In the code at the bottom of the previous page the central initialisation code has been grouped together.

> **Initialisation Reminder**
>
> *Code that makes sure the program runs in the same way each time by removing all traces of how it ran last time and setting up the sprite to operate in the same way.*

Code to trace over the square is grouped together on the left, and start drawing and stop drawing are left separate, so pupils can think about when they want to start and stop drawing in the flow of control.

Drawbacks

The main drawbacks of Parsons code is that it reinforces the erroneous idea that there is only one way of building the type of programming that you are focussing on. However, smart teaching can overcome this by making the point that this is only one way of achieving the goal you are focussing on.

'I hope you have enjoyed using the algorithm plan to assemble this program? Of course this is only one method of creating X: there are many more programming solutions to create x, some of which we will discover in primary and some in KS3 & 4.'

Summary

Parsons, problems are a useful tool for SEN pupils or any child who is still struggling to assemble code.

They are easy to adapt and make graduated versions that can be used with every child.

On their own they do not get pupils to think deeply enough about how code works, but combined with other strategies they are a useful tool in the computing teachers toolbox.

Further Reading

Raspberry Pi Quick reads Parsons Problems

http://raspberrypi-education.s3-eu-west-1.amazonaws.com/Qick+Reads/Pedagogy+Quick+Read+13+Parason's+Problems.pdf

---

[1] Distractors in Parsons Problems Decrease Learning Efficiency for Young Novice Programmers Kyle J. Harms, Jason Chen, Caitlin Kelleher

Paired Programming

Paired Programming
Working with a partner to program together with one person coding and the other giving directions. They are referred to as the driver and navigator.

Research Supported
Research from the US with secondary-aged students[1] has shown that this helps students within and below age-related expectations, but that it has less efficacy for students working above age-related expectations.

Swapping Roles
Studies suggest that swapping roles is important, so that both pupils have agency. In the classroom it is perfectly possible for one pupil to dominate the digital device, so having a clear mechanism for changing roles is important. Some advocate a set time (a 5 or 10 minute alarm), although that can lead to pupils swapping at a less helpful stage in learning where progress is being made and an interruption is a distraction. If pupils are using a structured approach such as investigate & Modify in PRIMM then swapping roles after every question is a less intrusive strategy.

Paired in PRIMM
Paired code comprehension is recommended as a part of PRIMM (see chapter 11 on Run & Investigate). Partner-supported programming rather than paired programming works best for this author's pupils when working on the final make task in PRIMM and is easier to assess. It also indicates to both pupils that they will need to work hard together in the earlier stages or they won't have the learning capital to create their own programming when they reach the Make stage.

Paired in Parsons Problems
Many pupils work well together to solve Parsons problems as a team. One holding and reading out the algorithm whilst they both search for blocks that are similar to build the code.

Paired in Create
Whilst I have outlined the problems with paired programming in the make stage of PRIMM as explained earlier, as an occasional strategy between pupils of similar ability who work well together it can be a real motivational strategy. Where the sum of both

pupils work is far greater than the work that would have been completed individually. It is however important to make sure that roles are regularly swapped if you are using this technique.

Choosing Pairs

This author has always advocated similar ability pairs in that pupils struggle together and one pupil does not dominate the learning. However, a study from 2013[1] suggested that friends coding together where one was more advanced made the most progress.

Restricting Factors

Teachers need to be aware of class dynamics when choosing or allowing pupils to choose a partner. Friendship with a partner can lead to greater progress, but every teacher knows that some friend ships are less productive. Also if the gap is too great the more advanced learner will become frustrated.

Strict Roles

Titling one person driver and one navigator can suggest that one person is passive whilst the other is active. This author would suggest that other than who is allowed to touch the digital device (driver), both pupils are encouraged to come up with solutions.

Overdoing Paired Programming

I visited a school that always worked in a strict paired manner, and pupils frankly were bored with the approach as it was used in every programming lesson. It is a useful strategy but should be used alongside other strategies such as solo programming or partner supported solo programming.

---

[1] Werner, L., Denner, J., Campe, S., Ortiz, E., DeLay, D., Hartl, A. C., & Laursen, B. (2013). Pair programming for middle school students: does friendship influence 53 Teaching programming in schools: Proceedings of the 44th ACM technical symposium on computer science education

PROCESSES

CHAPTER 21

Progression

Progression Factors
Three factors influence programming progression in primary education.

Programming Language Choice
This one is easy, as we are mainly looking at Scratch and other block-based programming languages in this book. However, we should note that if we were to choose a text-based programming language our progression might be different.

Age or Experience of the Programmer
Pupils in the UK typically start using Scratch in Year 3 (7 to 8-years old) and might continue on through primary into the first year or two of secondary education. During their time in primary school they will be introduced to negative numbers, greater than and less than and cartesian coordinates. They will become more fluent readers and faster writers. Their prior knowledge and understanding has to be taken into account when deciding on the order of programming concepts and the type of projects that can be used as exemplars.

Complexity of the Concept
Complexity in programming concept is reduced if we can link it to everyday ideas that we already have understanding about and increased if we do not have everyday links to connect to.

Repetition is a concept that primary pupils are likely to have everyday experience of whilst many primary pupils will have little experience or prior understanding or procedures or variables.

Complexity can also be increased by the number of elements involved in understanding a concept. You can examine these aspects in the individual chapters on programming concepts.

Progression Concepts

Sequence	chapter 1
Repetition	chapter 2
Selection	chapter 3
Procedures	chapter 4
Variables	chapter 5

Everyday Computing Primary Programming Progression
The only research based primary programming progressions are the excellent trajectories published by the everyday computing team in the United States. The three that I have found most useful are sequence, repetition and selection which are reproduced

Scratch IT – Teaching Primary Programming with Scratch

Best fit progression

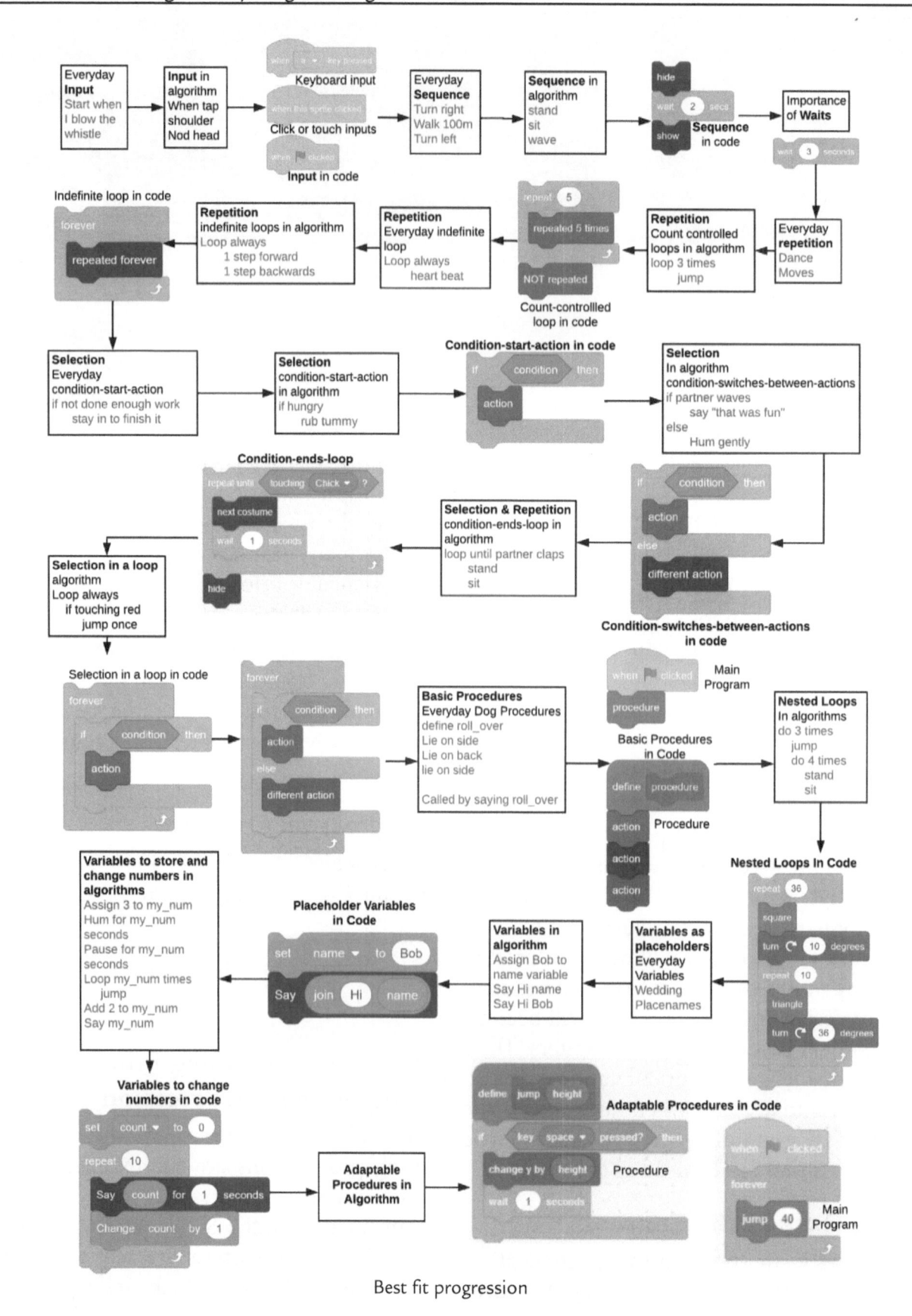

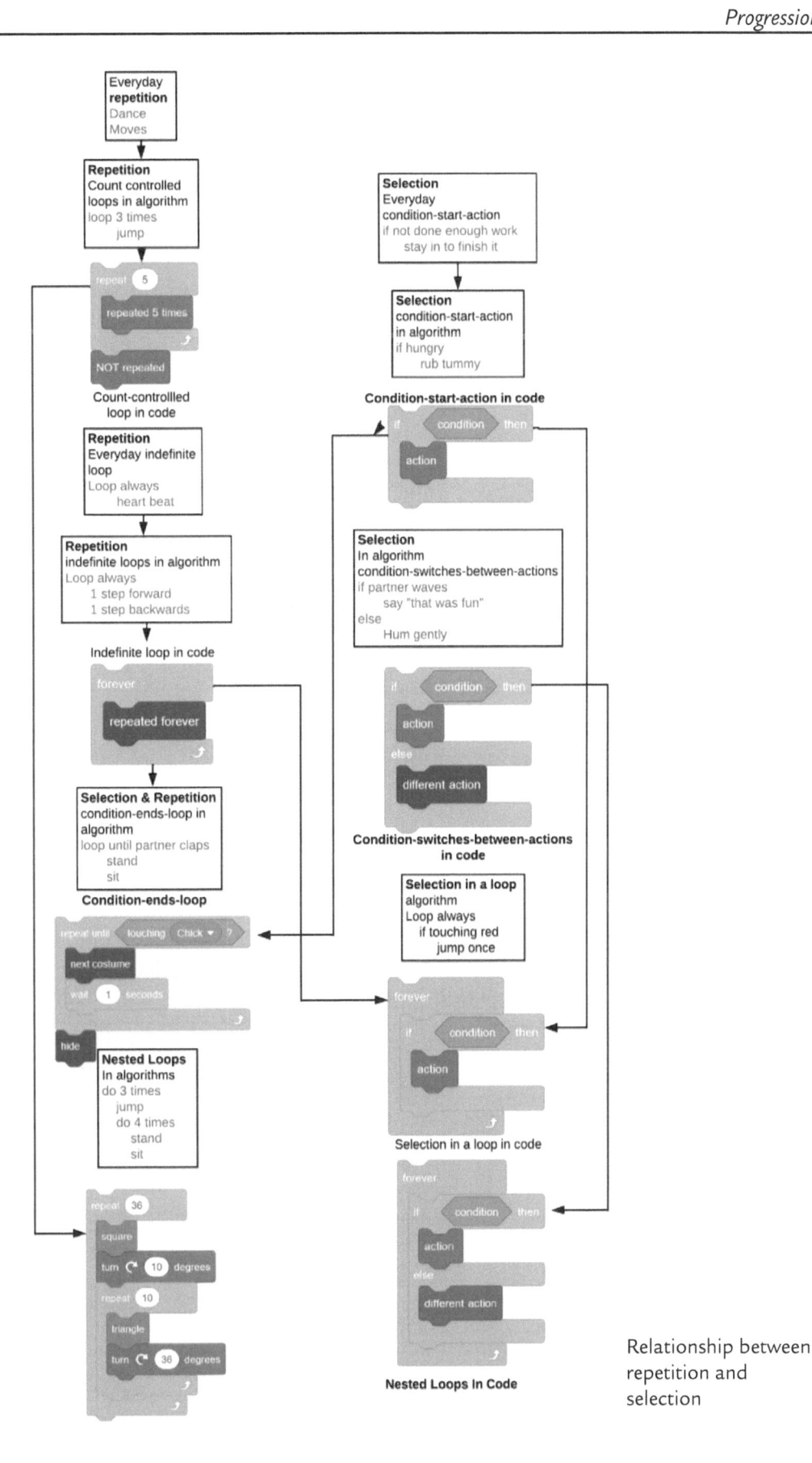

Progression

Relationship between repetition and selection

by kind permission in the chapters on these concepts.

Limitations

These deal with progression within an area such as repetition but do not look at progression between concepts. For that I have had to rely on best fit and the number of elements that you need to understand before you can fully understand a concept.

Best Fit Progression

On page 142 you can see a best fit progression influenced by Scratch, primary pupils prior knowledge, concept complexity, Everyday computing research trajectories and teaching programming using Scratch for 1000s of hours.

Adaptations

Indefinite loops ended by conditions are included in this progression but are less useful in projects.

Nested loops using procedures are included after basic procedures but if taught without procedures I would place them after place-holder variables.

I have included an example of everyday variables such as wedding place names but I am not always convinced that this example is universal enough to be useful with every class.

Relationship Between Repetition and Selection

As you can see from the diagram on page 143 selection and repetition have a close relationship.

Conditions can be used to end loops and loops can cause conditions to be checked over and over again.

Further Watching

You may also be interested in looking at research informed progression in programming concepts using Karl Matons semantic waves as a tool to introduce concepts over time.

http://code-it.co.uk/video

Further Reading

Everyday computing Trajectories

https://everydaycomputing.org/public/visulization

Collaboration

CHAPTER 22

Working in a Team
Contrary to the popular image of a lone software developer working in the dark, isolated from other humans, professional programming is a team sport.

Team Project
Most software projects are far too large to be worked on by just a single individual. Every programmer has responsibility to create a part of that whole.

Collaborating in the Primary Class
A simple method of collaborating in the primary classroom is to share code samples. This can be done by copying your code to a sprite and exporting it for others to import.

To be useful to another user this needs to be part of a bigger collaborative project.

Group Quiz
Year 5 pupils wrote maths questions for 20 minutes using different forms of conditional selection. They exported these sprites named after themselves into a shared folder on the network. They were then free to import questions from any other pupil in the class and use them in their own quiz. If they imported a duplicate question they had to either adapt it or delete it.

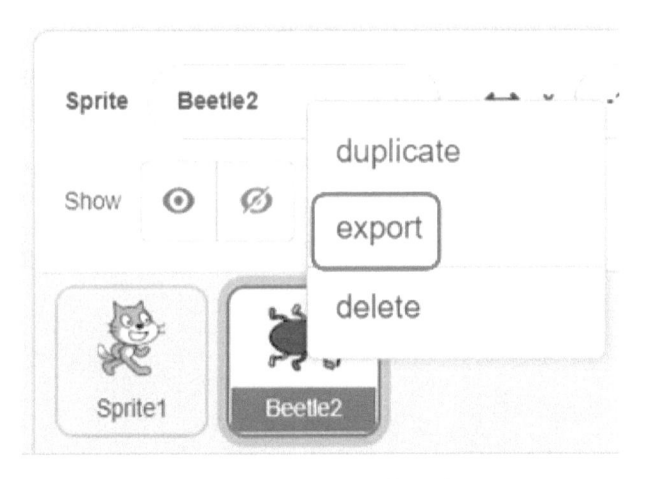

1 Export a sprite with code

2 Import that sprite with shared code

Adventure Game
Another collaborative project was one where pupils created different adventure

game encounters before sharing their code. They worked in small groups to plan out the encounters and consequences before dividing the work between the group members. Some pupils relished being part of a bigger collaborative project and some bemoaned their loss of solo autonomy.

Moving Code from Sprite to Sprite

To take part in this type of collaborative projects you also need to know how to move code from one sprite to another sprite.

First pick up the code and drag it over to the new sprite icon below the stage area.

Then hold your cursor over the sprite you want to copy the code too.

This will highlight and wobble the sprite. At this point release your left mouse or trackpad hold of the code. All the code dragged over will be copied over. Check that it has moved a copy of the code into the new sprite before moving on. It will sometimes be on top of other code.

Drag and drop code on the sprite on the next page shows part of the process.

Modularisation

Both projects described above work well for active group building because they are easy to modularise. In a quiz each question is a separate entity which can be written separately from every other question. In an

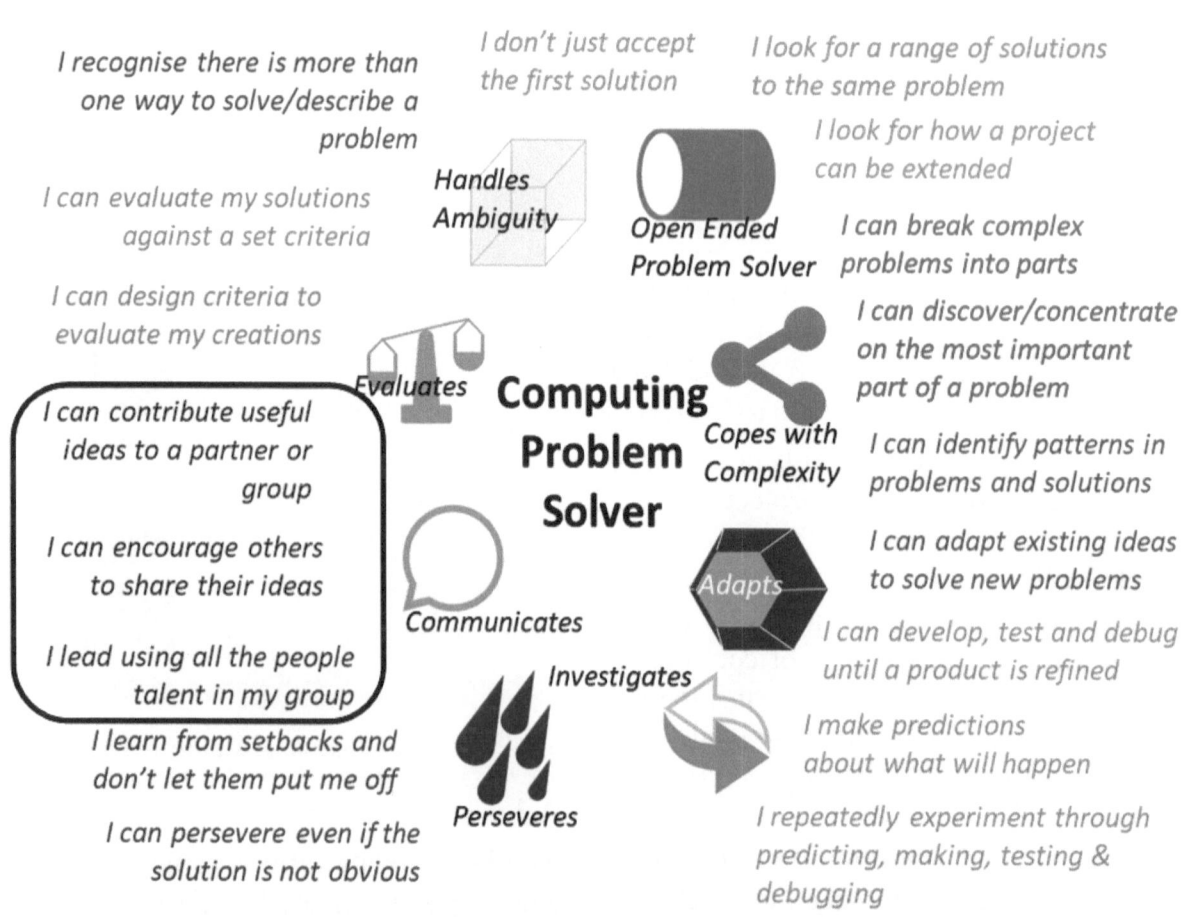

I recognise there is more than one way to solve/describe a problem

I can evaluate my solutions against a set criteria

I can design criteria to evaluate my creations

I can contribute useful ideas to a partner or group

I can encourage others to share their ideas

I lead using all the people talent in my group

I learn from setbacks and don't let them put me off

I can persevere even if the solution is not obvious

I don't just accept the first solution

Handles Ambiguity

I look for a range of solutions to the same problem

I look for how a project can be extended

Open Ended Problem Solver

I can break complex problems into parts

I can discover/concentrate on the most important part of a problem

Evaluates

Computing Problem Solver

Copes with Complexity

I can identify patterns in problems and solutions

Communicates

Adapts

I can adapt existing ideas to solve new problems

I can develop, test and debug until a product is refined

Investigates

I make predictions about what will happen

Perseveres

I repeatedly experiment through predicting, making, testing & debugging

Adapted from a problem solving rubric created by Mark Dorling & Thomas Stephens hosted at http://code-it.co.uk/attitudes/

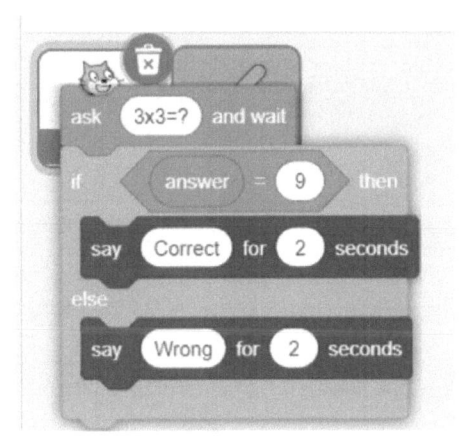

Drag and drop code on a sprite

adventure game every encounter can also be written separately. As long as the authors agree on common standards such as a theme or scoring, these separate code samples can be connected together like bricks in a tower. Teachers wishing to facilitate collaborative projects would do well to think about how easy or hard it would be to combine all the aspects of a collaborative project.

Collaboration in Problem-Solving Rubric

In the computing problem-solver rubric printed on the left, contributing useful ideas, encouraging others to share their ideas and leading using all the people's talents are important aspects of communication when collaborating.

Collaboration

Collaboration is a must-have skill for someone wanting to make a career in programming and a useful social skill for pupils to develop. However, let us use it when it can add value to a project rather than shoehorn it into every aspect of programming.

Chapter 23: Debugging

Debugging and Resilience

Computing isn't just about thinking, it's about doing. Learning to program means learning how to think about a problem, design an algorithm and then translate that algorithm into a form that the computer will understand. Like any creative process, it has lots of steps and many potential mis-steps. One of THE MOST IMPORTANT skills in practical computing is to be able to spot your errors, incorrect block order, logical errors and your wrong assumptions and to correct them. Debugging (so-called because of the story that errors in 1940s computer programs were caused by bugs and moths flying into the computers and short-circuiting the valves) is a learned skill of logical thinking and deduction. EB White (the author of *Charlotte's Web*) said that 'writing is rewriting' – it's just as true that 'programming is debugging'.

Debugging in the National Curriculum

Finding and fixing errors in algorithm and code is a key part of the 2014 computing curriculum. Pupils are exhorted to 'create and debug simple programs' in KS1 and 'detect and correct errors in algorithms and programs' in KS2. Importance of a process is in stark contrast to many pupil's experiences in ICT, where the finished product was often seen as paramount. Debugging is an excellent way to promote independence, resilience and move pupils away from learnt helplessness.

Don't Debug for Pupils

Everywhere I teach support and inspect I have seen teachers jump in and debug things for pupils. I think this often comes from fear that something really has gone wrong combined with too heavy a focus on the finished product over the process. If you do this you are denying your pupils essential problem-solving experiences and the opportunity to develop resilience. When I first started teaching computing science I had to train myself out of doing this. We need to facilitate pupils debugging themselves by suggesting strategies and giving them time to find errors themselves. Make it clear that you or their peers debugging their code or fixing their algorithms is not an option. The sense of achievement when they find errors is tangible. On a technical note we only debug code, but I have heard pupils talk about debugging their sentences or maths problems, and I don't correct their use of the word elsewhere as they have the essential sense of it.

Mistakes are Normal

When I first started teaching programming a Y6 pupil burst into tears. When I enquired as to what was wrong she informed me that she had never made a mistake in ICT before. Apart from the obvious horror at discovering a pupil who had gone through the whole of primary education without ever having been stretched enough in ICT to make a mistake, there is the need to reassure pupils that it is OK to make mistakes. I often find this can take quite a few weeks before pupils really believe me. As always they are judging to see if my words match up to my actions in the classroom. Once they realise that if is acceptable to make mistakes they take more risks and become better problem-solvers.

Praise Debugging

I save my highest praise for pupils who debug and problem solve. On occasion I have had younger pupils deliberately make and fix bugs just to get praise, but as long as the habit of debugging combined with the idea of personal responsibility to fix things themselves is ingrained I am happy.

Combatting Learnt Helplessness

In my experience learnt helplessness is particularly prevalent in computing. I define learnt helplessness as a strategy for getting other people to solve problems for you. In the classroom, for pupils, these others may be the teacher, LSA, classroom assistant or other pupils.

In computing learnt helplessness can be seen in various ways. Sweet helplessness often manifests to the teacher as a pupil putting on a sweet helpless voice and declaring they are stuck. Aggressive helplessness manifests with a cross tone and the implication that they think the work is 'stupid' or they don't get it. Being stuck is never a problem but if you ask what they are stuck on and the pupil cannot tell you or describe the problem or they give vague indications that they are stuck on everything then there is a good chance they are using learnt helplessness to get you to solve their problem. Similar strategies will often be used with their peers, tailored to make the problem solver feel valued, superior or pressured into helping.

The problem is that many teachers and pupils will respond to this strategy in Computing by solving the problem for the pupil. Often excellent teachers, who wouldn't dream of doing work for pupils in other areas of the curriculum, will jump in and solve the problem for the pupil. The fact that so many pupils use learnt helplessness suggests that it has been a successful strategy for many.

Getting someone else to do your work for you would be an issue in any subject, but it is the antithesis of computing science with its emphasis on problem solving and debugging. In fact to solve a problem for a child is to deny them the opportunity to debug code or fix algorithm and as such is debilitating.

How has it become so prevalent in computing? I suspect that it has grown out of teacher fear or unfamiliarity with the subject material coupled with a belief that pupils know more about technology than adults, combined with an emphasis on the finished product rather than the process. All of these factors lead teachers to fix things for pupils rather than steer them to find solutions for themselves.

Steps to counter learned helplessness

1. **Establish a positive class attitude** towards problem-solving. Computing science is very useful in that it calls errors bugs and

finding errors debugging. Although all bugs are caused by humans, the language is much more impersonal than mistakes, which imply blame or fault. Using bug and debugging language is helpful. It is also important to let pupils know that mistakes/bugs are a normal part of computing, that they are to be expected, that professional programmers write code that have bugs all the time and that you will not be cross or upset if their work has bugs/mistakes. This for me is a mantra for new classes for the first few weeks, and once they know I mean it there is a collective sigh of relief!

2. Promote the idea that it is **not your job to fix their algorithms or debug their code**. It is your job to promote useful strategies that they can use to fix things themselves, and we will come onto those very soon. So when they come to you they know they are looking for strategies to find and fix things themselves.

3. **Challenge pupils helplessness** and expose it for what it is. I have asked pupils; 'are you trying to get me to fix your code?' 'Are you trying to get me to solve the problem for you?' In the same way that we couldn't move on until we recognised the issue, some pupils won't either. Of course good teachers do this tactfully and with regards to pupils' known issues but an element of challenge is inevitable to identify the issue.

4. Recruit your pupils to combat helplessness. Encourage the class to join you in this by putting a **ban on doing things for other people**. They can describe what to do, but are not allowed to do it for them or give them a full solution to programming solutions. As you model this they will reflect this attitude to their peers. Having a ban on touching anyone else's mouse, keyboard or touchscreen is a good start. I often compare this to writing in someone else's maths or literacy exercise book.

5. **Move pupils away from language that personifies digital machines**. 'My computer hates me,' is typical. Computers are deterministic , which means that if all the inputs are the same you will always get the same output. Personification encourages pupils to think that an answer might not be available due to the capriciousness of the machine, an attitude that is anti-problem-solving and frankly incorrect.

6. **Don't neglect the other adults in the class**. All your good work could be being undone by your LSA or classroom assistant. Train them to help using good strategies and hints rather than solutions. If you are providing training on the new curriculum, don't neglect your classroom assistants: they are important.

Finally, you may notice learnt helplessness in teachers and learning support assistants. Is it worth the hassle to challenge this? As a parent I know that my children don't do what I say but what I do. I lead mostly by example, or lack of it, as my wife will testify. This is just as true in the classroom or computer suite. Of course we need to be tactful and recognise the good practice of teachers and the excellent problem-solving strategies in other curriculum areas, but if we don't identify the problem, nothing will change. I have found that talking about my own struggle to change has enabled others to do likewise.

Scratch Debugging Strategies

I do you do

Comparing their code with that of their neighbour or teacher to see if it is the same.

Looking for simple colour differences if using blocks. *'Are the colours of your blocks the same as the colours of teachers or neighbours?'*

Looking for different shapes. *'Are your code blocks the same shape as teachers or neighbours?'*

Looking for things that are missing. *'How many blocks have you got, is that the same as teachers or neighbours?'*

Looking for patterns that are different.

Suitable for all methods of teaching programming

Pupils read code aloud to see if it does what they wanted it to do.

Pupils read code to a partner to see if it sounds right or is in the right order

Pupils ask questions of the code that doesn't work. These can take the form of asking a question such as 'if I do x why doesn't y happen?' Or why doesn't this code section work all of the time?

Pupils step through more complex code which could include loops, selection and variables. They describe to a peer or teacher what is happening in each stage.

A variation on stepping through is to list what is happening at each stage. This is particularly useful when dealing with multiple variables or variables which change within loops.

Pupil cut out their code using screen capture software and draw on the flow of control to see if it is a flow of control error.

Pupils use strategies such as divide and conquer, breaking up longer sequences of code and running parts of it separately to try and find out where the error is.

Running each Scratch section of code separately to try and isolate the bug. This strategy can be difficult to use if parts of the code are dependent on other parts functioning correctly.

Pupils explain the code out loud to an inanimate object. Often called rubber ducking.

Common Pupil Bugs

Not enough time to run the code and show the changes.

Blocks that need waits between each step to show them on the screen.

Code that runs to quickly for changes to be seen

Waits missing in a loop. Here it changes from left leg to right so quickly it can hardly be seen.

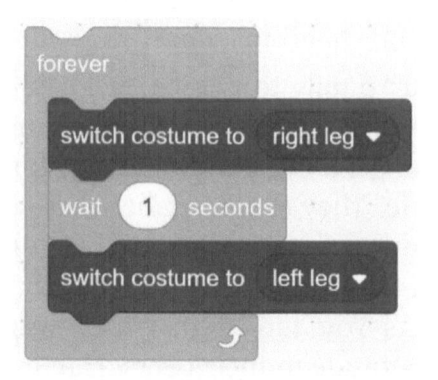

Wait block missing in a loop

Debugging

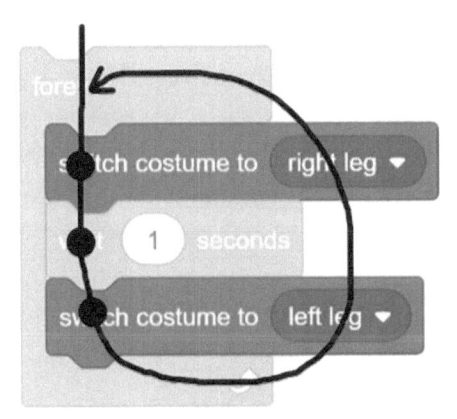

Drawing flow of control

Drawing the flow of control and tracing the instructions in real time with a very quick change after it switches costume to left leg.

This is what the code should look like.

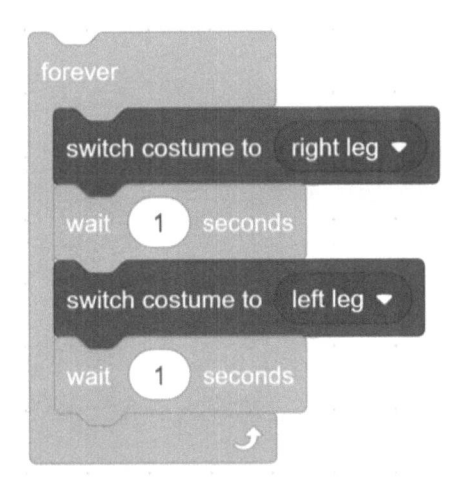

Debugged code

Leaving hide on the end of a sequence of code without remembering to make it show when initialising the code. This means that pupils sprites disappear.

A simple universal fix for very young pupils is to build sprite recovery code.

This will allow them to rescue sprites that have disappeared or gone off the screen.

You will still need to teach them about initialising code at some point so that it sets itself back to exactly where it was and what

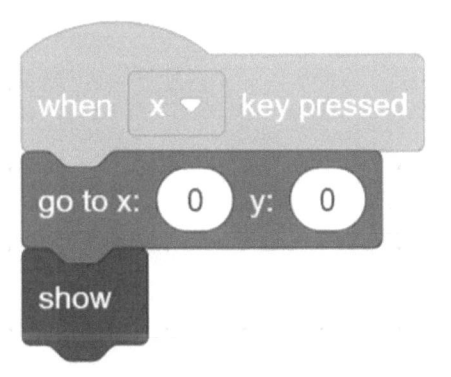

Sprite Recovery Code

it was doing when the program was written. In this case including a show when the sprite is started.

Another very common error in gaming modules are conditions that only check once.

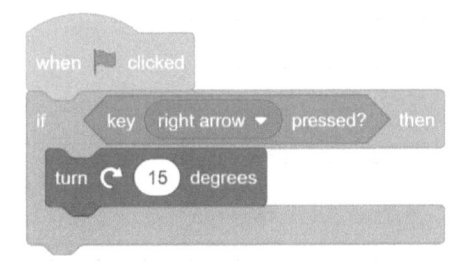

Here the pupil has forgotten to encase the condition within a loop. Often it is enough to ask them how many times the condition will be checked? However, drawing the flow of control can help as well as shown underneath.

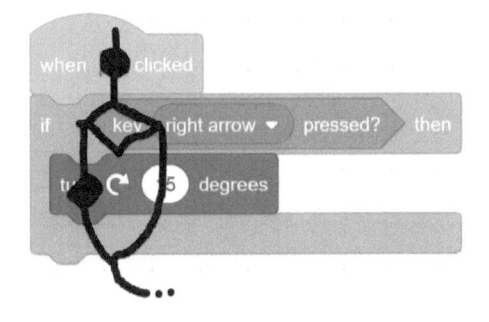

The code would need to look like this to work in a game.

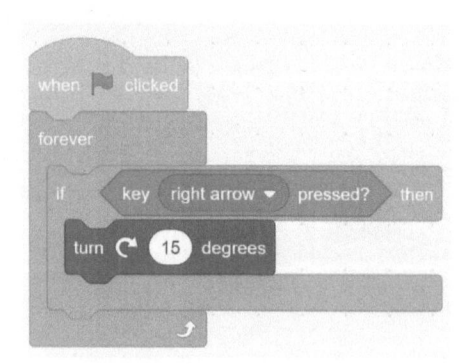

Edit and restore sprite is a very useful tool. Although if many other things have happened you may not be able to restore the sprite.

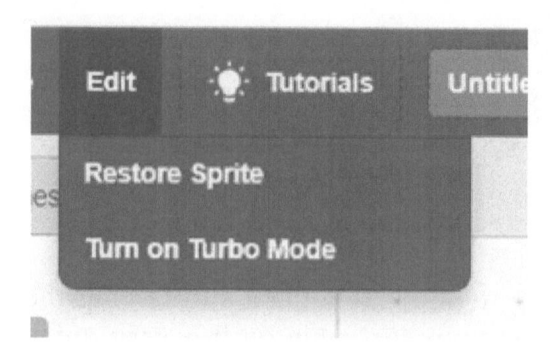

Deleting a sprite accidentally or on purpose, although not a direct bug is a pupil error that can cause problems for class teachers.

Knowledge

I can debug code that does not do what I want it to do

CHAPTER 24

Evaluation

Reflection

Undoubtedly, self-evaluation and reflection on work are crucial skills to develop to make progress in any area of life.

Have I made progress since I last checked? What areas do I still need to make progress in? Is there anything hindering or restricting my progress?

It is also something that most pupils will not do unless it is modelled or time is made available for it.

Encouraging Evaluation

The larger and more complex the programming project, the more it benefits from self, peer or teacher evaluation.

Self Evaluation

Checklists are a simple way of helping pupils to think about key aspects that they should include in a project. The key to writing a good checklist is to make sure it is relevant, easy to read and if there is flexibility within project outcomes the list is not too prescriptive.

When

Mid project is a good time to evaluate as pupils have time to adapt their project in light of feedback.

Quiz Checklist Example

Multiple types of questions such as

- Condition starts action question
- Condition switches between action question
- Multiple conditions checked in a single question
- Quiz is introduced
- Quiz has a theme

Quiz With Variables

- The score is collected within a variable in every question
- The score is set back to 0 at the start of the quiz (initialisation)

Game Project Checklist

- Game plan has a clear aim
- Game plan has list of objects
- Algorithm plan and code uses conditions checked within indefinite loops
- Game has user instructions
- Game code uses initialisation so sprites always start in same way or same place

WAGOLL

What does a good one of these look like? Asking this question mid-project will help you to create a useful checklist that pupils can use for peer or self-evaluation.

Peer Evaluation

Running a fellow pupils program and evaluating it is an essential part of the programming experience. Lots of software development sinks or swims on the strength of how easy people find to use it. Exposure to people's opinions and suggestions can provide you with lots of useful improvement suggestions.

Avoiding Peer Evaluation

Many teachers avoid programming peer evaluation out of fear that pupils' unguarded honest feedback will stop learning in its tracks. However, there are tried and trusted ways to avoid damaging feedback.

Two Stars and a Wish

Two positive comments and one suggested improvement can help to balance positive with negative.

Right to Teacher Arbitration

Many pupils are not fooled by two stars and a wish, and some pupils wrap up faint praise in such a way that it fools no one. A more useful strategy is the right to teacher arbitration. To explain your project choice to your teacher. Occasionally the peer-reviewing work will misunderstand what was intended. Having

I recognise there is more than one way to solve/describe a problem

I don't just accept the first solution

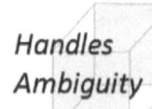

I look for a range of solutions to the same problem

I can evaluate my solutions against a set criteria

I can design criteria to evaluate my creations

Handles Ambiguity

Open Ended Problem Solver

I look for how a project can be extended

I can break complex problems into parts

I can contribute useful ideas to a partner or group

Evaluates

Computing Problem Solver

Copes with Complexity

I can discover/concentrate on the most important part of a problem

I can identify patterns in problems and solutions

I can encourage others to share their ideas

Communicates

Adapts

I can adapt existing ideas to solve new problems

I lead using all the people talent in my group

Investigates

I can develop, test and debug until a product is refined

I learn from setbacks and don't let them put me off

I make predictions about what will happen

I can persevere even if the solution is not obvious

Perseveres

I repeatedly experiment through predicting, making, testing & debugging

Adapted from a problem solving rubric created by Mark Dorling & Thomas Stephens hosted at http://code-it.co.uk/attitudes/

a right to teacher arbitration ensures that everyone can be heard.

More than one Peer Evaluator

If tick sheets and feedback is a short process, there may be room for more than one pupil to leave feedback on a project. Make sure that each new evaluation cannot read the previous evaluation to avoid pupils copying rather than evaluating. If this is avoided, then any points of convergent praise or similar recommendation will be even more impactful.

Teacher Informal Evaluation

There is a lot of value in informal teacher evaluations mid project. Providing pupils with feedback will often encourage those who are making progress to press on. Give mini targets to those who need a mid-project boost and tackle those who may be off target or underachieving.

This can be as simple as a midway verbal assessment of the summative assessment main areas.

'If I assess this next lesson, I will only be able to give you x or y, because you have not completed z. However, if you work on z you will achieve a and b.'

CHAPTER 25

More than One Method

Better Solutions

One of the reasons I love teaching and learning about programming is the plurality of solutions. Every time I learn about something new it opens up a pathway to a simpler or more elegant solution. There are always multiple solutions to the same issue. The more pupils learn the more they uncover more eloquent solution.

Steering Example

When working with programming novices, connecting keyboard commands with simple actions is a powerful way of indicating that the programmer can choose their own method of controlling a program rather than having to use someone else's method.

This method only works because behind the scenes these commands are in their own hidden loop. This complexity has been removed to help beginners connect keyboard inputs

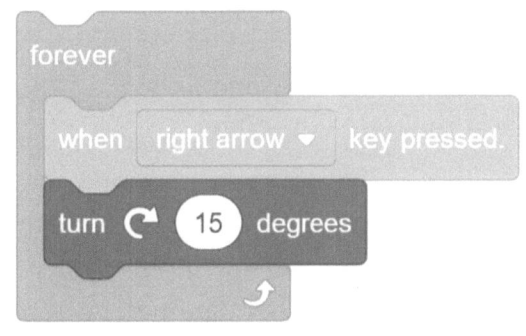

What is really happening?

to actions. This is what it really looks like behind the scenes.

With that in mind, it makes sense to move pupils on by explaining conditions and then how conditions can be checked within a loop as they are in this example.

We can also adapt the amount of degrees turned by using a variable as shown on the next page.

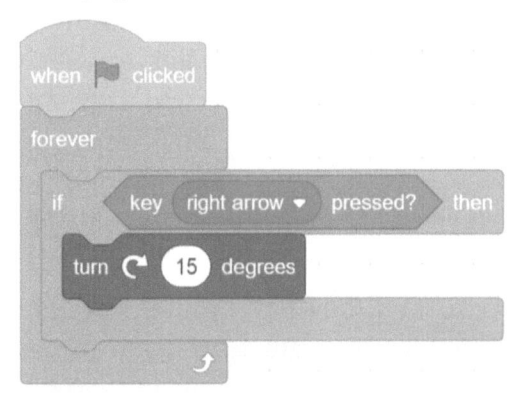

Steering for novice programmers

Condition that is checked repeatedly because it is within an indefinite loop

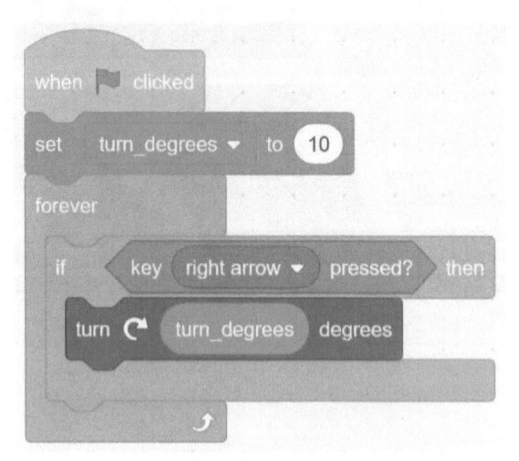

Steering using a variable

Steer right as a procedure version 1

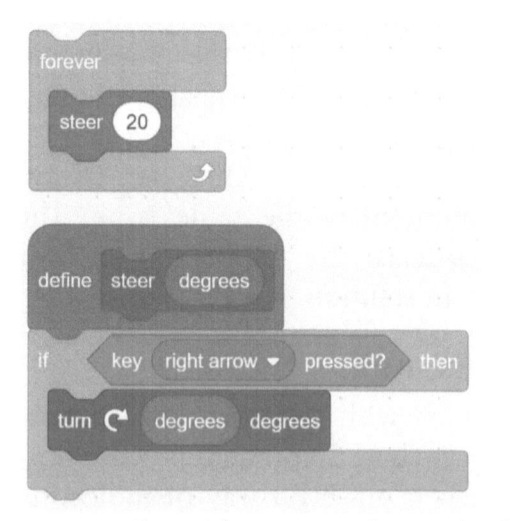

The variable can be assigned as it is in this example at the top of the code

set turn degrees to 10

or it could be assigned with different values in different levels of a game or simulation.

A procedure with a number parameter can be created and used with different values during different levels to vary the arc of the turn as shown on the right.

The loop can be part of the procedure as it is created below, or it can be wrapped around the steer 20 block that calls the procedure, as shown on the right.

The procedure can be created without a variable, as shown above and right middle, or with a variable as shown on the bottom.

The variable could also be used within the procedure, as shown bottom right, or within the block that calls the variable which has not been shown. If the steer 20 block that calls the variable was set to a negative number such as steer −15 then the block would turn left instead.

All of these methods have value, and as a whole they demonstrate how even something as simple as making a sprite turn can be created in a range of different ways.

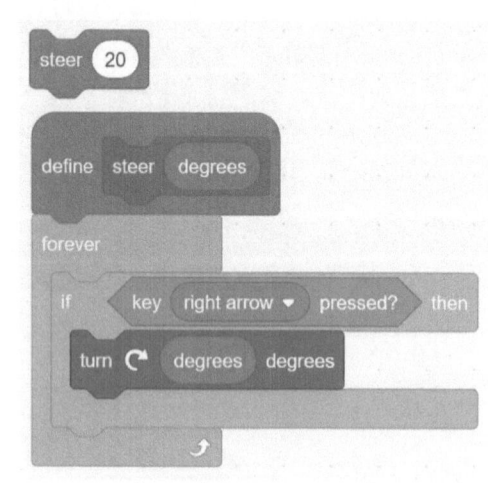

Steer right as a procedure version 2

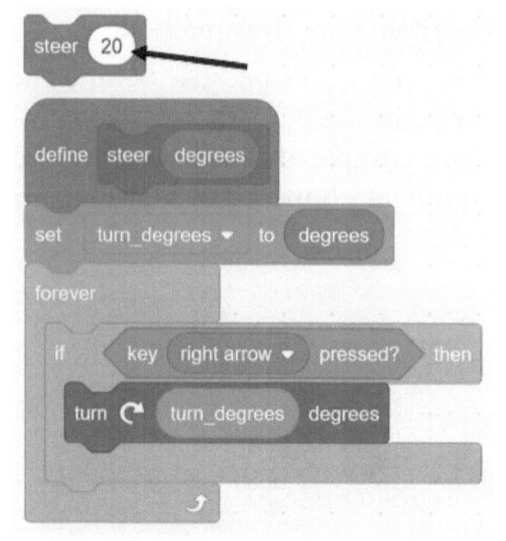

Steer right as a procedure that uses a variable

Solution Hierarchy

In these examples there is a definite hierarchy in the early stages, as we move away from solutions that cannot be replicated in other programming languages. Once we get to conditions that are checked within loops, it is much more about the needs of the project and the developing abilities of the programmers.

More Than One Solution

Modelling more than one solution and challenging pupils to find more than one solution enriches programming and pupils' problem-solving experience. If pupils are working on similar projects, sharing their different solutions with others can enrich and inform others.

I recognise there is more than one way to solve/describe a problem

I don't just accept the first solution

I look for a range of solutions to the same problem

I can evaluate my solutions against a set criteria

Handles Ambiguity

Open Ended Problem Solver

I look for how a project can be extended

I can break complex problems into parts

I can design criteria to evaluate my creations

Evaluates

Computing Problem Solver

I can discover/concentrate on the most important part of a problem

I can contribute useful ideas to a partner or group

Copes with Complexity

I can identify patterns in problems and solutions

I can encourage others to share their ideas

Communicates

Adapts

I can adapt existing ideas to solve new problems

I can develop, test and debug until a product is refined

I lead using all the people talent in my group

Investigates

I make predictions about what will happen

I learn from setbacks and don't let them put me off

Perseveres

I repeatedly experiment through predicting, making, testing & debugging

I can persevere even if the solution is not obvious

Adapted from a problem solving rubric created by Mark Dorling & Thomas Stephens hosted at http://code-it.co.uk/attitudes/

Chapter 26: Modularisation & Sub-Goal Labelling

Modularisation
Modularisation is the task of breaking a project into self-contained sections primarily so that it is easier to understand.

Sub-Goal Labelling
Sub-goal labelling[1] is a process where a section of code is explained or outlined in simpler language to reduce cognitive load.

Decomposition Process
Both are part of the decomposition process in which complex ideas are broken into parts to aid understanding.

Long Code Samples
If young pupils examine a long script of code they can become confused or overwhelmed by the amount of code. Sub-goal labels can help to reduce that.

Methods of Modularisation & Sub Goal Labelling

Basic Procedures
Modularisation can be accomplished in block based programming by using build your own block procedures. These procedures have not necessarily been created to be run multiple times, they are just a way of modularising the program, breaking it down into manageable chunks. The names of the procedures become descriptive labels.

Comments
Another method of sub-goal labelling in Scratch is to provide comments attached to the first block of a section of code.

Within Code Comprehension
One code comprehension adaptation is to give pupils a choice over code that has been already modularised or had sub-goal labels added and code that has not been amended in this way. Pupils can examine both and decide if they find the labels or modularisation useful or not.

Another way to use this within code comprehension is to ask pupils to add sub-goal labels using comments as part of the investigate phase.

They can also be useful in predictions where the code is more complex.

Within I Build You Build
A teacher can label sections of code after creating them as an aid to understanding, to exemplify the process taught and help pupils develop good commenting practice.

---

1 Sub-goal labelling is an idea by Margulieux, L.E., Guzdial, M. and Catrambone, R., 2012

Limit of What We Know

Classroom-based investigations with pupils aged nine and above suggest it can help some pupils comprehend the overall purpose of code more easily, especially if the code sample was long, More research is needed to see if modularisation labelling helps or hinders pupils if introduced at an even earlier stage, or even if it helps all pupils.

Limitations

My limited exploration has found it less useful with lower age primary pupils, as it is just one more thing to read and less useful with shorter code sections as pupils often do not need it.

Examples

The examples on this page and the top of the next page show the same program that has been modularised using procedures and comments.

The example on the bottom of the next page shows sub-goal labelling as part of helping pupils to predict what the code will do as part of PRIMM see chapter 10 for more details.

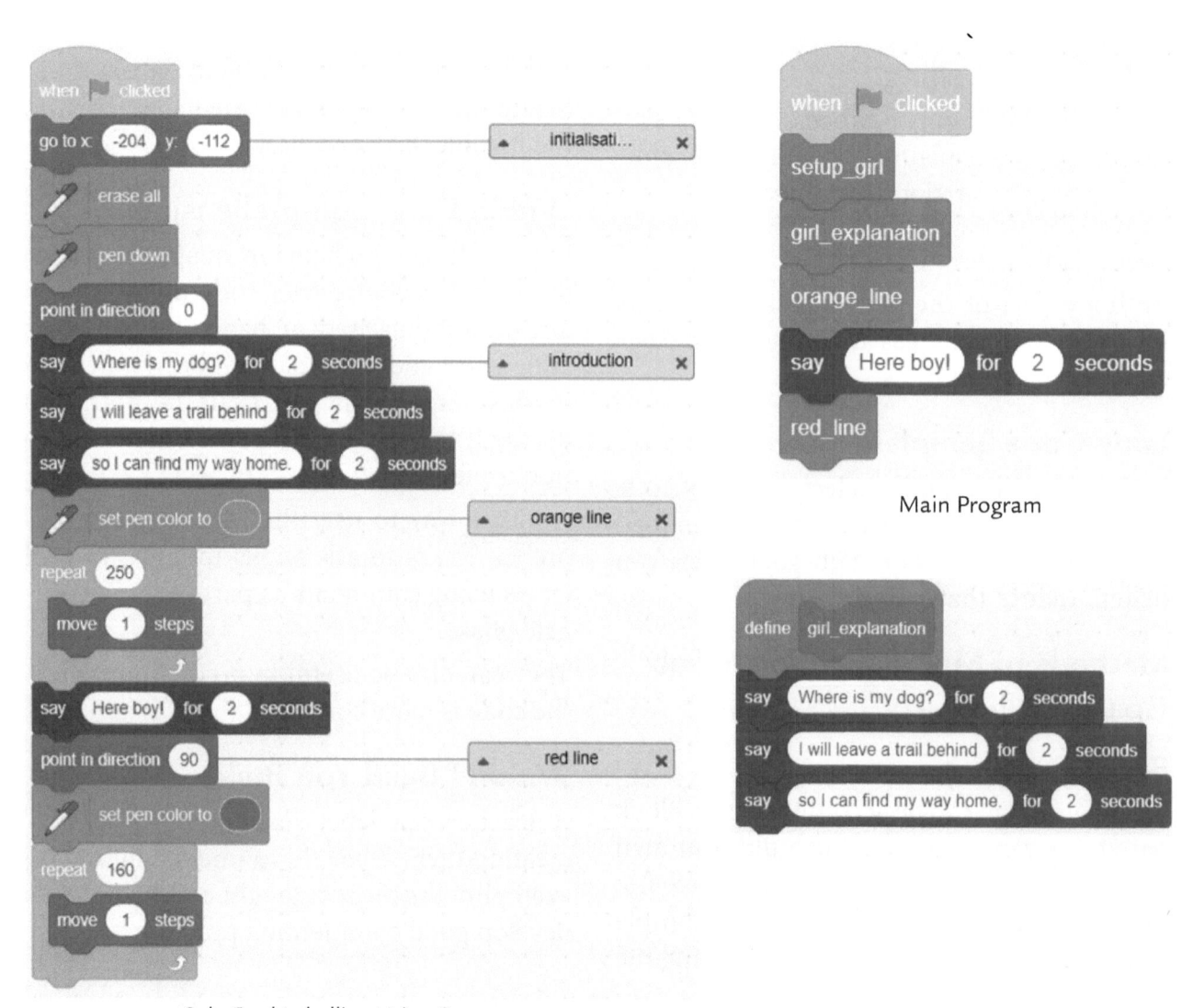

Main Program

Sub-Goal Labelling Using Comments

Modularisation & Sub-Goal Labelling

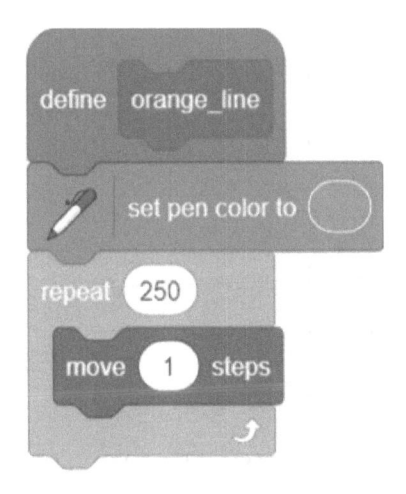

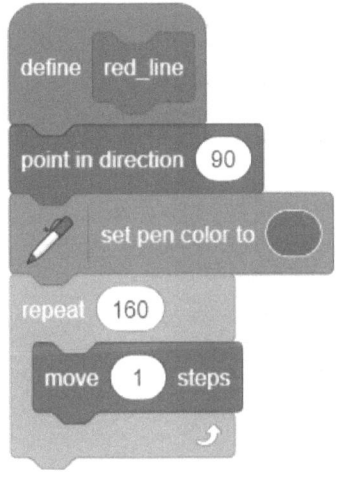

Modularisation Using Procedures

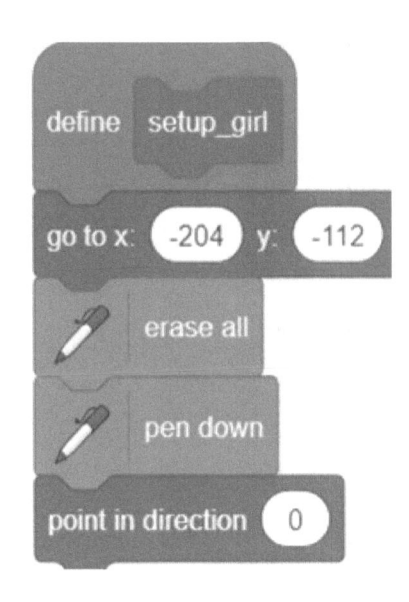

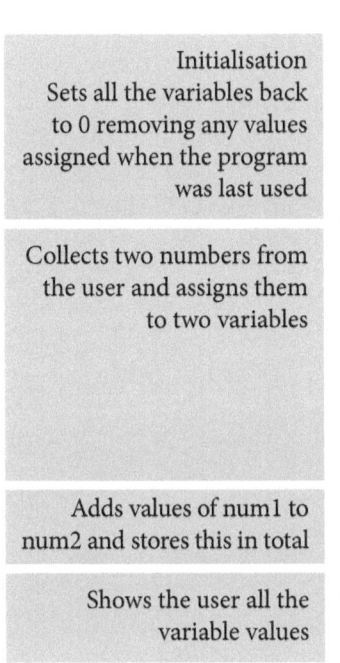

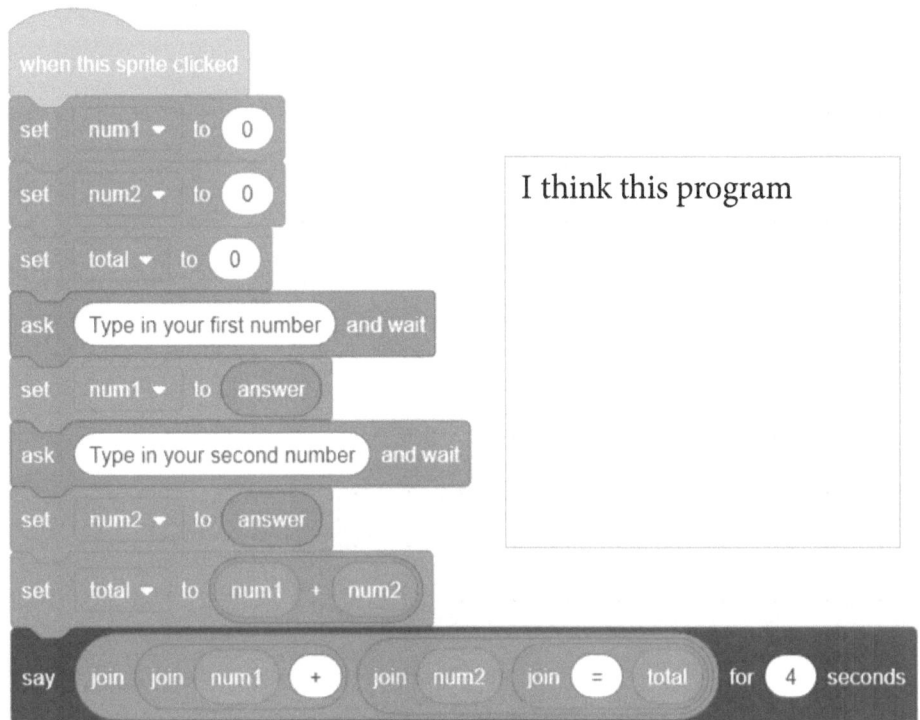

Initialisation Sets all the variables back to 0 removing any values assigned when the program was last used	set num1 to 0; set num2 to 0; set total to 0
Collects two numbers from the user and assigns them to two variables	ask "Type in your first number" and wait; set num1 to answer; ask "Type in your second number" and wait; set num2 to answer
Adds values of num1 to num2 and stores this in total	set total to num1 + num2
Shows the user all the variable values	say join join num1 + join num2 join = total for 4 seconds

I think this program

Sub-Goal Labelling in PRIMM Prediction

> **Further Reading**
> Computer Science in K-12 An A to Z Handbook on teaching programming edited by Shuchi Grover Chapter 23 Worked Examples and other scaffolding strategies especially p242

Flow of Control

CHAPTER 27

Flow of Control

Definition of 'Flow of Control'
The order in which programming commands are executed.

Alternate Naming
Sometimes computer scientists talk about control flow.

The Demise of Flowcharts
I am reliably informed that at one point you could spot a computer scientist at university by the flow-chart template poking out of their top pocket.

This invaluable aid was used to help them plan algorithms by drawing flow charts that would later be turned into code.

Please don't stop reading! I am not suggesting that we go back to flow charts, especially with primary pupils. I am suggesting that the real strength of a flow-chart algorithm is that it makes the flow of control really clear.

Many basic programming errors spring from misunderstandings about the flow of control. Many times I have seen pupils use an indefinite loop nested deep inside their code without realising that their flow of control would get stuck there or design a complex

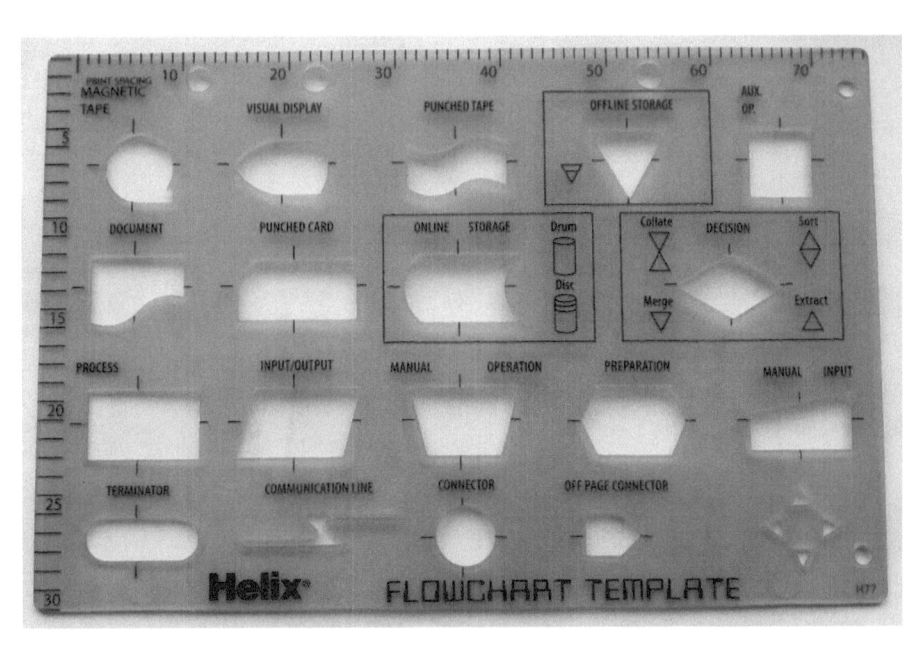

Scratch IT — Teaching Primary Programming with Scratch

set of decisions without embedding it within an indefinite loop so that the conditions are checked repeatedly.

Informal Flow Diagram?

Primary pupils have not got enough time to draw out formal flow charts, so I have developed simple notation to explore the flow of control in algorithms and in code.

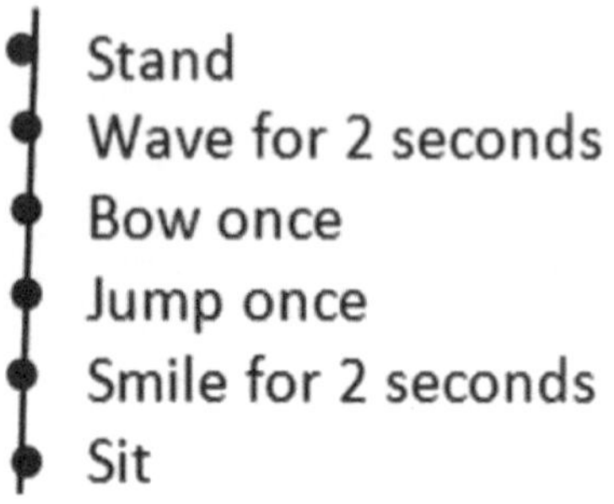

Simple Sequence

To illustrate the steps a program or algorithm takes we draw a line and put dots on the line to show actions.

Simple Count-Controlled Loops

The more I explore the flow of control around loops the more I am convinced that some pupils really struggle with this concept without seeing the flow of control.

Before drawing out the flow of control there are always a few pupils who will include the sit down inside the loop. This is despite labouring the use of an indent to show what is inside the loop. Working with the flow of control helps to reduce that number.

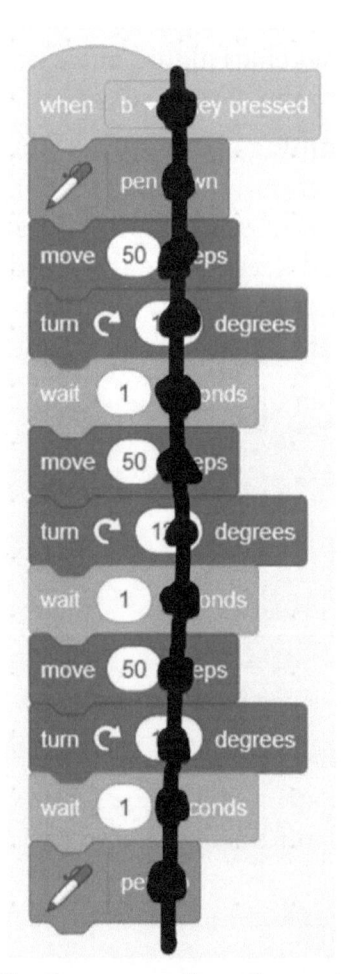

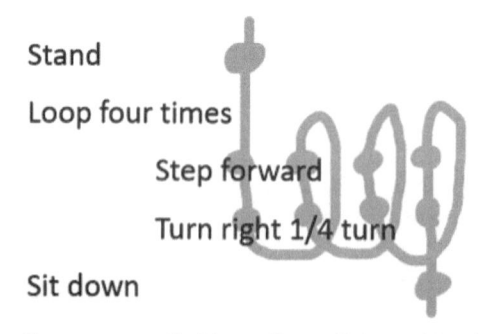

- Stand
- Wave for 2 seconds
- Bow once
- Jump once
- Smile for 2 seconds
- Sit

Simple sequence flow of control in algorithm

Stand
Loop four times
    Step forward
    Turn right 1/4 turn
Sit down

Count-controlled loop flow of control in algorithm

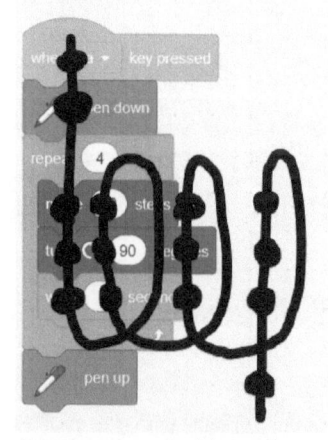

Simple sequence flow of control in code

Count-controlled loop flow of control in code

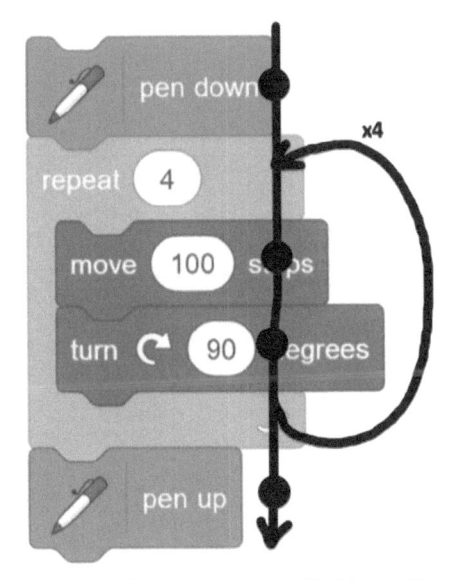

Flow of Control

More useful count-controlled loop flow of control

However, my notation become less useful once loops get too numerous. A more useful notation is the one above.

Avoiding Misconceptions

I always try to make it a visible loop shape and make it clear that the action dots are being drawn on the downward part of the loop cycle. This helps to avoid the misconception that the actions inside a loop can run from bottom to top.

It also helps to have actions after the count-controlled loop, as not all loops in Scratch can have actions after them.

Indefinite Loops

A simple arrow that loops back to the top demonstrates the simplicity of this indefinite forever loop.

Conditional Selection

The use of the diamond to show a decision links this notation to flow charts. Clearly drawing two paths and adding the actions to one of the paths enables you to explore the path when the condition is true and the path where it is false.

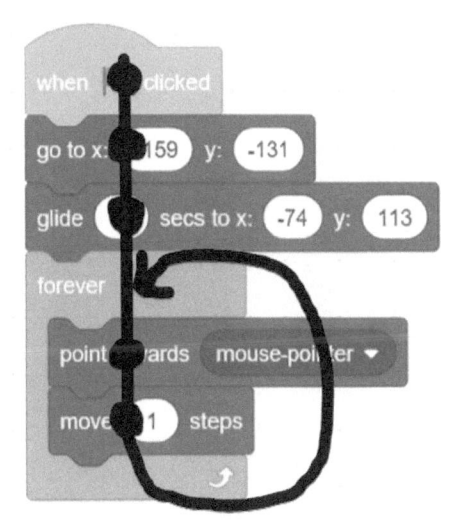

Indefinite loop flow of control

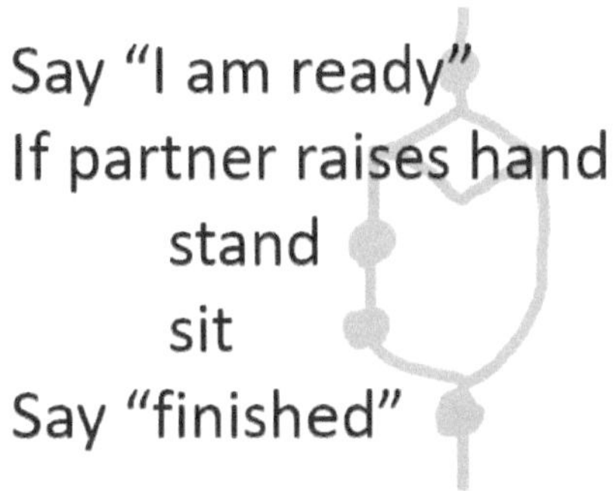

Say "I am ready"
If partner raises hand
    stand
    sit
Say "finished"

Condition selection flow of control in algorithm

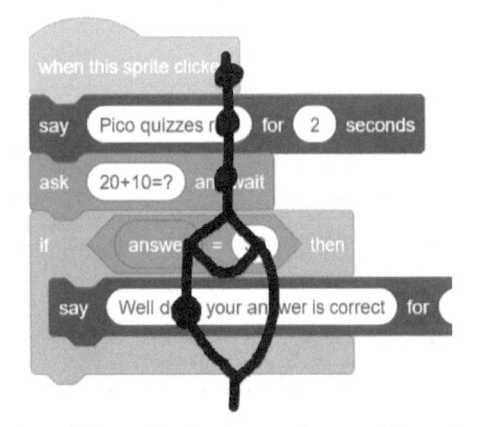

Condition selection flow of control in code

This notation is easy to adapt for if and else conditional selection. Here we can clearly see on the top of the next page that there are actions on both paths helping us to explain that actions can be run if the condition is false as well as true.

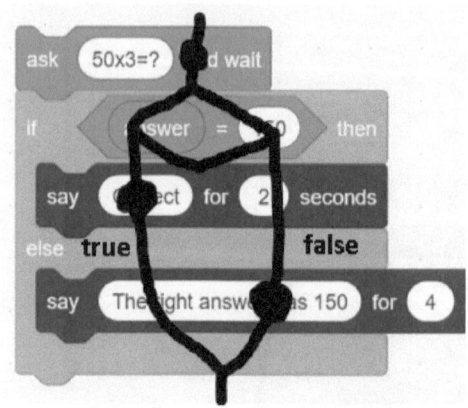

Scratch IT – Teaching Primary Programming with Scratch

If else flow of control in code

Conditions inside loops

Combining the decision diamond with the simple indefinite loop notation produces a clear representation of the flow of control.

This works equally well for simple notation such as the two examples below, but also for

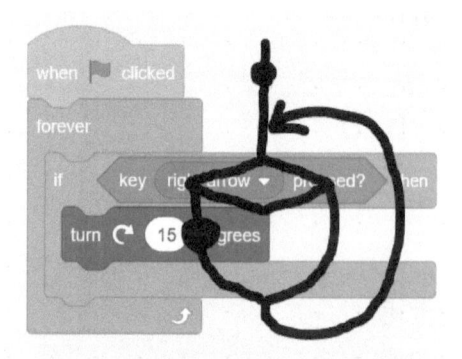

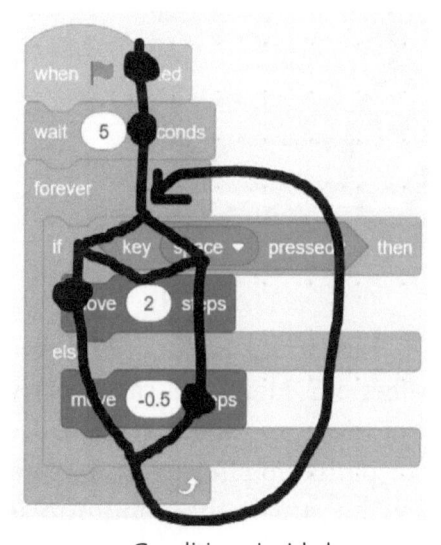

Conditions inside loops

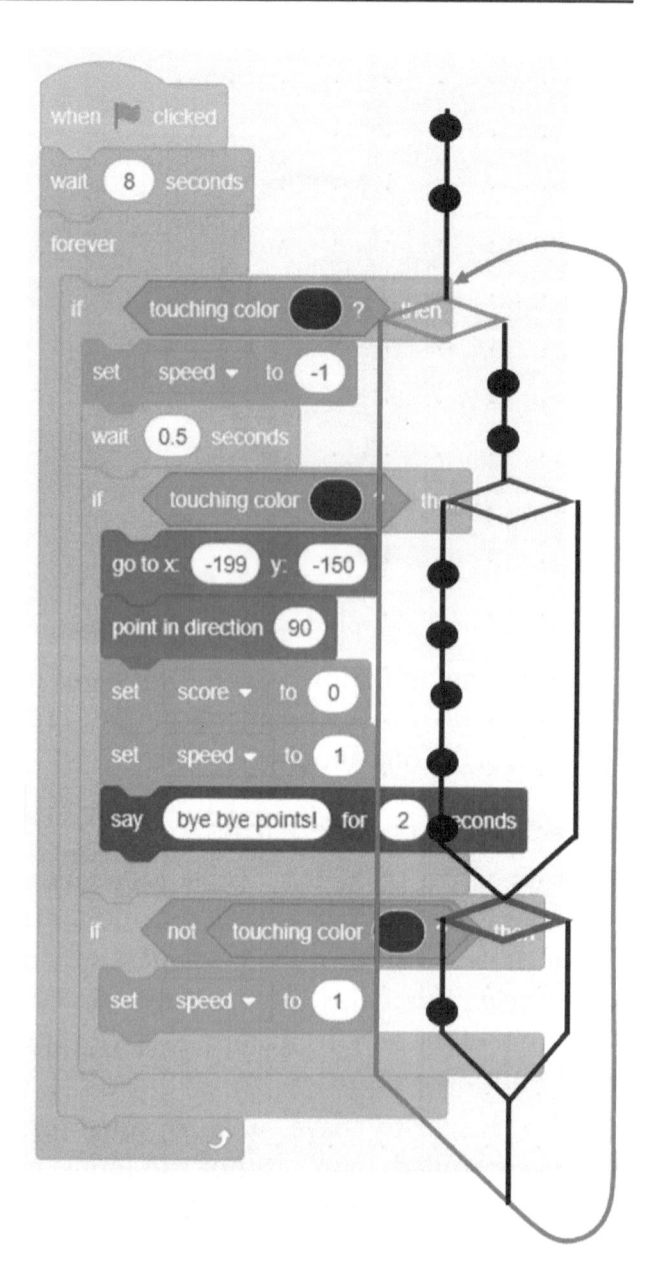

Complex flow of control

much more complex examples such as that above where conditions are nested inside each other.

Nested Conditions

In this more complex code, if the top green condition is false it bypasses all actions and through the indefinite red loop (forever loop) returns to check the top green condition again.

Flow of Control

If the top green condition is true it will carry out two actions and then check the second purple condition.

If the middle purple condition is true five actions will be carried out. If it is false no actions will be carried out.

Then a third blue condition is checked which if true will trigger a single action. Finally it returns to the red indefinite loop path and back up to check the green condition where it all happens again.

Condition Ends Loop

Can be drawn in this manner with the loop returning to the point where the condition also resides.

Both paths could also be drawn from right and left of the condition rather than from the bottom as shown.

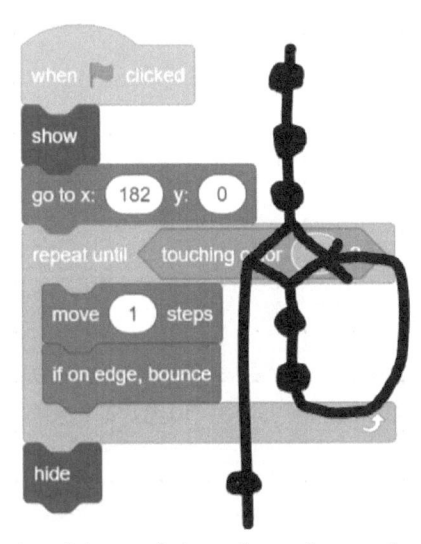

Condition ends loop flow of control

Procedures

A circle can be used to indicate a procedure and if multiple procedures need to be distinguished from each other then a letter in each one will accomplish this.

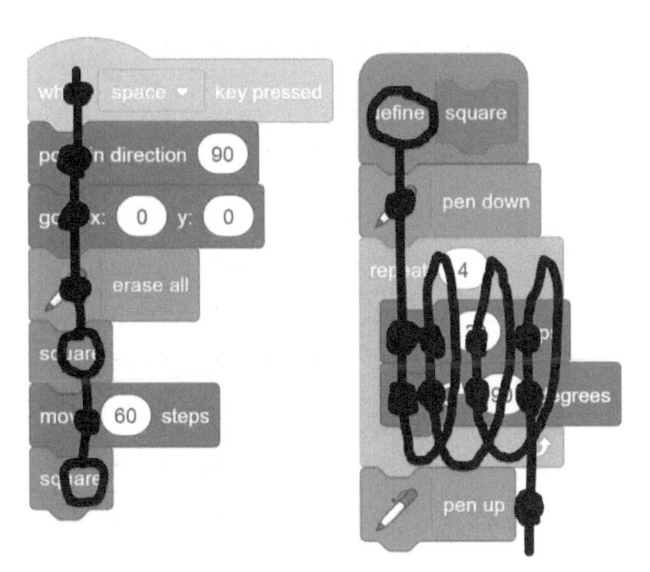

Flow of control to call a procedure

Variables

In this example on the next page the action dots on the flow of control diagram have been coloured orange. Pupils can write in the value of the variables alongside these dots to show that they understand how the variable value is being changed.

Tracing Live

I think the best way to learn about flow of control is to draw it live with your pupils.

The teacher can draw in on top of algorithms or on top of code using the many text inlay tools available via class display tools. They can use it to help them explain what the code does in the order that it will run.

Pupils can use the snipping tool or other screen capture software to quickly cut out code and annotate it with the flow of control notation.

If you have pre-prepared a flow of control examples get pupils to trace their finger over the flow of control and say what is happening at each stage.

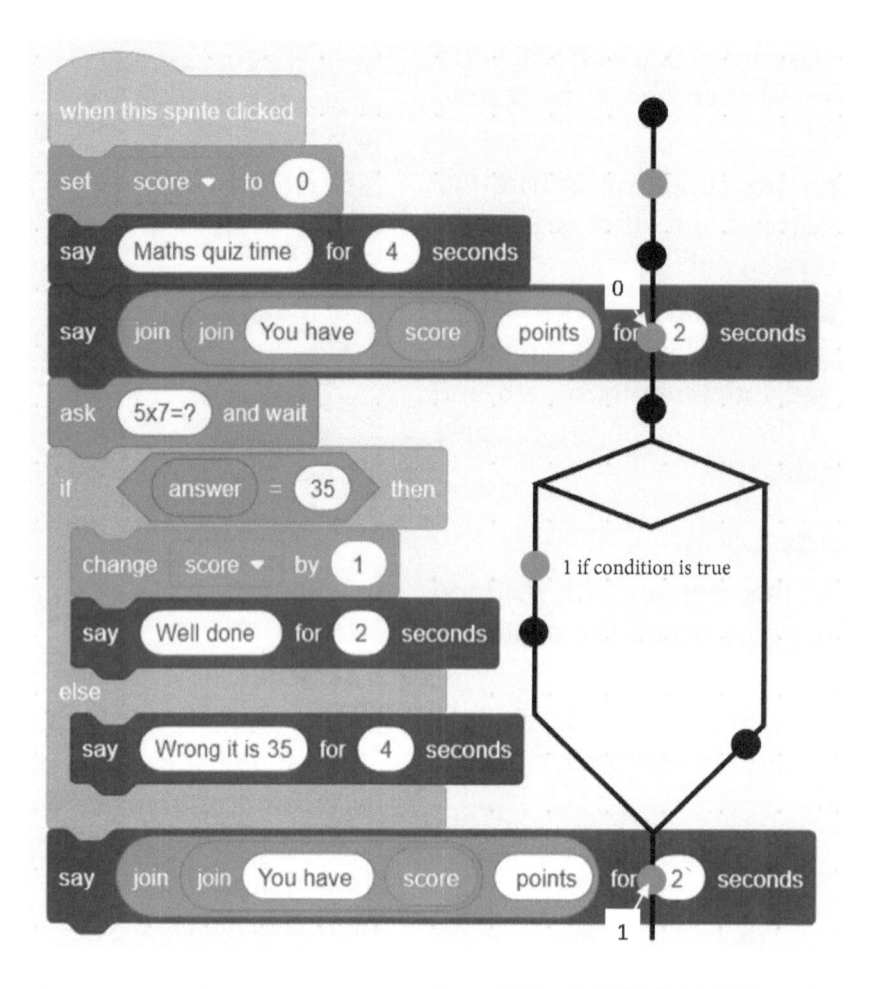

Flow of Control in Planning

Some pupils will choose to plan using a modified version of the annotation. It can definitely help them think through one aspect of their code.

Flow of Control in Debugging

Drawing the flow of control in a simple, quick way can help pupils see if they have any bottle necks or incomplete flows.

Flow of Control Research

As this is my invention I am going to name this the Bagge Block Flow method. I welcome any research into its efficacy.

Screen Capture Tools

On windows Ctrl-alt-delete will capture a picture of your whole screen

The snipping tool or Snip & Sketch

On a Mac https://www.cnet.com/how-to/mac-screenshots-4-ways-to-capture-your-macbooks-screen/

On an iPad https://support.apple.com/en-gb/HT210781

On a Chromebook type Ctrl + F5 on a standard keyboard. For a partial capture, press Ctrl + Shift first, followed by F5

Variability

CHAPTER 28

Multiple Examples

Variability is seeing the same concept in many different ways. If we show pupils how to use a type of connective in a sentence we then show them many different examples of how to use this to aid their understanding. Similarly, we might show pupils how to add numbers before using it with objects, money, more than two numbers, etc. This variability helps to establish the concept more firmly in our long term memory.

Aids Transfer

Sweller describes how variability aids the transfer of concepts from working memory to long-term memory after the concept has been introduced in the simplest way possible.

Balance

In the examples on the right the pupil is shown how the same condition starts action block can be used to check just one condition or two conditions one after each other. It is also possible to show pupils how two or more conditions might be checked in a single if statement as shown below, but teachers have to be careful not to introduce too many new concepts too early and cognitively overload pupils, hindering their transfer of concepts from working to short-term memory.

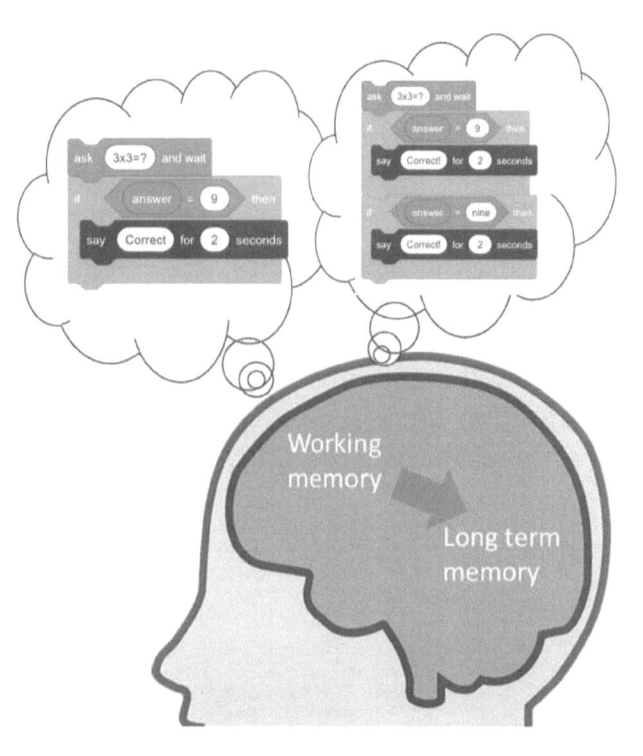

Variability in Code Comprehension

The educator choosing to use code comprehension strategies will want to create code to examine that illustrates the main concept introduced in multiple different ways to aid knowledge retention whilst still maintaining a coherence and purpose which makes it interesting, stimulating and inspiring when run.

Helicopter Example

In this gaming example, pupils were introduced to an indefinite loop before it was used in many ways throughout the game:

To make it look like the rotors are spinning using different costumes, as shown bottom left.

To steer and move the spite, as shown in the example on the top right.

To draw a black and grey dashed line, as shown by the example bottom right.

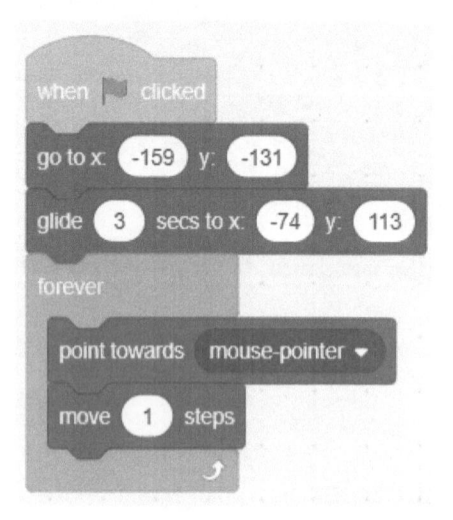

Limitations

It is tempting to just show pupils lots of sections of unconnected code that illustrate the concept introduced in a variety of different ways, but this is uninspiring and ignores programming's greatest asset in that it can make real things for real purposes.

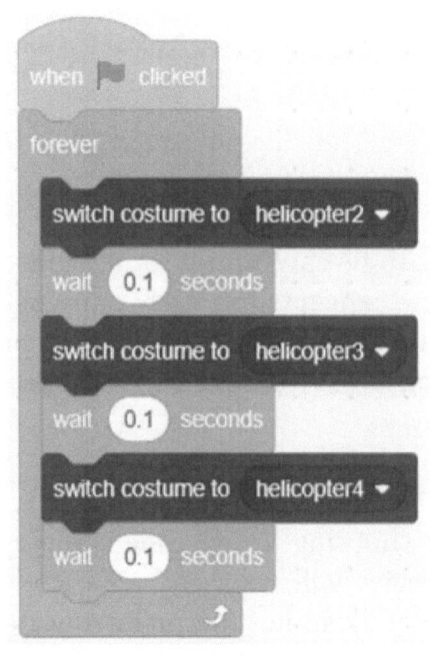

Move and Steer

Rotors Spinning Using An Indefinite Loop

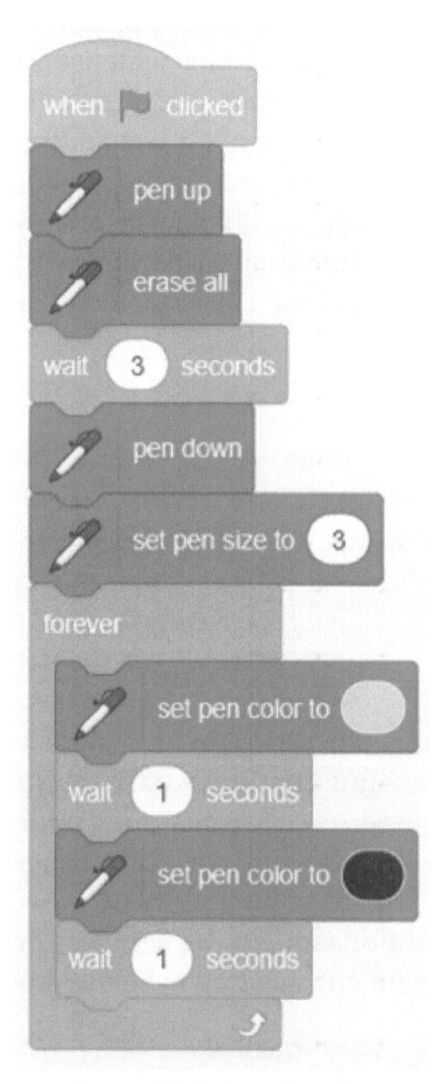

Draw A Black And Grey Line

Variability in I Build You Build

Variability can easily be built into the examples that educators choose to use to build and explore together with their pupils.

If the first examples are copied, the later examples can have more challenge by providing the code unconnected (Parsons) or providing hints as to how the concept can be used again to solve a similar but different problem.

In either methodology, careful thought is needed to avoid cognitive overload whilst encouraging variability of example.

Assessing Programming

CHAPTER 29

Formative Assessment

This is an important part of the computing teacher's skills. Checking to see if learning is happening in a specific area.

Formative assessment helps teachers to make value judgements during programming modules. If pupils have not grasped the learning, the teacher can provide corrective help. If they have grasped the learning quickly the teacher can provide enrichment. If they are working meaningfully towards understanding and are on task, teachers can give them more time.

Most commonly in primary programming practice this takes the form of teacher observation or questioning to avoid disrupting the flow of learning with more obtrusive methods. However on occasion a short written test or multiple choice test might be needed to check understanding.

The diagram on the right outlines the three possible outcomes.

A. Corrective help
B. More time to work (leave them to it)
C. Enrichment

Within Module Aims

The corrective and enrichment activities should always be within the scope of the module's objectives, as this avoids fragmented groups of pupils working on different areas who cannot easily re-join the class workflow.

Formatively Assess During All Activities

Do not be tempted to leave assessment to pupils' final programming project. Quality support and intervention may be too late by then.

Formative Assessment During Various Methods

I Build You Build

After demonstrating code-building or environmental skills, the teacher can travel the class looking to see if pupils are able to copy and adapt the programming demonstrated. This will help the teacher to determine if they are sharing too much or too little in each demonstration. It will also help them to identify any pupils who are off task, in need of a further demo or open to enrichment tasks.

Scratch IT — Teaching Primary Programming with Scratch

Formative Assessment Process

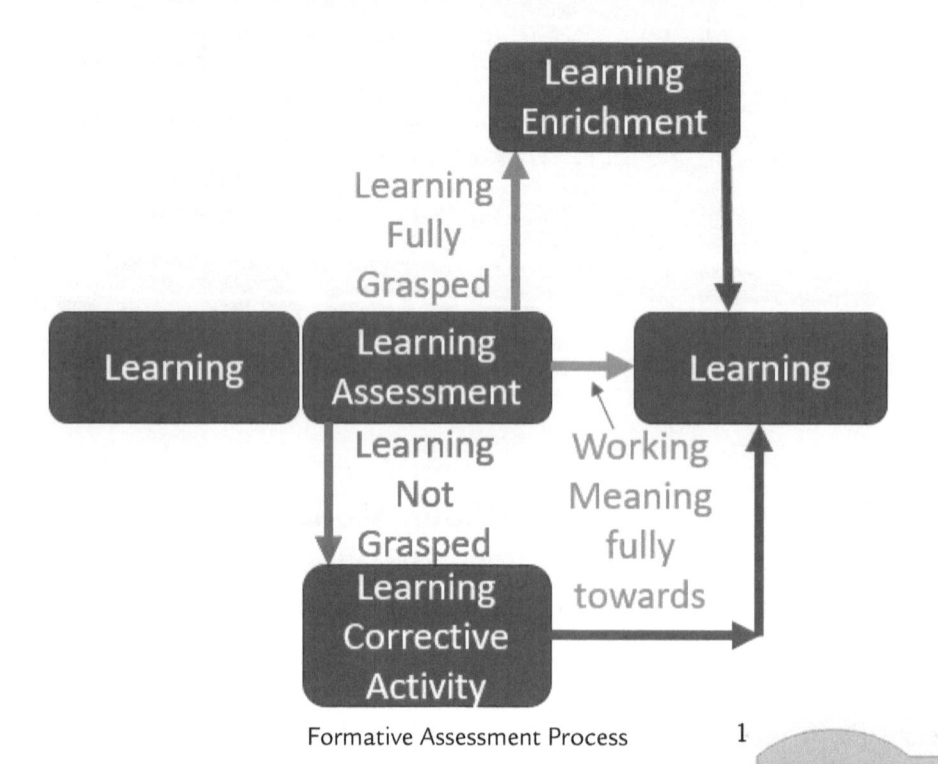

In the code the teacher has demonstrated how to snap the top two blocks and adapt them so that the 1 key moves 10 steps.

An Enrichment could be

A. Can you make the 2 key move 20 steps in a new code section?

B. I like the way you have programmed the 2 key to move 20 steps. Is that the only way to do that?

Which could lead to an answer similar to the third code block.

C. Can you make the 0 key program the sprite to move backwards using only the same blocks as before?

Which could lead to the fourth code block as a solution.

Corrective help at this stage will often be a slower or less packed repeat demo, or some reading support to help them find the blocks.

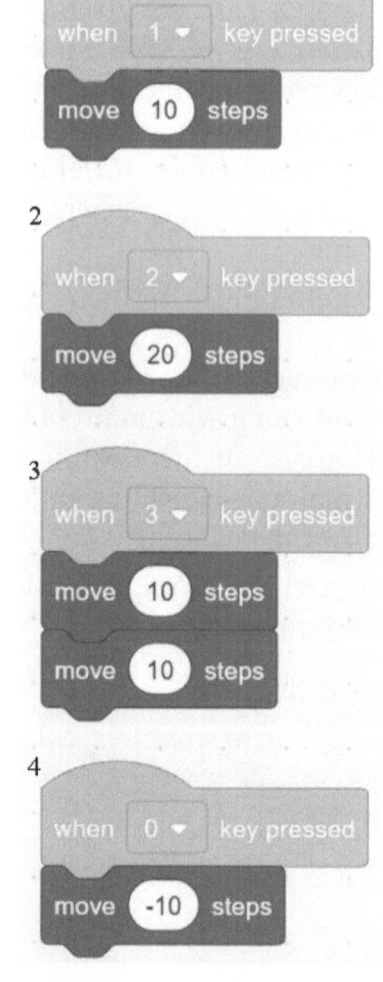

Concept Before Coding

Watching pupils roleplay sequences, loops or conditions will provide useful formative assessment information. Are any pupils slightly behind the actions in roleplay because they are copying their peers rather than reading and interpreting the algorithms themselves? When pupils get to the algorithm-writing stage this is an opportunity to check in on those pupils' understanding and provide **corrective** support reading, scribing or overlearning as needed.

Enrichment can be provided by encouraging longer algorithm writing with multiple elements or including other concepts learnt previously.

Code Comprehension

Collecting pupils' marks at all stages of code comprehension enables the teacher to check that the work is being done, the work is being marked and any pupils that struggled are being picked up and supported. There is far less need for enrichment as pupils can move on to the next, more complex, stage naturally without intervention.

Formatively Assessing Planning

Planning is there to aid quality code creation, so checking pupils' planning for key concepts can improve the quality of code.

For example, if you have just taught about conditions within indefinite loops, checking to see if algorithms are within indefinite loops will help the teacher to see if this key concept has been embedded before pupils code.

If you have just taught about initialisation, then looking for indicators that pupils have included it in the planning will help to check if they have understood this concept.

Faded Example

Opportunities for enrichment in faded examples are built into the concept, as teachers can remove scaffolding stages for those pupils who are demonstrating clear understanding.

Corrective help can involve going back to an early stage to see how much was understood or working with a pupil to add reading or writing support.

Summative Assessment

The marks collected for various stages of code comprehension can help to form a summative assessment of pupils' programming understanding, but nothing can replace assessing their actual programming creations to determine how much they have internalised and can use the key concepts taught independantly.

Three Strands Summative Assessment Focus

The table on the next page shows an example three-strand assessment grid that can be used to assess KS2 primary programming projects where they have been introduced to indefinite loops.

Has The Key Concept Been Used Successfully?

The first row assesses the key concept that was introduced, in this case simple indefinite loops (forever loops in Scratch).

There is a simple scale from no progress to concept mastery.

Teacher & Pupil Assessment Circle the stage that you think you have reached in each row. your teacher will check it.

Indefinite (forever) loops	Not used a forever loop	Copied a forever loop from the fish tank project	Copied and changed a forever loop idea	Used a forever loop in a way not shown
	0 Marks	1 mark	2 marks	3 marks
Used previous programming concept such as count-controlled loops			Not used previous programming concepts for real puipose	Used previous programming concepts for real puipose
			0 Marks	1 mark
Has a project theme in planning or code			No theme in planning or code	Has a theme in planning or code
			0 Marks	1 mark

Fish Tank Three Strands Summatiue Assessment For Pupils & Teachers for Year 4 (8-9) year old pupils

No progress

0, Not used concept

1, Copied concept

2, Adapted concept

3, New use of concept

Mastery

This is easy to assess in the lesson if you have examined the example program in detail before using it with your class.

Has Previous Learning Been Used?

Encouraging pupils to reflect on what they have learnt previously and continuing to use it, if it is appropriate, values their prior learning journey.

Is There a Theme or Purpose?

Programming is not just a mathematical problem solving exercise we write programs so that our users will enjoy running them. Recognising this is important. We could further divide this assessment strand into

No theme

A simple theme

A complex theme

But that is harder for pupils to self-assess.

Manageable Summative Assessment

There are lots of other things you can summative assess for but we need to keep primary assessment manageable for non subject specialist. These three strands can be easily assessed within lessons through checking what pupils have planned and coded.

The numerical values make it easier to track individual progress and compare progression across a class or year group.

Include Planning in Assessment

If we want pupils to value planning, then including it in our assessment will give it higher status. Tell pupils that for a single project you are going to assess their projects only

Assessing Programming

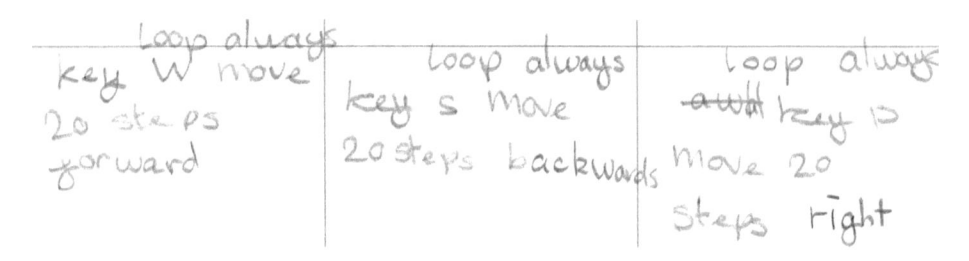

Example 1 Planning Algorithms Written for a game by Year 5 (9-10) year old pupil

through their planning. **Example 1** above was created by a Year 5 pupil after PRIMM.

The game that they examined did use steering but with 15 degrees so 2 marks for an adaptation and the movement was continuous and not controlled by keys so 3 marks for a new use not shown in the exemplars.

So overall you will give that project three marks for planning to use conditions within indefinite loops correctly and in a way not illustrated by the teacher.

The loop always in **Example 1** is indented to the left in every example, indicating that it was probably written on at a later date possibly after a prompt from the teacher such as

'That condition will be checked once and then the code will stop working, what can you do to make sure the condition is checked over and over again?'

The presence of such an indicator shows that effective formative assessment for that pupil was taking place in the lesson.

In **Example 2** on the previous page all three conditions are exactly the same as those in the exemplar project, but as they are all included within the same indefinite forever loop they are examples of planning that can also be given three points for demonstrating use in a new way not shown in the exemplar project.

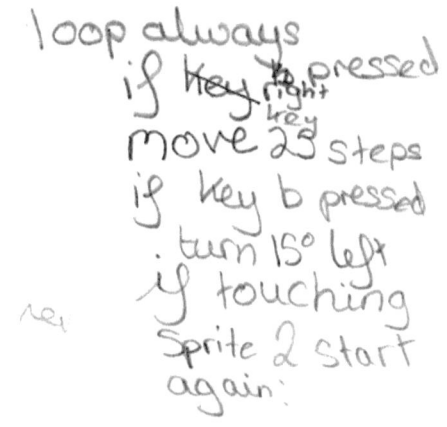

Example 2 Planning Algorithms Written for a game by Year 5, 9-10-year-old-pupil

Multiple Choice Retreival Practice

Multiple choice questions are useful for checking, what knowledge has been retained but don't tell you much about the quality of

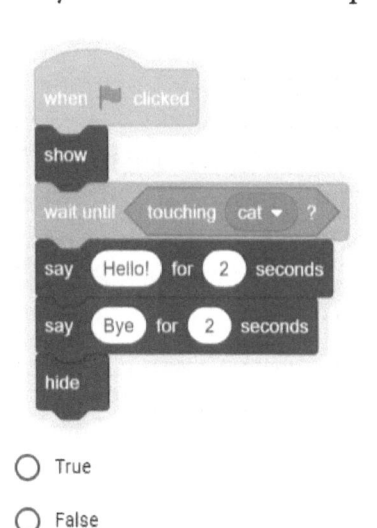

○ True

○ False

Code with a yellow outline is wrong code?
An example multiple choice retreival type question

Computing Problem Solver

I recognise there is more than one way to solve/describe a problem

I can evaluate my solutions against a set criteria

I can design criteria to evaluate my creations

I can contribute useful ideas to a partner or group

I can encourage others to share their ideas

I lead using all the people talent in my group

I learn from setbacks and don't let them put me off

I can persevere even if the solution is not obvious

I don't just accept the first solution

I look for a range of solutions to the same problem

I look for how a project can be extended

I can break complex problems into parts

I can discover/concentrate on the most important part of a problem

I can identify patterns in problems and solutions

I can adapt existing ideas to solve new problems

I can develop, test and debug until a product is refined

I make predictions about what will happen

I repeatedly experiment through predicting, making, testing & debugging

Handles Ambiguity — Open Ended Problem Solver — Evaluates — Copes with Complexity — Communicates — Adapts — Investigates — Perseveres

Adapted from a problem solving rubric created by Mark Dorling & Thomas Stephens hosted at http://code-it.co.uk/attitudes/

that knowledge. They do have their place in checking how much knowledge has been retained from week to to week.

Summative Assessment Errors

Do not be tempted to assess the amount of code produced. Whole segments of code can easily be copied. More is not necessarily better in programming.

Computational Attitudes

Attitudes to computing are arguably harder to assess than pupils work output, but we can engage pupils in self-assessment and peer assessment by focussing on a few problem-solving areas and asking pupils where they or the people they have worked with have made progress during a lesson. Pupils can record the problem solving skill and how they used it. These can provide helpful insight into pupils' attitude improvements at parents' evenings and end, of, year reports.

Limited Use

Once the vast majority of the class are demonstrating good problem-solving skills your focus on these could be phased out for most pupils.

MORE SUPPORT

Concrete Examples to Explain Abstract Code

CHAPTER 30

Away from the computer
A concrete example will be shared away from the computer through physical action such as roleplay, modelling, movement or simple drawing.

Links to existing schema
A concrete example is one anchored in a pupils' bank of everyday experience. An example they are likely to relate to because it is already common knowledge.

Abstract Concepts
Many aspects of how programming works are quite abstract.

Examples
Steps within a loop
If you drag out a move so many steps block and place it within an indefinite forever loop block as illustrated below you will observe the sprite moving across the screen when the code is run.

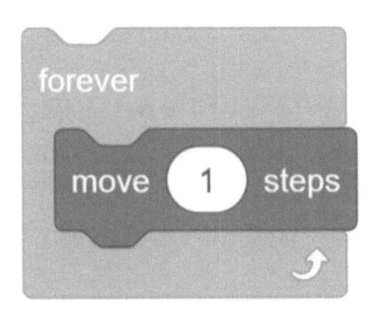

The move 1 step code is being repeatedly run over and over again which results in slow continuous movement for its sprite. Inside the loop it runs 30 commands per second.

Steps Within a Loop Roleplay
The teacher explains that they are the sprite and that they are inside an indefinite forever loop. Then they move one step saying move one step, and then repeat this movement and words until they encounter a physical object. When they encounter a physical object they continue to mime movement, comparing this to the sprite's actions when it reaches the edge of the screen. It is important to go in a straight line, as there is no turning or steering in this example.

Move More Steps
Teachers can model moving more steps at a time, making sure to do all the steps in the same amount of time so pupils can see how this will affect speed. Move two steps, move two steps, etc.

Move Backwards
Teachers can explain that when we move one step we are adding a step and if we want

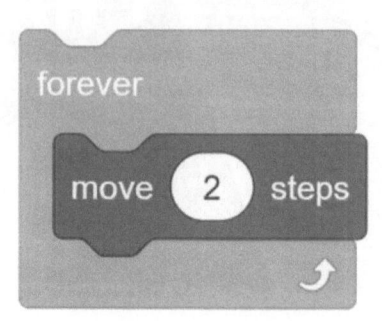

Moving two steps in the same amount of time

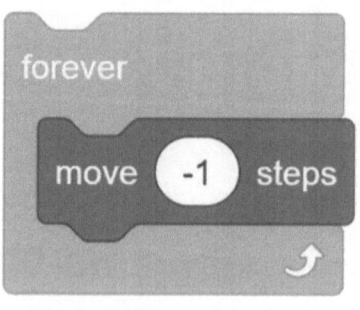

Moving minus 1 steps to go backwards

to move backwards we will need to do the inverse . Physically move backwards alongside the demo, as this adds to the value of the explanation. This will be enough for most pupils to start exploring how they will subtract a step. It helps to explain that when we add a step there is an invisible add sign in front of the number but when we subtract we need to put a visible subtract sign in front of the number.

Two Blocks

A further adaptation of this is to roleplay what happens when another block is added. Look at the code example underneath.

Two people are needed for this roleplay. Typically the teacher plays the sprite and another person plays the mouse pointer. The person playing the mouse pointer is instructed to not get caught by the person playing the sprite. The sprite person then moves one step before stopping and pointing towards the person playing the mouse pointer and turning towards them. This simple looped actions is carried out throughout the demonstration. The person sprite then moves around the floor chasing the person mouse pointer.

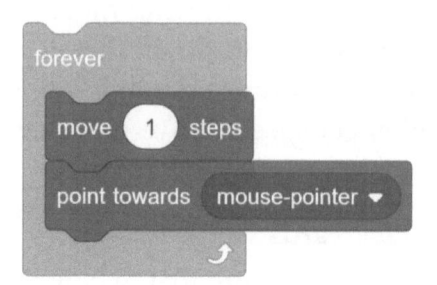

Pupils Roleplay

Pupils can act these out themselves, although part of the understanding comes through observing the roleplay actions of others rather than carrying them out themselves.

Flow of Control

Steps within a loop and all of its adaptations are fundamentally about the flow of control and occasionally about mathematical understanding. The indefinite forever loop block runs the blocks within and then goes back to the start of the loop to repeat the process. The handy arrow at the bottom of the loop points this out. The number can be changed to adapt the speed or move forwards or backwards.

Change Pen Colour Within a Loop

In this example we will start by showing a common coding error linked to time. The pupil wants to create a multi-coloured line that will

Concrete Examples to Explain Abstract Code

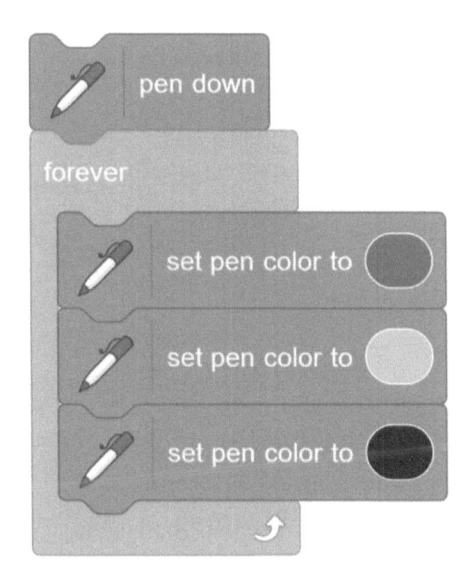

be drawn as the sprite moves about the screen and has created code as shown above.

They have also used the two blocks example shown on the left to make the sprite move and steer by following the mouse pointer. When this code is run the line is drawn as all one colour. The set pen colour blocks are run so quickly (34 times on my PC) that the colours blur into each other. Typically many instructions are processed per second, although this can be changed using turbo mode or if your computer redraws its screen faster. So in our example red, yellow and blue would be run ten times each whilst the sprite travels one pixel distance, one dot on the Scratch screen.

Age and experience variations
Younger Pupils
If working with lower KS2 pupils ages 7-9, then concrete modelling will help them to understand the problem. Get two or three different colour felt tip pens out, preferably of the same colours they used and ask them to place a dot of each colour on top of each other. They will see that the colours merge into each other. Now explain that each pen should make 10 dots in the same place, ten red, ten yellow and ten blue before you can move the pen on one dot width. Then ask how can we ensue that each colour stays for a longer period of time?

Older Pupils
Older pupils may not need the demonstration ,and an explanation will often suffice but if you get blank looks then modelling the abstract in a concrete manner will help. Eventually pupils will realise that the code needs to look like the code below with time waits.

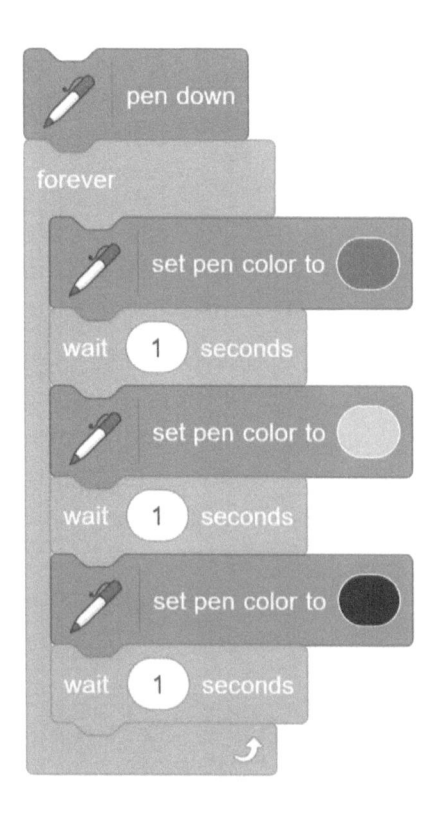

Developing Concrete Examples to Explain Abstract Code
First ask yourself if there is any aspect of the type of programming that you are teaching about or that pupils are using independently that could be modelled concretely? Do

any of the blocks have concrete everyday equivalents?

Motion Blocks

Many motion blocks are open to this process as they have everyday equivalents. We all turn right and left, although we are rarely precise in our degrees of turn.

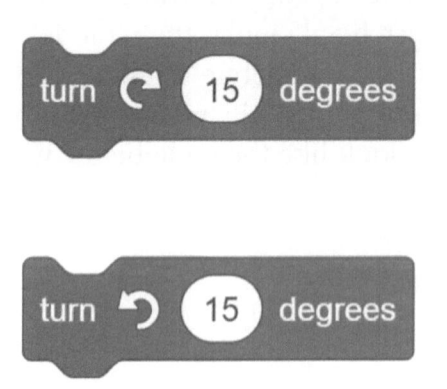

`turn ↻ 15 degrees`

`turn ↺ 15 degrees`

Younger pupils may not have explored degrees in depth, but often know about 90 degrees or a quarter turn. This is enough to explore turning and model it physically.

At first glance, going to a random position can seem easy to explain, but randomness isn't an easy concept to really understand. Simplifying the concept down to six possible locations and rolling a die to determine which one is chosen can help reduce the concept to manageable proportions.

`go to random position ▾`

Point in direction comes with a draggable dial so even if you don't understand degrees in a circle you can point where you want the sprite to go.

`point in direction 90`

Labelling parts of the playground or classroom floor can help pupils to understand what point in direction is doing as well as reinforce the importance of degrees outside of a purely mathematical context.

Looks Blocks

Say and think blocks are open to this process through speech or drawn speech bubbles, although if pupils haven't created or observed these they often think these involve sound rather than speech bubbles.

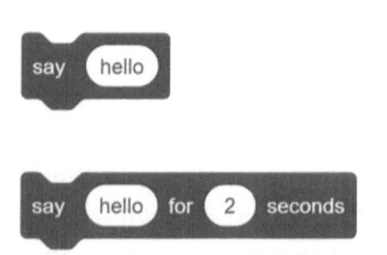

`say hello`

`say hello for 2 seconds`

Say blocks with and without time elements

Show and hide rarely need this process directly unless a pupil is struggling with flow of control issues. It can be enough to show an object and hide it behind your back.

Drawing simple objects different sizes on whiteboard or paper can illustrate size changes effectively even for pupils whose grasp of percentage is tenuous.

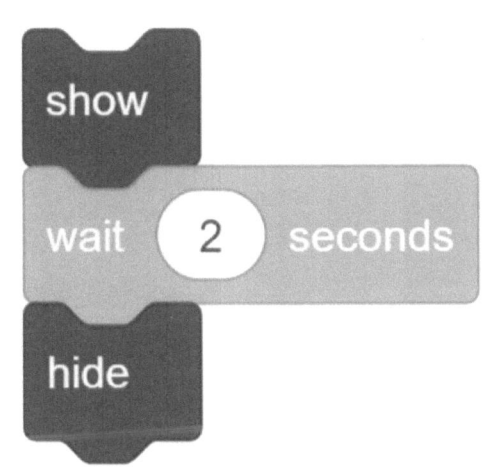

Concrete Examples to Explain Abstract Code

Show and hide

Size changes

Size changes drawn

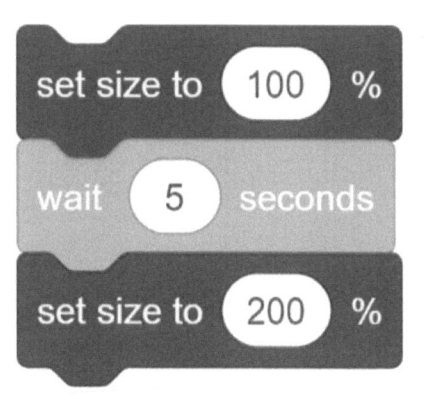

Drawings don't need to be mathematically exact, it just has to be obvious that the size has changed.

Things to consider

Teachers need to be aware that the concrete example may introduce misconceptions. Looking out for these may convince you to use another strategy or determine to address the misconceptions of these at a later stage.

Sometimes it is more effective to just observe what code does in the program than take the process away from the computer. See the chapter on **More Clues**.

The explanation away from the computer needs to be as simple or simpler than the code it is explaining. It is possible to explain many things with concrete examples but not all will lower pupils cognitive load.

Chapter 31

Trace and Explain

Trace and Explain
Trace and explain is a strategy for talking through what code is doing block by block. Trace because we make it very clear which part of the code we are explaining by pointing to it.

To Whom
Trace and explain can be delivered to one pupil, a small group or the whole class.

Good Questioning
Ensuring active attention often includes involving pupils through good questioning. If you are working with the whole class then asking pupils to tell their partner the answer or write it on a whiteboard helps to improve concentration, as they know they may be asked questions.

Code Confidence
I have observed that a small percentage of pupils, when faced with a large amount of code, can give up or go off task. Trace and explain can be a useful strategy for building code confidence with these pupils. If they persevered independently they would have been able to read it successfully but were put off by the size of it.

Key Element
Sometimes there is one part of the code that most of the class will benefit from having traced and explained, e.g. a particularly novel outworking of a concept already introduced or code where lots of hidden things are taking place such as variables or inputs.

Combined
Trace and explain can be combined with other strategies on occasions.

Teacher Knowledge
Teachers needs to know what is happening in the code themselves before being confident to trace and explain. In the curriculum books there are plenty of examples of trace and explain in particular contexts to explore.

Examples
The following are examples of trace and explain without contexts. The rows are numbered for easy book reference, as a teacher would point these out on his or her interactive whiteboard, touch screen tv or computer screen. Running the code or a part of the code is always part of this process. Visual references are created in italics.

Limitations

As always, cognitive overload can be an issue with this approach. If we are attempting to introduce a new concept then there are better strategies. As a reinforcement tool and a support tool more commonly for individuals or small groups and occasionally for the whole class it has a useful place.

Moving Character

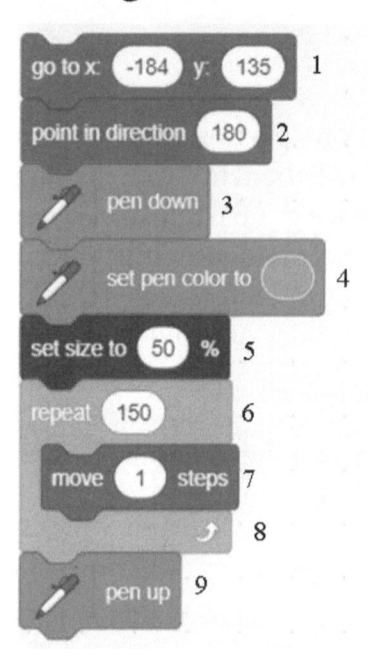

Teacher: Lets look at this code together.

Action: Teacher runs code.

Action: Teacher drags out block one and moves the sprite to a new position on the screen.

Teacher: When we left click this block to run it on its own, we can see that it moves the sprite to a set place on the screen. The numbers tell the computer where on the screen. You will study how those numbers work next year in Maths.

Action: Teacher replaces line 1 of code.

Action: Teacher points to line 2 and left clicks inside 180 to reveal 360 pointer.

Teacher: Tell your partner which direction 180 degrees will make the sprite point?

Teacher: Did you agree that the sprite would point down? The arrow clue helps.

Action: Points to arrow clue

Action: Points to line 3. Picks up a pen and mimes it touching the screen.

Teacher: Here a pen is placed on the screen to start drawing. Lines will only be seen once the sprite moves.

Action: Points to line 4.

Teacher: Note how the Americans who made Scratch spell colour without a U.

The line colour is now set to pink.

Action: Point to line 5.

Teacher: The sprite is now reduced in size to half size, 50 being half of 100.

Action: Points to lines 6, 7 & 8.

Teacher: How many times will move 1 step be run inside this count-controlled loop? Write it down on your whiteboard and show it when asked.

Teacher: Well done, move one step will be repeated 150 times. This makes the sprite look like it is slowly moving across the screen.

Teacher: Tell your partner how you might make the sprite move faster?

Teacher: Well done increasing the number of steps will make it move faster and further.

Action: Increase steps to 2 and run code.

Action: Points to line 9.

Teacher: Finally the pen is removed from the screen to stop it drawing.

More questions could be asked, but teachers need to take into account the length of pupils attention span and the value of trace and explain against hands-on experience or other support strategies.

Backdrops

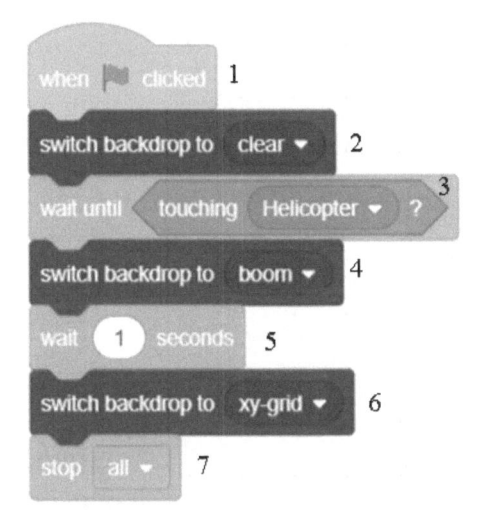

Teacher: Let's look at this code together.

Action: Points to line 1. Clicks on green flag runs the code.

Teacher: The green flag block starts the code.

Action: Points to line 2.

Teacher: The stage backdrop called clear is shown on the screen.

Action: Navigates to stage and point out backdrop 1 called clear marked A.

Teacher: Most of this code is switching between these three stage backdrops.

Action: Click on A, B and C to show how these change what is displayed on the stage.

Action: Returns to the code.

Action: Points to line 3.

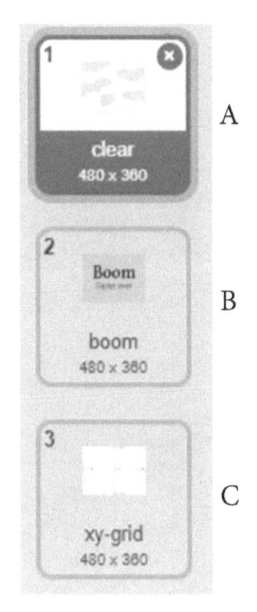

Teacher: The code then waits for the sprite to touch the helicopter sprite. This might happen straight away, later on, or never happen. It is affected by what the user does.

Teacher: Once the sprite has touched the helicopter, tell your partner what will happen next?

Action: Point to line 4.

Teacher: Correct, It will switch to showing the boom backdrop.

Action: Points to line 5.

Teacher: Pauses for 1 second.

Action: Points to line 6.

Teacher: Shows the x and y grid backdrop on the screen.

Action: Points to line 7.

Teacher: Finally this code stops all the code, as it is the end of the game.

Teacher: Let's look at this code together.

Action: Points to line 1 code.

Teacher: The script is started when it is clicked on using a mouse or trackpad or touched if using a tablet.

Karaoke

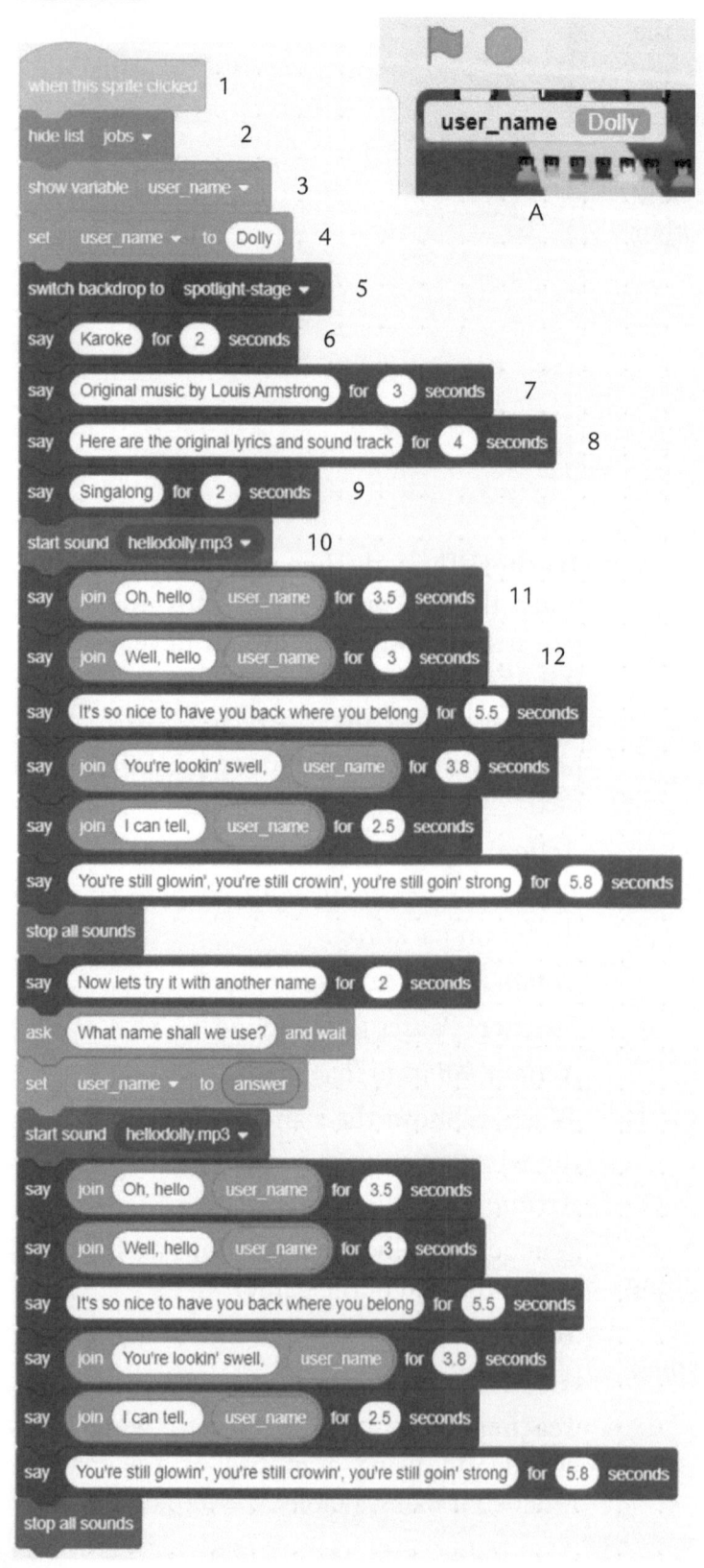

```
when this sprite clicked                              1
hide list jobs                                        2
show variable user_name                               3
set user_name to Dolly                                4
switch backdrop to spotlight-stage                    5
say Karoke for 2 seconds                              6
say Original music by Louis Armstrong for 3 seconds   7
say Here are the original lyrics and sound track for 4 seconds  8
say Singalong for 2 seconds                           9
start sound hellodolly.mp3                           10
say join Oh, hello user_name for 3.5 seconds         11
say join Well, hello user_name for 3 seconds         12
say join It's so nice to have you back where you belong for 5.5 seconds
say join You're lookin' swell, user_name for 3.8 seconds
say join I can tell, user_name for 2.5 seconds
say You're still glowin', you're still crowin', you're still goin' strong for 5.8 seconds
stop all sounds
say Now lets try it with another name for 2 seconds
ask What name shall we use? and wait
set user_name to answer
start sound hellodolly.mp3
say join Oh, hello user_name for 3.5 seconds
say join Well, hello user_name for 3 seconds
say join It's so nice to have you back where you belong for 5.5 seconds
say join You're lookin' swell, user_name for 3.8 seconds
say join I can tell, user_name for 2.5 seconds
say You're still glowin', you're still crowin', you're still goin' strong for 5.8 seconds
stop all sounds
```

A — user_name Dolly

Action: Points to line 2 code.

Teacher: This code hides a jobs list that might be visible after running another script attached to a different sprite. It is an initialisation block.

Action: Points to line 3 code.

Teacher: This block makes the variable name and value visible on the screen as shown here.

Action: Points to A.

Action: Points to line 4.

Teacher: The value Dolly is assigned to the variable called user_name.

Action: Points to line 5.

Teacher: This code changes the stage to spotlights-stage backdrop.

Action: Points to lines 6, 7, 8 & 9 and read the lines out as shown in the first example below.

Teacher: Say Karaoke for 2 seconds.

Action: Repeat for lines 7, 8 & 9.

Action: Points to line 10.

Teacher: The script starts to play the sound track hellodolly.mp3.

Action: Points to line 11.

Teacher: The spite now says 'Oh hello and then looks to see what value has been assigned to the variable named user_name. We can see in line 4 that the value assigned to user_name variable is Dolly so that is the name read out. Oh, hello Dolly'.

Action: Points to line 12.

Teacher: The spite now says 'Well, hello' and then looks to see what value has been assigned to the variable user_name. We can see in line 4 that the value assigned to user_name variable is Dolly so that is the name read out. Well, hello Dolly.

At this point some pupils may look like this has helped, so you might send them back to whichever independent task or challenge they are working on, whilst working with those who may need more trace and explain.

Labouring how each variable works can seem long-winded and slow, but it can really help some pupils to understand how a variable can be used as a placeholder within a program.

CHAPTER 32

More Clues

More Clues

Block-based programming languages like Scratch and Snap often provide you more visual clues than just what displays on the programming screen when the code is run. Being able to help pupils access and interpret these extra clues, when they are needed, is a powerful way to support their programming needs.

Costumes and Backdrops

If pupils are using sprites with multiple costumes such as the famous Scratch cat, shown below, then reminding them where the costumes can be viewed (sprite, costume tab) and manually swapping between them by clicking on costumes such as costume1 and costume2 can help them understand that these are pictures that the programmer can change with the right instruction. A few seconds pointing out where these are can often help with animation type programming that use the switch to next costume blocks or switch to a specific costume blocks.

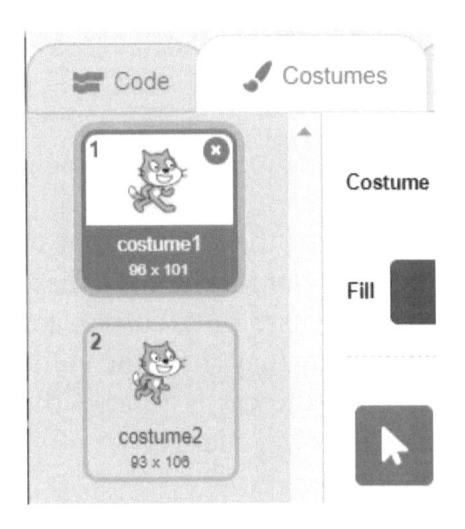

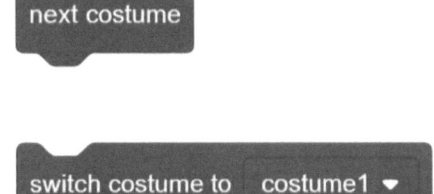

The stage area can have many backdrops, which can be viewed by clicking on stage and then clicking on the backdrop tab. Each backdrop will also have a unique name, so that it can be programmed. In Scratch 2 & 3, backdrops can be programmed from within a sprite or in the stage area. In Scratch 1.4, backdrops called backgrounds can only be programmed in the stage area.

As with sprite costumes, a few seconds reminding pupils where these are can help them to make more sense of the code that controls these.

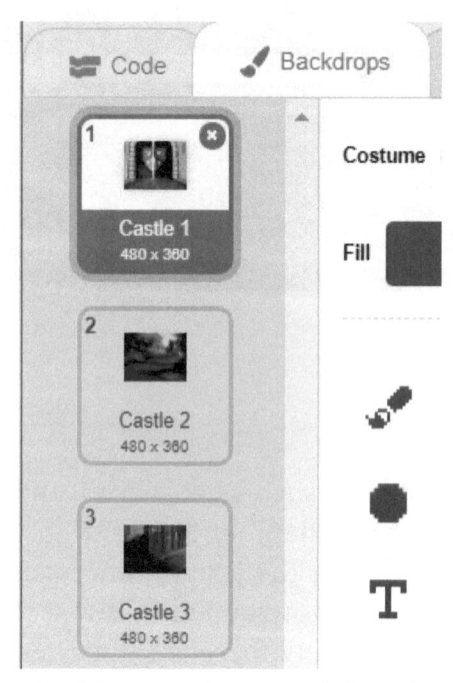

Backdrops can be accessed through the stage and backdrops tab

Only One

Sometimes it is not the code that is the problem but the fact that there is only one costume or backdrop and pupils are trying to use next costume or next backdrop to change to a non-existent costume or backdrop.

Hidden Variables

Pupils may know how they can see the value assigned to a variable displayed on the screen by ticking a box in the code area next to the variable as shown.

This then displays the value in an adjustable box on the screen which can look like this.

There are many other values that are hidden variables. You can see and change the values but you can't rename these.

The built in variable available in Scratch 3

It can really help pupils to see what these hidden variable values are.

If pupils need the value before they are ready to be introduced to variables then there is no need to mention that these are variables, just that the tick box shows for example the direction the sprite is pointing towards.

Hidden Motion Variables

In the motion blocks we have x position, y position and direction.

These will display on the screen as shown below.

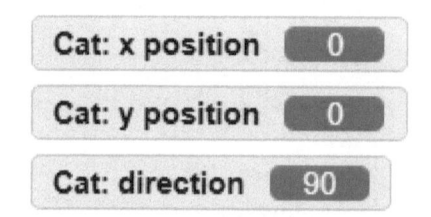

Notice that the name of the sprite is put in front of the value. For your information these are local variables that are only correct for that sprite, which is why they show the name of the sprite first. As the cat is rotated the value of **Cat: direction** will change.

Hidden Looks Variables

Costume and backdrops both have an assigned number which you can see on the previous page in the top left-hand corner of the description square. Tick to show these on the screen. You could program these to change with numbers via variables.

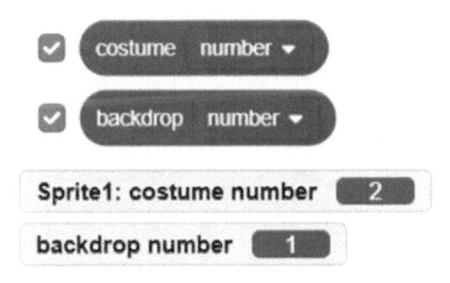

Of more use to younger programmers is the size value.

Hidden Sound Variables

Volume

Hidden Sensing Variables

By far the most useful sensing variable for younger programmers is the answer block. This variable holds the value inputted through the ask block. This value can then be acted on immediately, as shown below or stored in a variable for long-term use.

Ticking it will show the value assigned on the screen.

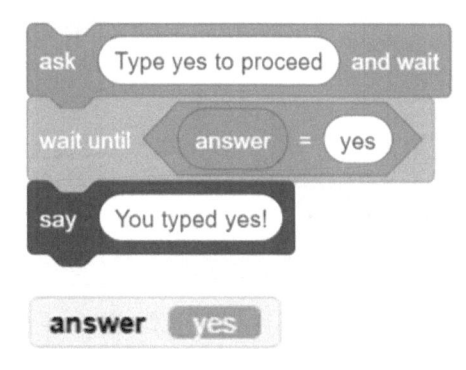

Sensing blocks have other hidden variables that all link to external information that pupils can view and use: **loudness** which records information through an attached microphone if you have one. A built –in **timer**, your **username** if you are using Scratch via the website and a **date**.

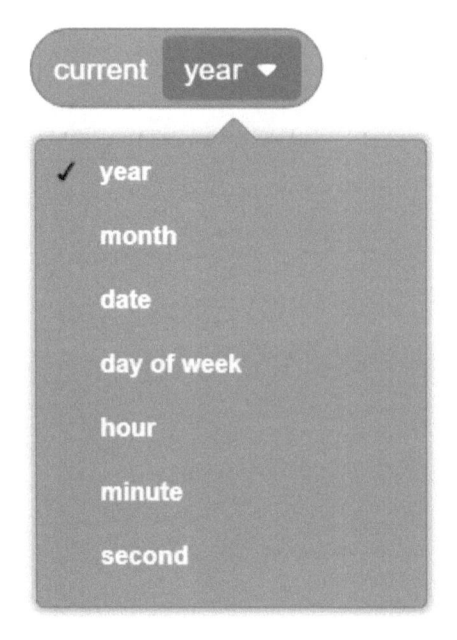

All of these can also be shown on the screen by ticking them.

Extension blocks also have hidden variables, such as tempo in sound and language in translation.

It is only the work of a moment to remind pupils to tick the box and view the value currently assigned. They can always untick it when they are finished, if it ruins the aesthetic of their program.

Language Clues

You may have a pupil whose struggle is not with programming concepts but with the language itself. Maybe English is a second language. Showing them how they can view Scratch in their native tongue may be the support they need.

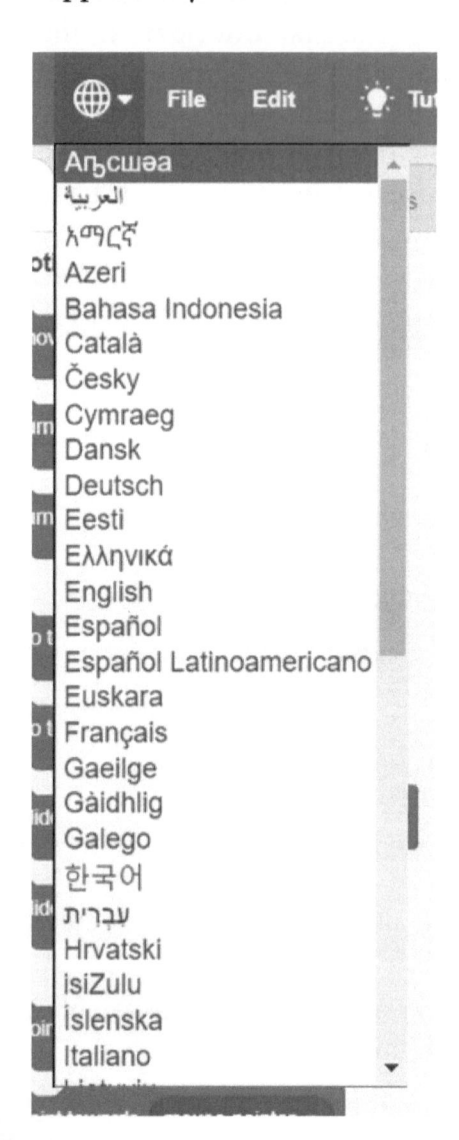

Look for the world icon, top left of the Scratch environment and select the language you want.

When teaching to pupils with English as a second language, I teach in English, as I wanted them to learn English, but at the end of demos I would switch the screen to their language for a minute or two.

I got them to program in English using the change language option as a support mechanism if they didn't understand a word. This seemed to work well.

Sound Files

If pupils have not created the program themselves, they may not be aware that sound blocks play sound files that are linked to specific sprites.

Directing them to the sounds tabs so they can view or edit a sound file may help them make sense of the program they are running, adapting or modifying.

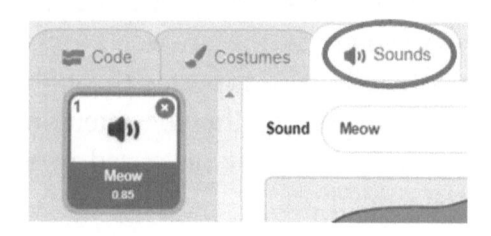

Read Aloud

Read Aloud

Read aloud is a support strategy that asks pupils to read their code, planning, algorithm aloud rather than just internally.

Rubber Duck

Reading code aloud is not a new support technique. In the book *The Pragmatic Programmer*[1] a programmer carries around a rubber duck and explains their code line by line to the duck.

Many programmers have experienced fresh insight when explaining an idea to a colleague, and the rubber duck seeks to emulate that when another person is not available.

Debugging Only?

Whilst talking to an inanimate object is primarily linked to debugging, fresh insight at any stage of programming project can be gained by reading your code, algorithm, task, objects list or initialisation aloud.

Effective Initial Support Strategy

Encouraging a pupil to read their work aloud can be a very efficient initial support strategy. It doesn't take long for a teacher to do this, and it is obvious if a pupil complies with the request.

Many schools have strategies where support is sought from other sources before a teacher is consulted.

It would be sensible to include reading work aloud in these types of strategies we adapt for computing.

Stuck?

Read it aloud.

Explain to a partner.

Get a partner hint.

Ask your teacher for a hint.

Read chapter 23 on effective support and debugging to understand how to use this and other independent peer-support strategies effectively without making peers more helpless.

---

[1] The Pragmatic Programmer David Thomas & Andrew Hunt.

Support Cards

CHAPTER 34

Support Cards

There are many different types of support cards or sheets. In this chapter we will look at different types and analyse the benefits and drawbacks of each approach.

Why use support cards

Support cards or sheets are often welcomed by teachers of large classes as a way of sharing the support burden. Trying to get round 32 support-needy pupils who have just begun programming can be a daunting task. A desire to impart help that pupils can use away from the teacher, thus freeing the teacher to help with more complex issues, is an admirable aim. A realisation that many of the challenges and problems pupils encounter when programming are common to many pupils means that some issues can be anticipated and planned for through support cards and sheets.

Common Ingredients

Most support cards use pictures, diagrams or code samples alongside text to help users visualise the problem or solution. Many try to keep text to a minimum. Most of them also focussed on solving just one problem or issue rather than multiple ones.

Folded Cards Adapted

Some of the following examples were originally designed to be folded after being printed. This meant that half the card was upside down as shown on the example on the next page. Other sample folding cards in this chapter have been adjusted so that information is easier to read.

How are these used?

These can be given out by the teacher when a need is spotted. They can be placed in an identified location for pupils to use when needed. A set can be given out for use by a particular table or group of pupils. Pupils could access them online if they are linked in an accessible location as PDF viewers allow easy rotation.

Original Examples Remade

Some examples have been remade using Scratch 3 to match the book theme.

Copy Code Cards

Copy code cards identify an issues and provide one possible solution. Code is shown fully connected for pupils to copy.

Context

This example on the right went alongside another skills card with instructions on how

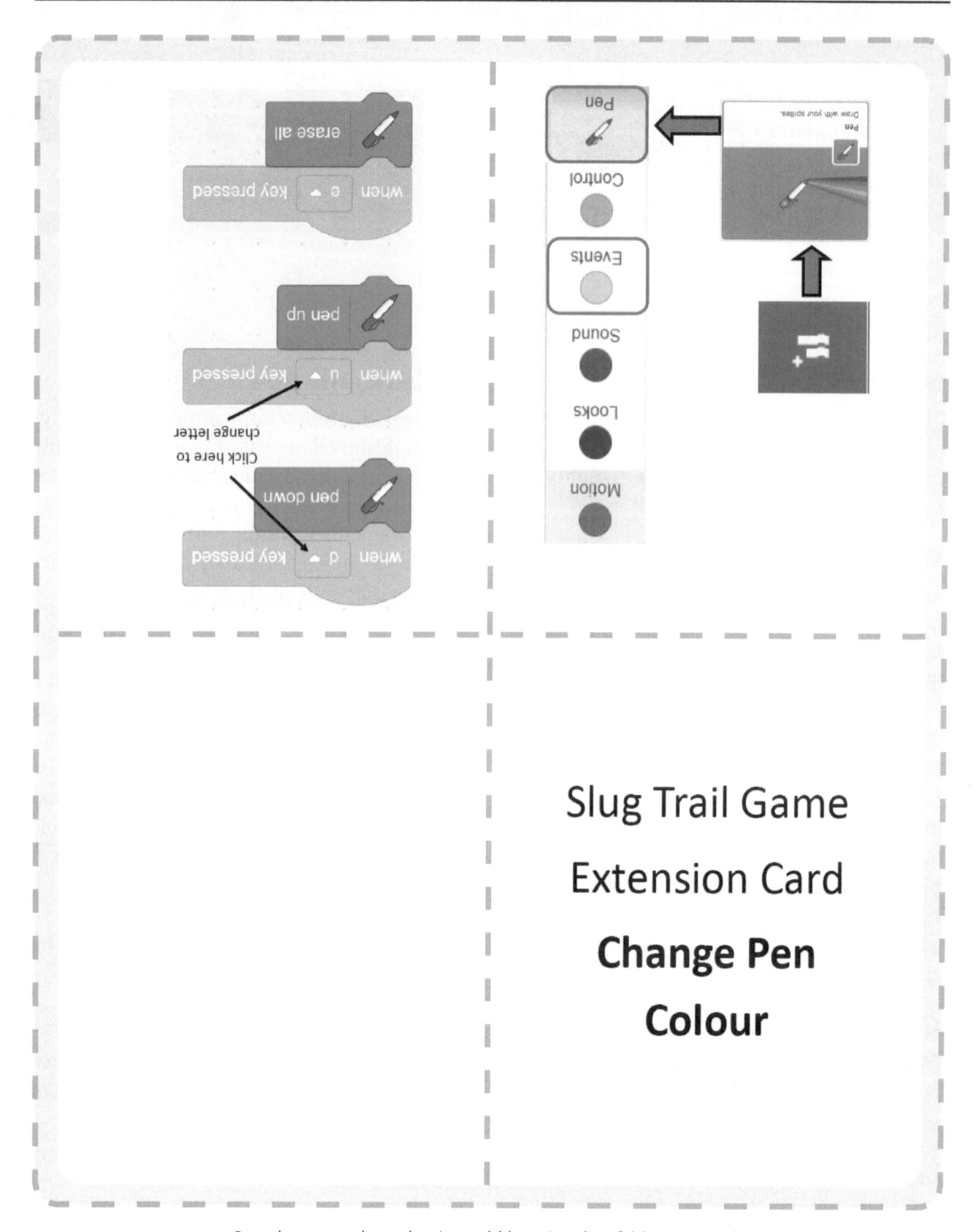

Scratch IT – Teaching Primary Programming with Scratch

Slug Trail Game

Extension Card

Change Pen Colour

Sample copy code card as it would be printed to fold into a booklet

to import a backdrop. It was included in a module designed for Year 3 pupils who were 7 to 8 years old. It wasn't widely used by many pupils.

Benefits

Identifying where code blocks can be found by linking the blocks to the location is beneficial to some pupils. Being able to hold up a code sample and compare it to what you have created can be useful for some struggling pupils.

Drawbacks

Pupils can build this code without really engaging in what it does or how it works. Some pupils who are poor readers copy the shape of the blocks without reading what it does. It only promotes one solution.

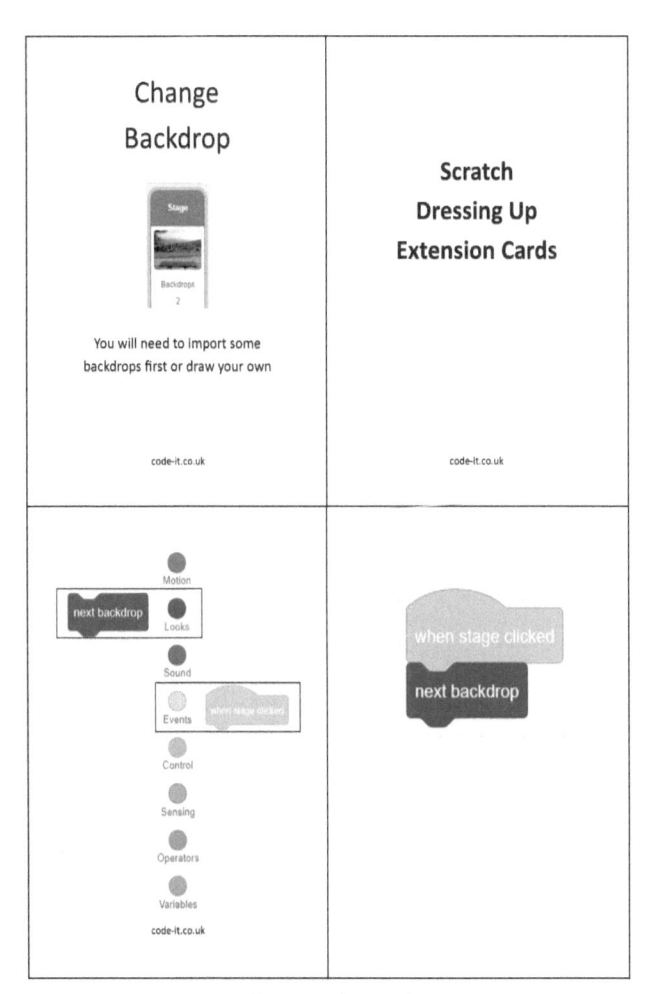

Recommendations

There are better ways to create support cards which make pupils think harder about programming solutions. However the Scratch coding cards below might be a good way of introducing programming environmental basics such as sprite and background creation.

Good Examples

The Scratch coding cards are examples of well made copy code cards.

https://resources.scratch.mit.edu/www/cards/en/imagine-cards.pdf

Parsons Code Cards

These cards contain the exact type and number of blocks needed to create one possible solution. They are presented unconnected, so pupils have to puzzle out how to connect them.

Context

This example on the next page went alongside a module of work to build a Crab Maze game.

Benefits

Limiting the number of blocks can be an effective support strategy enabling pupils to focus on just the code that is needed, thus reducing the time taken to solve the problem.

Drawbacks

Although the code can be used to create steer right or steer left blocks, it is still limited to only one possible interpretation of either.

Copy code card

Scratch IT – Teaching Primary Programming with Scratch

Recommendations

Teachers have always sought to reduce complexity by limiting the options available which lowers the cognitive load of an approach. Alongside other approaches this can be an effective support strategy which lowers complexity whilst still retaining some challenge.

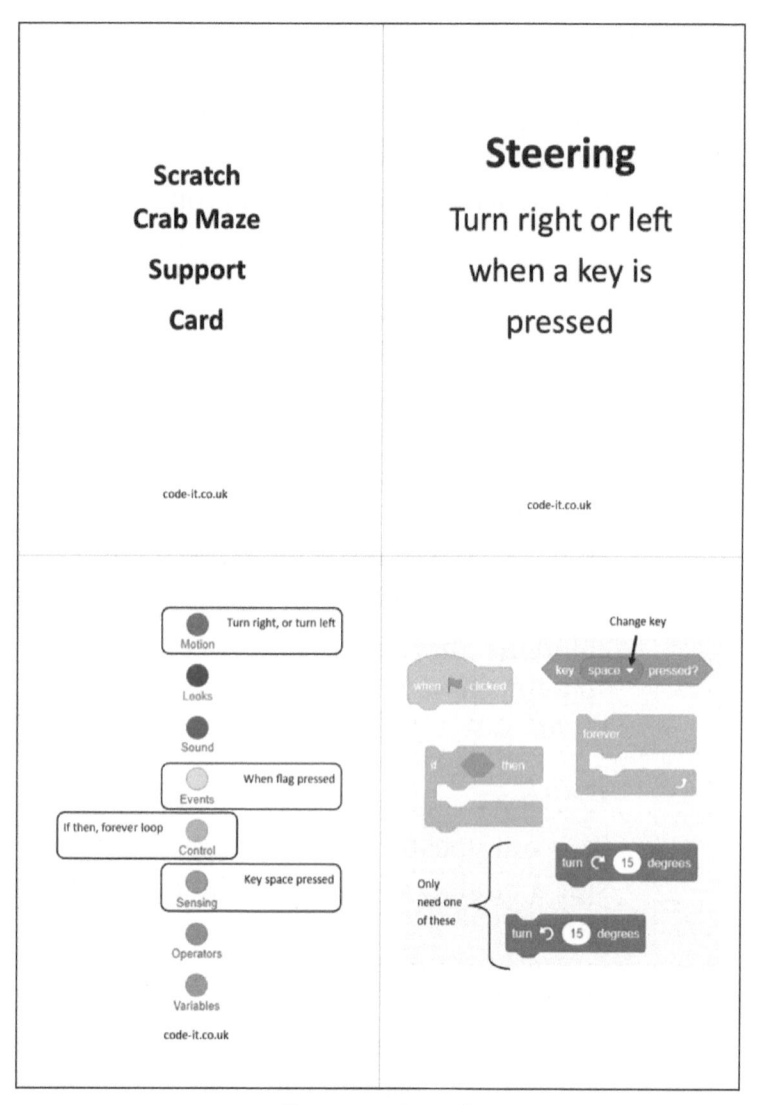

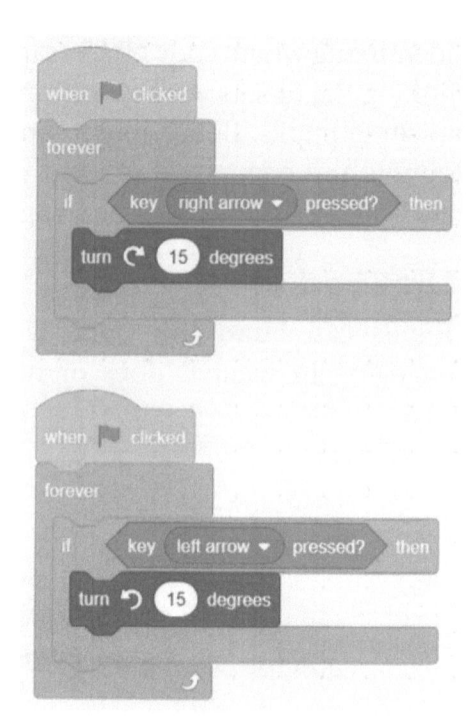

Scratch Crab Maze Support Card

code-it.co.uk

Steering

Turn right or left when a key is pressed

code-it.co.uk

Correctly connected code would assemble like this

Parson code card

Parsons Code Cards with Algorithm

This card is similar to the Parsons code cards on the previous page with the added extra clue of providing an algorithm. The example below uses a simple flow chart, but this could be swapped for a text only algorithm, such as the one below.

```
Start
Loop always
        If the distance sensor detects
        something within 50 mm
                Turn the motor on
        Else
                Turn the motor off
```

Solution

Although there was a solution inside the card, the card was stapled shut and pupils were instructed to only force the card open as a last resort. None of them, to the best of my knowledge, ever did!

Context

This example went alongside a module of work linking DT and computing by designing, building and programming an ensuite bedroom toilet fan using Lego WeDo.

Benefits

We already know from the previous page that reducing choice can be an effective support strategy to reduce cognitive load. This version also has the added bonus of having a solution that is there in case pupils need it.

Drawbacks

As well as the drawback listed on the previous page, many pupils also need to have been introduced to algorithms in a simpler format to accurately read more complex examples such as those shown here.

Recommendations

The ready-made solution alongside the instruction to try and avoid using it is a very effective challenge. A worthwhile strategy if used in moderation.

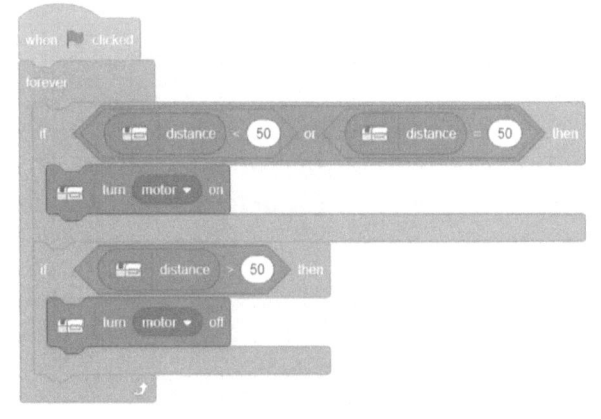

An alternate solution impossible to build with the blocks provided

Device Cards

These cards contain information about one type of programmable device. They provide the pupil with more than one type of information about the device. Pupils can place their Crumble microcontroller attached to an optional Crumble playground on top of the card. Turn it so the sockets match up and then use this to work out how to plug in a specific device, in this case a Sparkle programmable light. Elsewhere on the card are useful code blocks that the pupil may wish to use with this programmable light, as well as helpful information you may need to know to program it. On the back of the card, shown in the top right in this illustration, is more information.

Context

This example, alongside many other Crumble cards can be found at http://code-it.co.uk/cards/

Fully Connected Code Samples

Some Crumble device support cards also have examples of fully connected code for pupils to copy. Some pupils found these example programs helpful especially if the device could be programmed using more complex concepts such as variables. The author tried to keep the sample code simple enough so that pupils gained a flavour of how it could be used whilst avoiding providing ready-made solutions that could be copied without any modification that would demonstrate understanding and creativity.

Benefits

A well-crafted card can become a one-stop shop for many different types of support issue. In this example, connection, code sample and information about similar devices are all included on the same card.

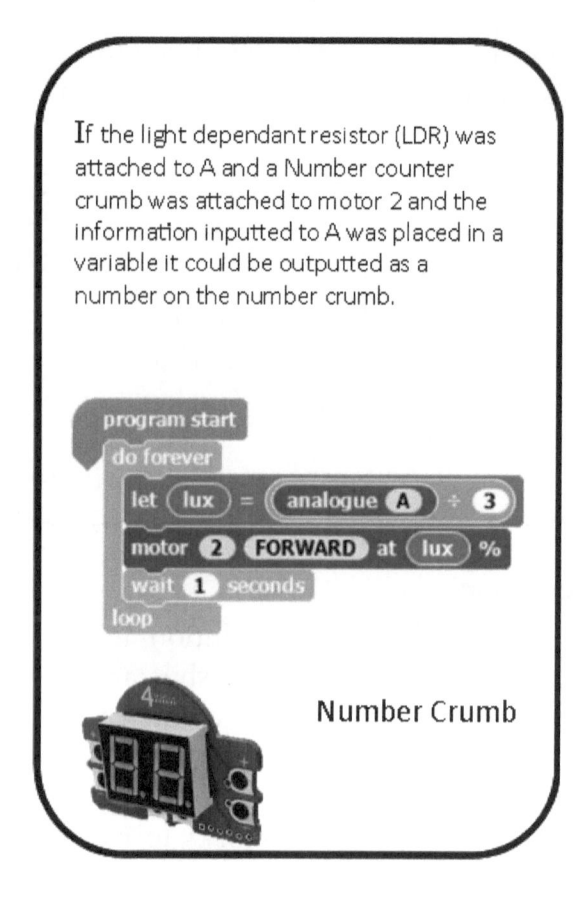

Drawbacks

Too much information can put some pupils off from reading the cards.

Recommendations

This type of cards can be very useful especially for more confident readers. Teachers will need to know what is on the cards for those times that pupils haven't really read or studied the card. An indication, of where the information they need is situated is often the only prompt some pupils need. Device cards could be created where Scratch plugs into external devices such as the Microbit.

Support Cards

Crumble Playground Programmable Lights

MC01

More Information

Lights are outputs. Programmable lights can be very bright. You can reduce this by covering the light with a translucent cover such a piece of white paper.

Lights can be daisy chained together.

4Tronix who make this programmable light call it a flame. The Crumble software calls it a Sparkle.

You can program multiple lights on one device with these adaptations of the basic Sparkle.

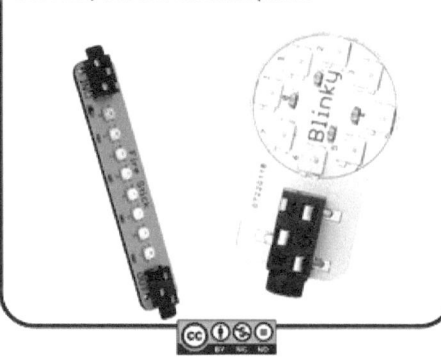

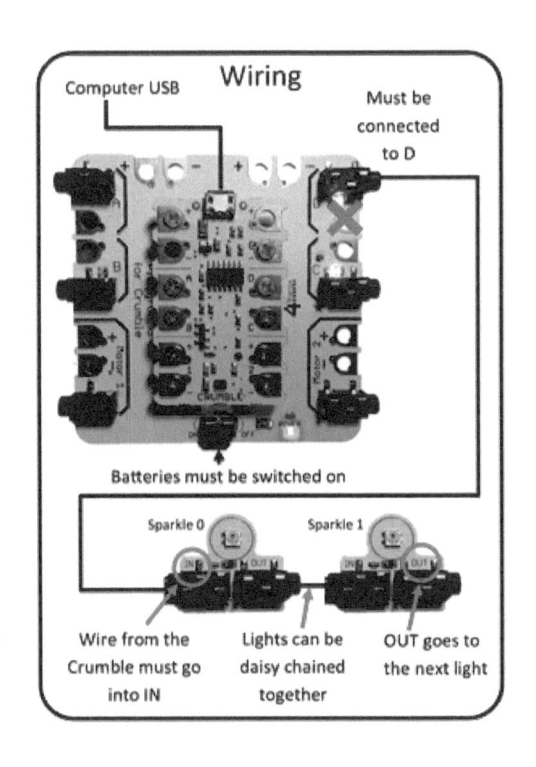

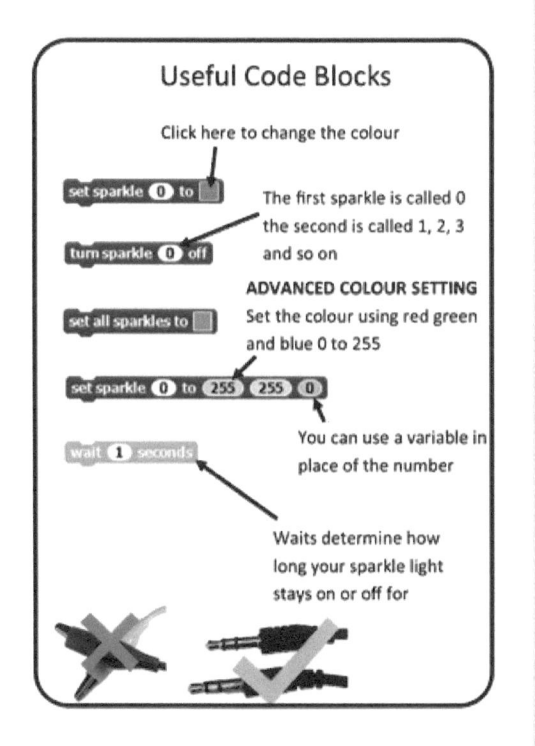

Wiring

Computer USB

Must be connected to D

Batteries must be switched on

Sparkle 0 — Sparkle 1

Wire from the Crumble must go into IN

Lights can be daisy chained together

OUT goes to the next light

Useful Code Blocks

Click here to change the colour

`set sparkle 0 to ▢`

The first sparkle is called 0 the second is called 1, 2, 3 and so on

`turn sparkle 0 off`

ADVANCED COLOUR SETTING
Set the colour using red green and blue 0 to 255

`set all sparkles to ▢`

`set sparkle 0 to 255 255 0`

You can use a variable in place of the number

`wait 1 seconds`

Waits determine how long your sparkle light stays on or off for

Device cards

Skills Cards

These cards contain step-by-step information on how to control, manipulate or make something that is not intuitive or easy. It might show in pictures how to snap blocks inside each other or how to create a variable or make a procedure using build a block. These cards don't replace the rich information that comes from a well-described demonstration, but they can trigger memory and remind pupils of a process explained and part forgotten.

Context

This example (top right) goes through the steps to create a variable called count. It was originally part of a counting machine module of work created to work with Scratch 1.4. This updated version uses connected bubbles rather than text to indicate the steps in order.

Benefits

This type of cards can be very useful as an aid to remembering complex processes that pupils may only have done a few times before. Most pupils find them easy to use, although the choice of a coloured line can be a difficult one when referencing multicolour blocks.

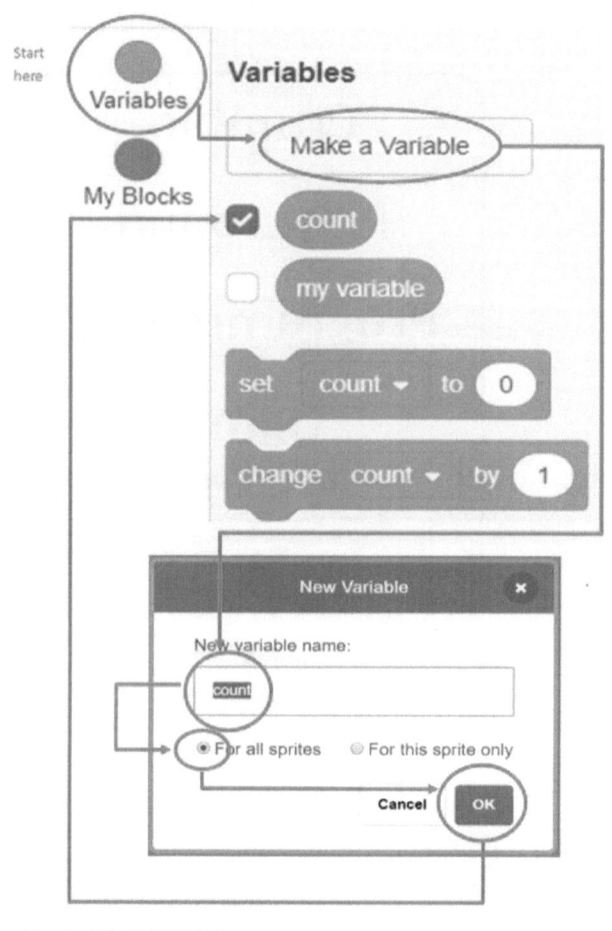

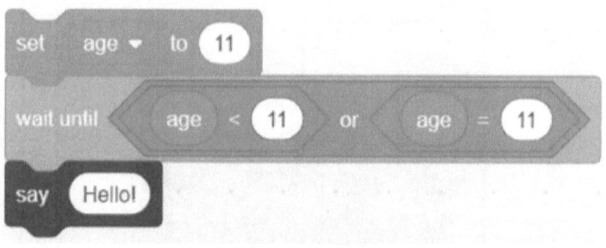

A simple example showing how a complex condition might be used

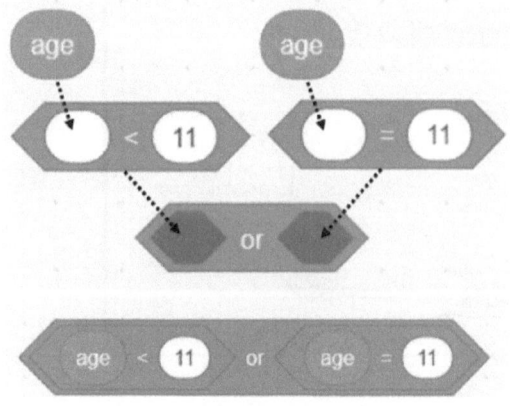

Drawbacks

There are no significant drawbacks with this card, apart from a belief by teachers that they can be used in place of demonstration or example.

Recommendations

A good type of card to have and use when needed.

Part of a skills card showing how complex conditions can be created

Concept Cards

These cards contain theory and examples about an aspect of programming. They might show examples of what algorithmic planning might look like. The example at the bottom has two forms of algorithmic plan, text on the left and a flow chart on the right.

They might contain everyday examples that pupils already know about in order to help them make a connection with a more abstract programming concept, as shown on the right.

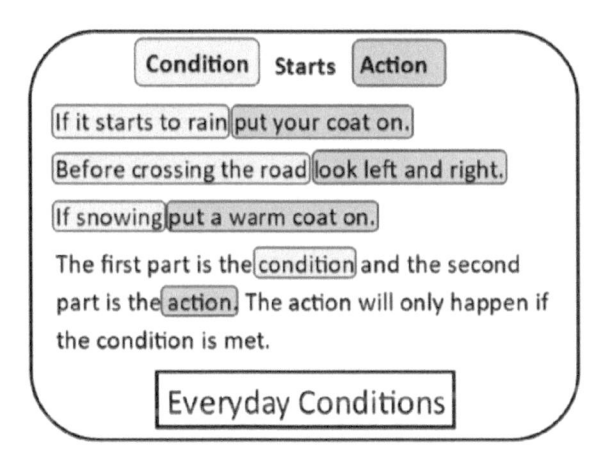

Context

These examples are from two different cards explaining types of conditional selection. They were designed to be used as a reminder when pupils are programming independently. Pupils were not surveyed about their usefulness.

Benefits

The bottom example helps to correct a common misconception that conditions will be checked many times through the picture and commentary about how loops work with conditions.

Drawbacks

There is a lot to read on these cards, which may discourage casual browsing. More research is necessary to determine their usefulness.

Recommendations

Useful as a follow-up resource that triggers prior learning.

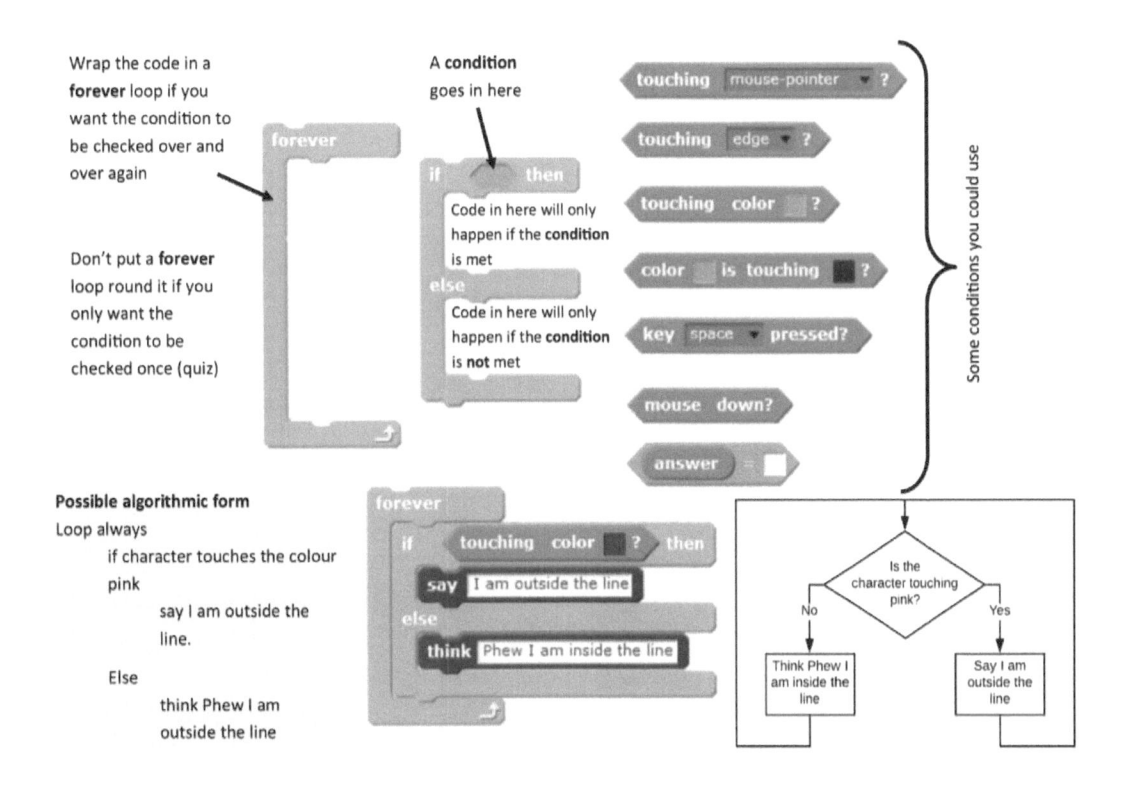

GLOSSARY

abstraction
The skill of reducing complexity by hiding irrelevant detail and focussing on the most important element

accessibility
Making a program or technology easy to use for everyone, including those with disabilities

algorithm
A list of steps (or rules) to do something

Algorithmic evaluation
To compare two algorithms to decide which one is best

Assign
Give a value to a variable

block-based programming language
A programming language that allows a user to code by connecting blocks. Scratch is the most popular of these

Browser
Short for web browser, a program designed to enable a user to interact with the world wide web and other internet services

bug
An error in a program or an unfinished program that does not run as it should

call (a variable)
Code that reads the name of the variable but acts on the value assigned to the variable (see variable)

call (a procedure)
Code that starts a procedure (see procedure)

code
The language that programmers create and use to give instructions to a digital device

computational thinking
A set of critical thinking skills useful in computing (algorithmic thinking, decomposition, generalisation, abstraction, etc.)

conditions
If statements that can either be true or false, met or unmet

Condition-starts-action
Another name for if then conditional selection commands that don't include an else

Condition-stops-loop
Another name for a loop that is ended by a condition called a repeat until block in Scratch

Condition-switches-between-actions
Another name for if-then-else conditional selection commands that start actions if the condition is TRUE or FALSE

count-controlled loop
A definite loop (we know how many loops) controlled by a number

cyberbullying
Using technology to make another person feel angry, sad, or scared.

data
Information without context such as text, graphics, video, sound

debugging
Finding and fixing problems in code

decompose
Break a problem down into smaller parts to solve each part separately

Desktop publishing
A document that combines graphics and text for print or web publication

digital citizen
Everyone who communicates or connects online

digital device
Any device controlled by programming from the smallest microchip-controlled toy to the largest supercomputer

digital footprint
The information about themselves that digital citizens leave behind whilst communication and connecting

DNS (domain name service)
The service that changes URLs into IP addresses.

double-click
Press the mouse or trackpad button very quickly twice

drag
Click a mouse button or trackpad button and hold it down as the cursor is moved

fiber optic cables
A cable that uses light to pass information

Firewall
A program to check incoming internet data and exclude harmful data. Can also be hardware that only runs software that does this role in a large organisation.

Forever loop
Scratch name for an indefinite infinite loop

Generalisation
A computational thinking skill to adapt a solution that solved one problem to solve another

Keyboard shortcuts
Key combinations which, when pressed at the same time, carry out other jobs than the one on the key. Ctrl + C copies highlighted text and documents Ctrl + V pastes highlighted text and documents

Indefinite loop
Any loop where it is hard to predict how many times the loop will be run either because it never ends or because it is ended by a condition (see infinite loop)

Infinite loop
An indefinite loop with no way of ending built in. In Scratch this is called a forever loop.

input
A way to give (put in) information into a computer.

Internet
A group of computers and servers that are connected to each other all around the world

IP address
A number assigned to any digital device that is connected to the Internet

iteration
Another name for repetition

Glossary

loop
Doing something over and over again.

online
Connected to the Internet.

Online safety
Knowledge needed to keep yourself and others safe when using online services

output
Digital device putting out information (sound, text, light and data, etc.) Common outputs are screens, printers, speakers

packets
Small chunks of information split up to pass over the internet and recombined in a browser

Parameter
An extra piece of information passed to a procedure to adapt it

pixel
Screens are made up of pixels which are dots containing a single colour. The Scratch 3 screen has 480 horizontal pixels and 360 vertical pixels, 480×360=172,800 pixels to program with.

placeholder variable
A variable assigned data that will stay the same throughout the program. It can be changed but is not. Often users assign their name to a placeholder variable through the ask and answer Scratch blocks

procedure
a set of instructions bundled together to complete a part of a program that can be called (run) many times

program
An algorithm that has been turned into code to run on a digital device. A set of instructions written in a language a digital device can read and act on

programming
Thinking through a problem creatively and solving it with code

repeat
Doing something again

Router
A device to route data across the internet and networks

Run or running (program)
A program that has started and not stopped

Shortcut
A small user-created file that directs the user to another place when it is run

search engine
A program on the world wide web that looks through giant databases of websites to help a user find the right website

servers
Computers that provide services to other computers and users connected to them. See web servers

Simple procedure
A procedure without parameters (see parameters)

Switch
A device to route data around a local network

Taskbar
The bar on computers containing commonly used menus and shortcuts

Text-based programming language

A programming language where you have to type all the commands (see block based programming language)

Toolbox

A collection of digital tools grouped together as icons (pictures)

URL (universal resource locator)

An internet address that is easier to remember than the IP address (code-it.co.uk)

Username

The name a user uses on a network or website to identify themselves to the system

Variable

used to store information to be referred to and changed in a computer program or algorithm

Website

A collection of linked web pages on the world wide web

Wi-Fi

A method of sending information using radio waves that does not use wires

Word-processing

Manipulating text on a digital device